Scott Foresman

Reading

Grades 4-6

Phonics Workbook
Blackline Master
and Answer Key

Scott Foresman
Phonics System
™

Scott Foresman

Editorial Offices: Glenview, Illinois • New York, New York
Sales Offices: Reading, Massachusetts • Duluth, Georgia • Glenview, Illinois
Carrollton, Texas • Menlo Park, California

Skill	Page Numbers

Editorial Offices: Glenview, Illinois • New York, New York
Sales Offices: Reading, Massachusetts • Duluth, Georgia • Glenview, Illinois
Carrollton, Texas • Menlo Park, California

ISBN 0-673-61433-6

345678910-CRK-06050403020100

© Scott Foresman 4-6

Name _____

The letter *a* stands for the short *a* vowel sound in these words.

stamp   hanger   demand

Circle the words that have the short *a* vowel sound spelled *a*. Then write the word that names each picture.

label	rabbit	apple	candle	angle
dancer	trailer	garden	sandwich	weather
basket	rattle	branch	cabin	display

1. _____

2. _____

3. _____

4. _____

5. _____

6. _____

7. _____

8. _____

9. _____

10. _____

Notes for Home: Your child identified and wrote words with the short *a* vowel sound.
Home Activity: Begin with a short *a* vowel word such as *pan*. Take turns with your child making rhyming words: *pan, can, man, bran, plan, than.*

The letter *a* can stand for the short *a* vowel sound in words.

Write the word with the short *a* vowel sound in each sentence.

1. Min Lei sat on the park bench. _____

2. The sale price is written on the tag. _____

3. The answer to the question is easy. _____

4. The baby napped for one hour. _____

5. Mrs. Miki put a package in her suitcase. _____

6. The plane landed about two hours ago. _____

7. Bart is the last one in line. _____

8. Heavy snow began to fall near the lake. _____

9. Dane did his homework after dinner. _____

10. We walked along the sandy beach. _____

11. The catcher gave the pitcher signals. _____

12. Everyone agrees that it is a beautiful day. _____

13. The dog wagged her tail wildly. _____

14. We ate breakfast in a cafeteria. _____

15. A sprinter must make a fast start. _____

 Notes for Home: Your child identified words with the short *a* vowel sound in sentences.
Home Activity: Have your child write a sentence using at least one short *a* word. Then ask your child to draw a picture illustrating his or her sentence.

The letter *e* stands for the short *e* vowel sound in these words.

tr**e**nd   l**e**sson   **e**ffect

Circle the words that have the short *e* sound spelled *e*. Then write the word that names each picture.

fender   engine   monkey   medal   beaver

pencil   seven   cheese   saddle   melon

teammate   letter   enter   telephone   blender

1.   _____

2.   _____

3.   _____

4. 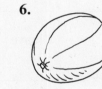 _____

5.   _____

6.  _____

7.   _____

8.  _____

9.   _____

10.  _____

 Notes for Home: Your child identified and wrote words with the short *e* vowel sound.
Home Activity: Have your child write sentences using two or more of the short *e* words on the page.

Name _____

The letter *e* can stand for the short *e* vowel sound in words.

Write the word that completes the sentence and has the short *e* sound spelled *e*.

1. We flew over the ocean in a _____.

            jet   plane

2. Mario found a _____ on the beach.

           whale   shell

3. Ava wants to be a _____ of the club.

           leader   member

4. Our math _____ is tomorrow.

           final   test

5. This morning I ate _____ and toast.

           eggs   cereal

6. Our class must _____ at one o'clock.

           end   leave

7. Many fish were caught in the _____.

           current   net

8. Samir stood in the _____ of the circle.

           center   middle

9. Mom noticed a _____ in the car fender.

           dent   hole

10. Kent was the _____ person in line.

           eighth   tenth

Notes for Home: Your child wrote words with the short *e* vowel sound to complete sentences. **Home Activity:** Start with a short *e* word such as *bed*. Take turns with your child naming rhyming words in which *e* stands for the short *e* sound: *red, fed, led, sled, shed*.

© Scott Foresman 4-6

Name _____

The letter *i* stands for the short *i* vowel sound in these words.

bridge   inform   magic

Circle the words that have the short *i* vowel sound spelled *i*. Then write the word that names each picture.

visor	muffin	kitten	billion	picture
ribbon	pickle	violin	scissors	robin
chicken	bridle	writer	pitcher	chimney

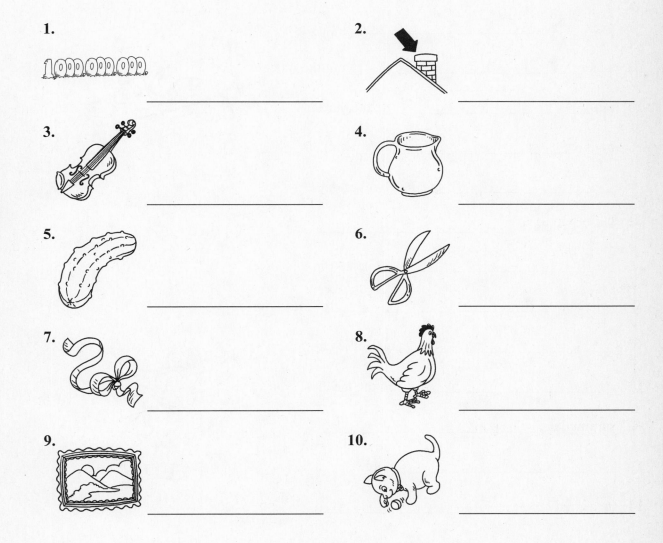

1.

2.

3.

4.

5.

6.

7.

8.

9.

10.

Notes for Home: Your child identified and wrote words with the short *i* vowel sound.
Home Activity: Think of a riddle for one of the short *i* words on the page. Have your child answer the riddle and then think of a short *i* word riddle to ask you.

The letter *i* can stand for the short *i* vowel sound in words.

Use the words with the short *i* sound to complete the phrases.

inches	twist	finger	pop	find	silver
glided	middle	high	white	dripped	slipped
wood	trip	around	chilly	brick	ninth
leaked	fifth	vacation	twigs	into	tick
bright	dig	end	miles	chime	ankle

1. the _____ of the room

2. pack for a _____

3. water _____ from the faucet

4. ran _____ the yard

5. built a _____ wall

6. _____ October day

7. heard the clock _____

8. the _____ person in line

9. collected _____ for the campfire

10. _____ off bottle cap

11. _____ on the ice

12. sprained my _____

13. _____ a hole

14. measured six _____

15. a new _____ car

Notes for Home: Your child wrote words with the short *i* vowel sound to complete phrases. **Home Activity:** Using a road map or an atlas map for your home state, have your child look for cities, rivers, lakes, mountains, and parks whose names have the short *i* vowel sound spelled *i*.

The letter _o_ stands for the short _o_ vowel sound in these words.

d**o**dge   c**o**ttage   resp**o**nd

Circle the words that have the short _o_ vowel sound spelled _o_. Then write the word that names each picture.

rosebud	harmonica	watermelon	hotel	octopus
bottle	locker	teapot	lobster	shoulder
robin	flowers	doctor	dollar	rocket

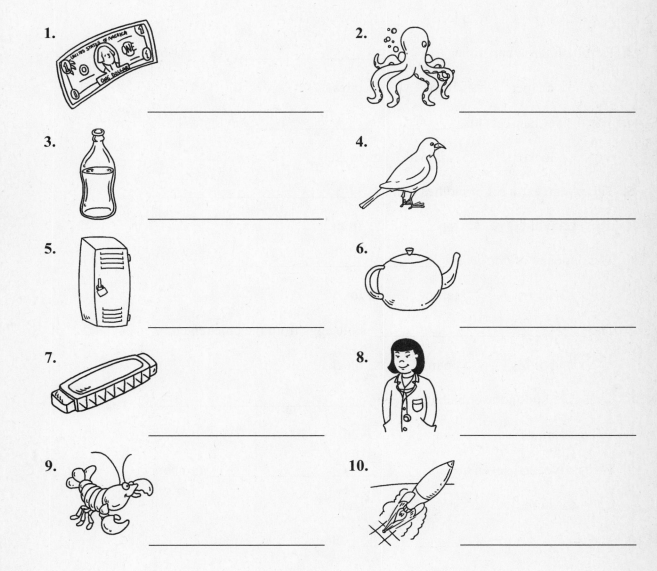

1. _____

2. _____

3. _____

4. _____

5. _____

6. _____

7. _____

8. _____

9. _____

10. _____

Notes for Home: Your child identified and wrote words with the short _o_ vowel sound.
Home Activity: Have your child write sentences using two of the short _o_ words from the page in each sentence.

The letter *o* can stand for the short *o* vowel sound in words.

Fill in the ovals by the short *o* words. Then write the short *o* word that completes the sentence.

⬭ rod   ⬭ hole   ⬭ pot

1. Martina made soup in a large _____.

⬭ pocket   ⬭ color   ⬭ robber

2. Put your wallet in the _____ of your pants.

⬭ jog   ⬭ job   ⬭ joy

3. Elizabeth has a part-time _____ after school.

⬭ copper   ⬭ crops   ⬭ crows

4. The farmer harvests his _____ in the fall.

⬭ locker   ⬭ sailboat   ⬭ rocket

5. Tito put an extra set of clothes in his _____.

⬭ pond   ⬭ top   ⬭ front

6. The opposite of *bottom* is _____.

⬭ frog   ⬭ fellow   ⬭ fox

7. The _____ stole eggs from the chicken coop.

⬭ bottles   ⬭ boards   ⬭ blocks

8. Catherine built a tower using wooden _____.

⬭ mock   ⬭ odd   ⬭ old

9. Three, five, and seven are all _____ numbers.

⬭ store   ⬭ stop   ⬭ shop

10. The toy _____ closes at 5:00 P.M.

Notes for Home: Your child wrote words with the short *o* vowel sound.
Home Activity: Have your child find a magazine advertisement, read the ad aloud to you, and identify short *o* vowel words that he or she finds in the ad.

The letter _u_ stands for the short _u_ vowel sound in these words.

br**u**sh   **u**ntie   waln**u**t

Circle the words that have the short _u_ vowel sound spelled _u_. Then write the word that names each picture.

bucket	runner	cruise	muffin	bathtub
umpire	puppet	button	tulip	umbrella
numbers	cube	music	pumpkin	utensil

1. 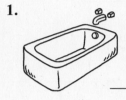 _____

2. 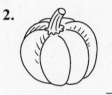 _____

3.  _____

4.  _____

5. _____

6.  _____

7.  _____

8. _____

9.  _____

10.  _____

Notes for Home: Your child identified and wrote words with the short _u_ vowel sound.
Home Activity: Have your child add syllables to the following short _u_ words to make new short _u_ words: _sun (sunny); sum (summer); pup (puppy, puppet); fun (funny, funnel); bud (budget, buddy); shut (shutter, shuttle)._

© Scott Foresman 4–6

The letter *u* can stand for the short *u* vowel sound in words.

Draw a line from each short *u* word to the phrase it completes. Write the word.

musical
under
much
mustard
trunk
funny
useful

1. thank you very _____

2. ketchup and _____ on a hot dog

3. look _____ the bed

4. suitcases in the _____ of the car

5. a _____ cartoon

puddles
umbrella
uniform
dust
July
successful
summer

6. a colorful striped _____

7. blew _____ off the old books

8. a hot _____ day

9. _____ formed after the rain

10. a _____ campaign for president

juice
supper
butter
rusty
purple
crumbs
unfold

11. enchiladas for _____

12. extra _____ on the popcorn

13. _____ the tablecloth

14. wiped _____ off the table

15. a _____ car fender

Notes for Home: Your child wrote words with the short *u* vowel sound.
Home Activity: Using the movie section from the newspaper, have your child identify short *u* words in movie titles, theater names, movie theater locations, and so on.

The long *a* vowel sound can be spelled *a*-consonant-*e*, *ai*, and *ay*.

sh**ade**   afr**ai**d   aw**ay**

Use the letters and one of the long *a* vowel patterns—*a*-consonant-*e, ai,* or *ay*—to make a word that names each picture. Write the word.

1. b r c l e t

_____

2. d s y

_____

3. c r o n s

_____

4. s c l s

_____

5. g r n

_____

6. m i d d

_____

7. q u l

_____

8. g r p s

_____

9. s p r

_____

10. s h p s

_____

Notes for Home: Your child wrote words in which *a*-consonant-*e, ai,* or *ay* stands for the long *a* vowel sound. **Home Activity:** Write *a*-consonant-*e, ai,* and *ay* as headings on a sheet of paper and have your child write each word from the page under the correct heading.

Name _____

The long *a* vowel sound can be spelled *a*-consonant-*e*, *ai*, or *ay*.

para**de**   **fai**nt   tod**ay**

Underline the words in the box that have the long *a* sound spelled *a*-consonant-*e*, *ai*, or *ay*. Then write each of the words in the correct column below.

sample	straight	gadget	replace	valley
contain	rapid	napkin	delay	praise
away	became	subway	escape	breakfast
poached	maybe	sailor	happy	drapes
graceful	canyon	planet	detail	essay

a-e   as in par**ade**

1. _____

2. _____

3. _____

4. _____

5. _____

ai   as in **fai**nt

6. _____

7. _____

8. _____

9. _____

10. _____

ay   as in tod**ay**

11. _____

12. _____

13. _____

14. _____

15. _____

Notes for Home: Your child wrote words in which *a*-consonant-*e*, *ai*, or *ay* stands for the long *a* vowel sound. **Home Activity:** Have your child cut out magazine or catalog pictures of things whose names have the long *a* vowel sound. Have your child sort the pictures according to the patterns that spell the long *a* sound: *a*-consonant-*e*, *ai*, *ay*.

The long _e_ vowel sound can be spelled _ee, ea, e,_ or _y._

qu**ee**n   l**ea**ves   mayb**e**   nois**y**

Use the letters and one of the long _e_ vowel patterns—_ee, ea, e,_ or _y_—to make a word that names each picture. Write the word.

1. w r t h

_____

2. m

_____

3. n d l e

_____

4. f i f t

_____

5. z b r a

_____

6. b v e r

_____

7. j n s

_____

8. g s e

_____

9. a s l p

_____

10. f e r r

_____

Notes for Home: Your child wrote words in which _ee, ea, e,_ or _y_ stands for the long _e_ vowel sound. **Home Activity:** Have your child circle the letters that stand for the long _e_ sound in each word he or she wrote on the page.

© Scott Foresman 4–6

The long *e* vowel sound can be spelled *ee, ea, e,* or *y.*

asl**ee**p   **ea**sy   **z**ebra   wind**y**

Write the word that goes with each clue and has the long *e* sound. Then circle the letter or letters that stand for the long *e* sound in the word.

contest	cereal	trees	promise	thirteen
between	empty	thanks	pants	middle
eggs	wheels	trophy	east	perhaps
bridge	leaves	maybe	circles	seesaw
please	ferry	open	insects	secret
poles	jeans	west	twelve	ball

1. floats from one side to the other   _____

2. comes as a pair   _____

3. not yes, not no   _____

4. something that squirrels like to climb   _____

5. comes after eleven   _____

6. one end goes up, one end goes down   _____

7. filled with nothing   _____

8. they go around and around   _____

9. often eaten for breakfast   _____

10. something you might win   _____

11. turn colors in the fall   _____

12. where the filling in a sandwich is   _____

13. not north or south   _____

14. something you must keep   _____

15. a nice thing to say   _____

Notes for Home: Your child wrote words with the *ee, ea, e,* and *y* patterns for the long *e* vowel sound. **Home Activity:** Have your child identify outdoor things whose names have the long *e* vowel patterns—*ee, ea, e, y.*

© Scott Foresman 4–6

The long *i* vowel sound can be spelled *i*-consonant-*e, ie, igh,* or *y.*

inv**ite**   tr**ie**d   fl**igh**t   repl**y**

Use the letters and one of the long *i* vowel patterns—*i*-consonant-*e, ie, igh,* or *y*—to make a word that names each picture. Write the word.

1. s t r p s

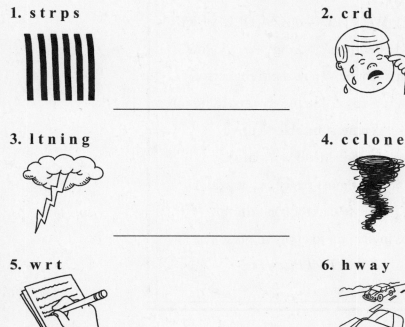

_____

2. c r d

_____

3. l t n i n g

_____

4. c c l o n e

_____

5. w r t

_____

6. h w a y

_____

7. u n t

_____

8. d i v d

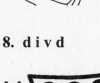

_____

9. s m l

_____

10. m u l t i p l

11×22

_____

Notes for Home: Your child wrote words in which *i*-consonant-*e, ie, igh,* or *y* stands for the long *i* vowel sound. **Home Activity:** Write *i*-consonant-*e, ie, igh,* and *y* on a sheet of paper and have your child write a word that has each pattern.

Name _____

The long *i* vowel sound can be spelled *i*-consonant-*e, ie, igh,* or *y.*

      wr**i**t**e**   un**tie**   br**igh**t   den**y**

Circle the long *i* words in the help wanted ad. Then write each word in the correct column below.

> HELP WANTED—PIZZA DELIVERY
> Tried other jobs? Boring? Pay too low?
> Then maybe you're the right person
> for this fun-filled and highly rewarding job.
> You must be able to drive
> and available to work nights,
> and you must really like pizza!
> If we can rely on you,
> we invite you to apply in person at
> *Love That Pizza Pie!*

Long *i* spelled *i-e*

1. _____

2. _____

3. _____

Long *i* spelled *igh*

4. _____

5. _____

6. _____

Long *i* spelled *y*

7. _____

8. _____

Long *i* spelled *ie*

9. _____

10. _____

Notes for Home: Your child wrote words in which *i*-consonant-*e, ie, igh,* or *y* stands for the long *i* vowel sound. **Home Activity:** Have your child look for long *i* words in the want ads in a newspaper. Try to find at least two words for each letter pattern—*i*-consonant-*e, ie, igh, y.*

The long *o* vowel sound can be spelled *o*-consonant-*e, oa, oe,* or *ow.*

| alone | co**a**st | t**oe** | yell**ow** |

Use the letters and one of the long *o* vowel patterns—*o*-consonant-*e, oa, oe,* or *ow*—to make a word that names each picture. Write the word.

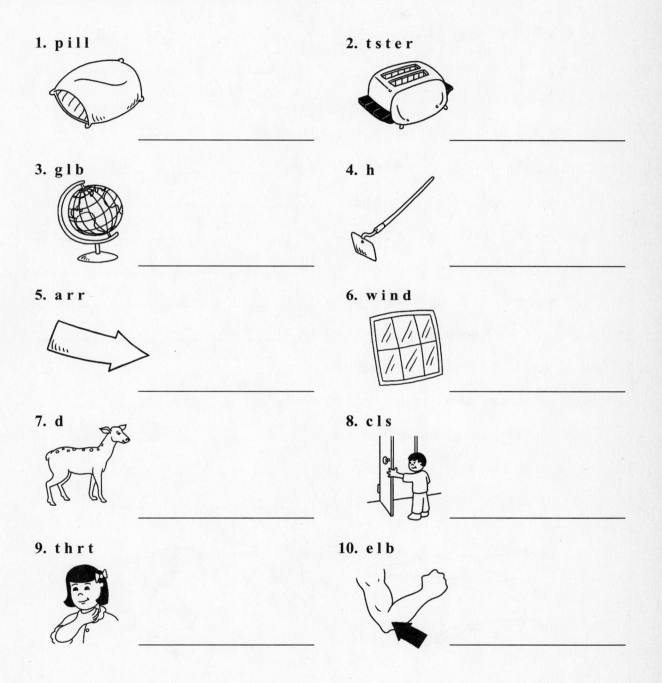

1. p i l l

_____

2. t s t e r

_____

3. g l b

_____

4. h

_____

5. a r r

_____

6. w i n d

_____

7. d

_____

8. c l s

_____

9. t h r t

_____

10. e l b

_____

Notes for Home: Your child wrote words in which *o*-consonant-*e, oa, oe,* or *ow* stands for the long *o* vowel sound. **Home Activity:** Have your child write a sentence using each long *o* word on the page.

Name _____

The long *o* vowel sound can be spelled *o*-consonant-*e*, *oa*, *oe*, or *ow*.

       gl**obe**   thr**oa**t   d**oe**   thr**ow**

Write the word with the long *o* sound in each sentence. Then circle the letters that stand for the long *o* sound.

1. The glow from the fire could be seen for miles. _____

2. Angelica's favorite flowers are roses. _____

3. Rodney turned the soil with a hoe. _____

4. Mrs. Ramirez cut the loaf into two portions. _____

5. The young man wrote a wonderful song. _____

6. Holly put the books on the lowest shelf. _____

7. The long road curved around the mountain. _____

8. I suppose I could ask everyone in town. _____

9. We know how to use the Internet properly. _____

10. Drive slowly past the school to see who is there. _____

11. Who forgot to put a stamp on the envelope? _____

12. Sonya used pink polish on her toenails. _____

13. That box isn't big enough for all those bottles. _____

14. Looking at his work made Monty groan. _____

15. Leon sailed the boat across the pond. _____

Notes for Home: Your child identified and wrote words in which *o*-consonant-*e*, *oa*, *oe*, or *ow* stands for the long *o* vowel sound. **Home Activity:** Have your child find long *o* words in an article in the travel section of a newspaper. Encourage your child to find one example for each long *o* pattern—*o*-consonant-*e*, *oa*, *oe*, *ow*.

Name _____

The long *u* vowel sound can be spelled *u*-consonant-*e* or *u*.

am**use**   p**u**pil

Use the letters and one of the long *u* vowel patterns—*u*-consonant-*e* or *u*—to make a word that names each picture. Write the word.

1. n i f o r m

_____

2. m e n

_____

3. c b

_____

4. b g l e

_____

5. f e l

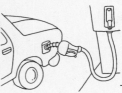

_____

6. m l

_____

7. r e f s

_____

8. c c u m b e r

_____

9. p e r f m

_____

10. m s i c

_____

Notes for Home: Your child wrote words in which *u*-consonant-*e* or *u* stands for the long *u* vowel sound. **Home Activity:** Help your child make a list of other long *u* words with the *u* and *u*-consonant-*e* spelling patterns.

Name _____

The long *u* vowel sound can be spelled *u*-consonant-*e* or *u*.

              use   **u**nit

In each set of words, circle the words that have the long *u* sound <u>*and*</u> the same pattern for the long *u* sound—*u-e* or *u*. Then use the circled words to complete the sentences.

1. reuse   rug   huge   2. mule   mouse   museum

3. suit   useful   menu   4. cute   cut   commute

5. perfume   true   amuse   6. sauce   universe   muse

7. mug   music   mule   8. blue   bugle   humid

9. fruit   future   refusal   10. applause   accuse   announce

11. I was so excited when a _____ whale surfaced near our boat.

12. Every day at sundown, a lone soldier blows a _____.

13. Austin's _____ to work takes him 45 minutes on the train.

14. When Anita said no, Joelle would not accept her _____.

15. The scent of strong _____ makes me sneeze.

16. Cars will be able to navigate themselves in the _____.

17. Houston is very hot and _____ in the summer.

18. Plastic containers are something you can _____ many times.

19. I wanted to take the _____ little puppy home with me.

20. It is hard to think of ways to _____ a small child.

Notes for Home: Your child identified and wrote words in which *u*-consonant-*e* or *u* stands for the long *u* vowel sound. **Home Activity:** Have your child look for long *u* words in a magazine or newspaper article. Check the words in a dictionary to make sure they are long *u* words.

Many words have this pattern of letters: consonant + vowel + consonant + *e* (CVCe). Usually the vowels in words with this pattern stand for the long vowel sounds.

CVCe	CVCe	CVCe	CVCe
f a c e	k i t e	n o t e	c u t e

Circle the word in each row that has the CVCe pattern. Then write the example word (*face, kite, note,* or *cute*) that has the same vowel sound as the circled word.

1. please   vase   best   _____

2. bread   time   rock   _____

3. mule   limb   mouse   _____

4. hoe   hop   hope   _____

5. need   nose   nail   _____

6. cage   curl   coal   _____

7. four   file   feet   _____

8. girl   goat   gate   _____

9. cube   crab   crib   _____

10. even   leave   five   _____

Notes for Home: Your child identified words with the consonant-vowel-consonant-*e* (CVCe) pattern. **Home Activity:** Write these word forms on a sheet of paper: __*a*__*e*, __*i*__*e*, __*o*__*e*, __*u*__*e*. Have your child add consonants to make words with the CVCe pattern.

These words have the consonant + vowel + consonant + *e*, or CVCe, pattern.

face	kite	note	cute

Write the CVCe word that names each picture. Then circle the letters that stand for the vowel sound.

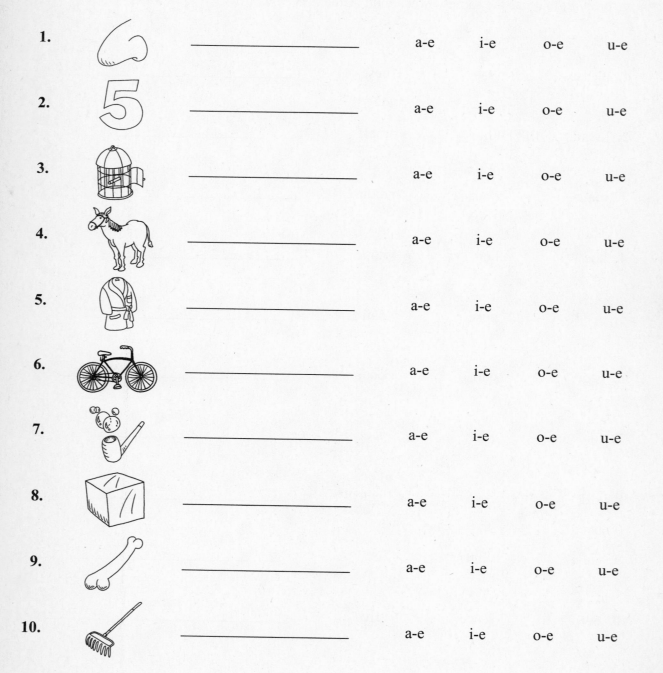

1. _____   a-e   i-e   o-e   u-e

2. _____   a-e   i-e   o-e   u-e

3. _____   a-e   i-e   o-e   u-e

4. _____   a-e   i-e   o-e   u-e

5. _____   a-e   i-e   o-e   u-e

6. _____   a-e   i-e   o-e   u-e

7. _____   a-e   i-e   o-e   u-e

8. _____   a-e   i-e   o-e   u-e

9. _____   a-e   i-e   o-e   u-e

10. _____   a-e   i-e   o-e   u-e

Notes for Home: Your child wrote words with the CVCe spelling pattern.
Home Activity: Have your child look through a newspaper article and highlight words that have the CVCe pattern.

© Scott Foresman 4–6

Name _____

These words have the consonant + vowel + consonant + *e*, or CVCe, pattern.

        take   kite   vote   cube

Find and write the CVCe word in each phrase.

1. wash your face   _____

2. cute pink slippers   _____

3. found the right size   _____

4. rode the horse   _____

5. choose a ripe pear   _____

6. huge grizzly bear   _____

7. a single red rose   _____

8. dig a large hole   _____

9. bake an apple pie   _____

10. lost the final game   _____

11. refuse to change seats   _____

12. ripped the note in half   _____

13. pleased to be alone   _____

14. invite a friend to stay   _____

15. follow the parade route   _____

Notes for Home: Your child identified and wrote words with the CVCe pattern.
Home Activity: Have your child write words that rhyme with some of the CVCe words he or she wrote on the page.

Name _____

Many words have this pattern of letters: vowel + consonant + consonant + vowel (VCCV). This pattern will help you divide the word into syllables.

V C C V
p i c / t u r e

V C C V
f o l / l o w

Underline the word with the VCCV pattern in each row. Then write the VCCV word and divide it into syllables.

1. soccer   shiver   _____

2. book   chapter   _____

3. after   above   _____

4. dollar   shape   _____

5. sandwich   picnic   _____

6. advice   heavy   _____

7. wheat   harvest   _____

8. daytime   evening   _____

9. butter   peanut   _____

10. atlas   thesaurus   _____

11. compete   comedy   _____

12. pilot   doctor   _____

13. summer   autumn   _____

14. salad   dessert   _____

15. ceiling   carpet   _____

Notes for Home: Your child identified syllables using the VCCV pattern in words.
Home Activity: Have your child find the VCCV pattern in the names of at least four sports or activities. Examples: tennis, basketball, swimming, soccer, stamp collecting.

These words have the vowel + consonant + consonant + vowel, or VCCV, pattern. This pattern will help you divide the words into syllables.

pic/ture   **fol/low**   **fif/te**en

Circle the words in the box that have the VCCV pattern.

patch	rabbit	classroom	carpet	wonder
debated	problem	situation	morning	cookie
signal	around	winter	closet	pepper
tomatoes	button	hamster	under	ready

Choose a circled word from above to complete each sentence. Write the word in syllables.

1. I was late for school this _____.

2. The _____ dug a burrow in our garden.

3. The traffic _____ changed from green to yellow.

4. I _____ why cats sleep so many hours a day.

5. Carol puts plenty of _____ in the sauce.

6. Angelo looked _____ the bed for his missing shoe.

7. They chose a gold _____ for the living room.

8. Erich goes cross-country skiing in the _____.

9. Does anyone know the answer to the fifth math _____?

10. I noticed that I had lost a _____ off my jacket.

Notes for Home: Your child identified and wrote words with the vowel + consonant + consonant + vowel (VCCV) pattern. **Home Activity:** Encourage your child to think of at least three household objects whose names contain the VCCV pattern. Examples: carpet, mirror, dresser, pillow.

© Scott Foresman 4-6

Name _____

The vowel digraphs *au* and *aw* stand for the vowel sound in these words.

s**au**cer   h**aw**k

Underline the words in the box that have the vowel sound you hear in *saucer* and *hawk*. Then write each underlined word under the picture whose name has the same pattern for the vowel sound.

fault	awful	drawn	aware	author
cruise	amuse	beauty	shawl	barrel
crawl	pause	shared	assume	applaud
audio	faucet	straw	because	lawn
awake	lawyer	waffle	laundry	music

1. _____

2. _____

3. _____

4. _____

5. _____

6. _____

7. _____

8. _____

9. _____

10. _____

11. _____

12. _____

13. _____

14. _____

15. _____

Notes for Home: Your child wrote words with the vowel digraphs *au* and *aw*.
Home Activity: Encourage your child to think of two more *au* and *aw* words and write them in sentences.

The vowel digraphs *al* and *all* stand for the vowel sound in these words.

almost   sm**all**

Fill in the oval by the word that completes each sentence and has the vowel sound in *small*. Write the word and circle the letters that stand for that vowel sound.

1. Iko used _____ to draw a picture.   _____
   ⬭ chalk   ⬭ charcoal

2. Morris puts _____ on his scrambled eggs.   _____
   ⬭ pepper   ⬭ salt

3. I can't _____ the ingredients I need for the stew.   _____
   ⬭ recall   ⬭ remember

4. We _____ like ice cream for dessert.   _____
   ⬭ also   ⬭ both

5. Michelle is several inches _____ than Stefan.   _____
   ⬭ shorter   ⬭ taller

6. On Saturdays Kara plays _____ with her friends.   _____
   ⬭ soccer   ⬭ baseball

7. They _____ on the phone last night.   _____
   ⬭ talked   ⬭ spoke

8. Dayna _____ new kitchen cabinets.   _____
   ⬭ built   ⬭ installed

9. Grandpa _____ wears a hat to keep his head warm.   _____
   ⬭ always   ⬭ sometimes

10. Our annual _____ averages only ten inches.   _____
   ⬭ rainfall   ⬭ precipitation

Notes for Home: Your child wrote words with the vowel digraphs *al* and *all*.
Home Activity: Have your child make a list of other words with the vowel digraphs *al* and *all*.

The vowel digraphs *au, aw, al,* and *all* stand for the vowel sound in these words.

author   **aw**ful   **al**most   sm**all**

Circle the words in the box that have the vowel sound you hear in *small*. Then combine each circled word with a word below to make a compound word. Write the compound word and circle the letters that stand for the vowel sound you hear in *small*.

law	blow	ball	walk	stand
tale	draw	auto	suit	fall
allow	straw	pull	saw	shallow
slaw	huge	chew	sauce	salad

1. water_____   _____

2. _____berry   _____

3. side_____   _____

4. _____graph   _____

5. cole_____   _____

6. _____suit   _____

7. _____pan   _____

8. basket_____   _____

9. _____bridge   _____

10. _____dust   _____

Notes for Home: Your child wrote words with the vowel digraphs *au, aw, al,* and *all*.
Home Activity: Have your child use each circled word in a sentence with another word that has the same pattern for the vowel sound.

© Scott Foresman 4–6

The vowel digraph *ea* can stand for the short *e* vowel sound.

feather

Write the letters *ea* to complete each word. Then write each word in the group where it belongs.

1. br_____d

2. sw_____ter

3. h_____d

4. br_____kfast

5. tr_____sure

6. dr_____dful

7. thr_____d

8. st_____dy

9. m_____sure

10. m_____dow

11. dinner, lunch, _____

12. needle, scissors, _____

13. shirt, pants, _____

14. muffins, rolls, _____

15. shoulders, neck, _____

16. wealth, riches, _____

17. weigh, estimate, _____

18. field, pasture, _____

19. terrible, awful, _____

20. regular, even, _____

Notes for Home: Your child wrote words in which *ea* stands for the short *e* vowel sound.
Home Activity: Have your child write groups of related words for the *ea* words *tread, wealth,* and *pleasant.*

Name _____

The vowel digraph *ea* can stand for the short *e* vowel sound.

br**ea**d   f**ea**ther

Write the word that completes the phrase and has the short *e* sound spelled *ea*.

fleece
1. a coat made of _____   leather

meadow
2. wildflowers growing in the _____   field

sweater
3. knitted a _____   vest

pleasing
4. spoke in a calm, _____ voice   steady

able
5. finally _____ to go   ready

breakfast
6. eggs and toast for _____   dinner

measure
7. use a ruler to _____   reach

jewels
8. a search for buried _____   treasure

pleasant
9. a mild, _____ day   peaceful

heavy
10. a very _____ suitcase   empty

Notes for Home: Your child wrote words in which *ea* stands for the short *e* vowel sound.
Home Activity: In a five-minute time period, have your child list as many words as possible
that rhyme with *head*.

Name _____

The vowel digraphs *ie* and *ei* can stand for the long *e* sound.

p**ie**ce   c**ei**ling

Circle the word in each phrase in which *ie* or *ei* stands for the long *e* sound. Then write each circled word under the picture whose name has the same pattern for the long *e* sound.

1. not nice to deceive people

2. a belief in myself

3. a knight's sword and shield

4. a gleeful shriek of surprise

5. too conceited to see reality

6. need a receipt to return the present

7. seized the beagle's leash

8. a beautiful green field

9. the greedy leader of the thieves

10. a favorite leisure activity

11. _____

16. _____

12. _____

17. _____

13. _____

18. _____

14. _____

19. _____

15. _____

20. _____

Notes for Home: Your child wrote words in which *ie* and *ei* stand for the long *e* vowel sound.
Home Activity: Have your child choose two or more *ie* or *ei* words from the page and write them together in a sentence.

The vowel digraphs *ie* and *ei* can stand for the long *e* sound.

field   **cei**ling

Underline the words in the box that have the long *e* sound spelled *ie* or *ei*. Then write the underlined words to complete the sentences.

brief	receive	seized	greed	relief
succeed	media	agree	receipt	these
speak	believes	legal	repeat	deceived
leisure	sweet	shield	niece	beige

1. A knight carried a sword and a _____ into battle.

2. My little sister _____ in the tooth fairy.

3. You need a _____ to get a refund from the store.

4. Many people are _____ by get-rich-quick schemes.

5. I visited my _____ and nephew in Chicago.

6. David _____ the barking dog by its collar.

7. Flo wrote a _____ one-paragraph summary of the story.

8. Did you _____ the letter I sent you last week?

9. My favorite _____ activities are reading and tap dancing.

10. It was a _____ to see the train had not yet left.

Notes for Home: Your child wrote words in which *ie* and *ei* stand for the long *e* vowel sound. **Home Activity:** Have your child sort the circled words on the page according to the vowel pattern that spells the long *e* sound.

The vowel digraphs *ew, ui,* and *ue* stand for the vowel sound in these

           gr**ew**   s**ui**t

Circle the letters in each word that stand for the vowel sound you he
words to answer the clues.

cruise	flew	threw	chew	
blue	drew	bruise	juice	fruit

1. color of the sky _____

2. trip on a boat _____

3. something to drink _____

4. apple or banana _____

5. not false _____

6. use your teeth for this _____

7. injury to the body _____

8. what the artist did _____

9. what the pitcher did to the ball _____

10. what a bird did _____

Notes for Home: Your child wrote words with the vowel digraphs *ew, ui,* and *ue.*
Home Activity: Have your child choose five words from the page and write a story using
them.

© Scott Foresman 4-6

_____

...igraphs *ew, ui,* and *ue* stand for the vowel sound in *threw, bruise,* and *glue.*

...e the word or words in each book title that have the same vowel sound as *threw, bruise,* ...ue. Write the word or words and circle the letters that stand for the vowel sound in *threw,* ...se, and *glue.*

1. Someone Stole the Queen's Jewelry

_____

2. Mr. Fix-It and His Magic Screwdrivers

_____

3. The Crew of the Haunted Cruise Ship

_____

4. The Clue to the Missing Jewels

_____

5. True Tales About Fabulous Fruit

_____

6. The Night the Wind Blew the Lights Out

_____

7. The Knight Slew Seven Dragons

_____

8. Stewart Seton's Secret Stew

_____

9. The Stranger in the Blue Suit

_____

10. The Man Drew a Line in the Sand

_____

Notes for Home: Your child wrote words with the vowel digraphs *ew, ui,* and *ue.*
Home Activity: Have your child write clues for five words on the page for you to answer.
Then write clues for your child to answer.

Choose the word that has the same vowel sound as *threw, bruise,* and *true*. Write the word to complete the sentence.

1. Moss _____ under the shady tree.

   grew   ground   died

2. A diamond is a precious _____.

   jelly   jewel   gem

3. Dave wore his new _____ to the graduation ceremony.

   sure   shirt   suit

4. The artist _____ a picture of the sunset.

   painted   drew   dream

5. We enjoyed our _____ through the Panama Canal.

   cruise   coast   trip

6. The dog likes to _____ on old slippers.

   choke   chew   chow

7. Kelly _____ the candles out after dinner.

   blew   lit   put

8. Oranges are Oscar's favorite _____.

   flavor   fruit   taste

9. Rosa used _____ to reattach the cup's handle.

   look   glue   paste

10. On a warm spring day the sky can be clear and _____.

   blue   bright   bluff

 Notes for Home: Your child wrote words with the vowel digraphs *ew, ui,* and *ue*.
Home Activity: Challenge your child to think of five words that rhyme with words he or she wrote on the page.

Name _____

The vowel digraph _oo_ stands for the vowel sound in these words.

w**oo**d   s**oo**t

Add the vowel digraph _oo_ to each word in the box. Then write the words to answer the clues.

l___k	st___d	h___k	cr___ked	c___kies
c___k	f___t	b___k	t___k	sh___k
g___d	cr___k	h___d	w___den	br___k

1. opposite of _bad_   _____

2. something to read   _____

3. moved quickly up and down   _____

4. past tense of _stand_   _____

5. at the end of your leg   _____

6. head covering   _____

7. a small stream   _____

8. prepare food   _____

9. to see   _____

10. sweet treats   _____

11. a criminal   _____

12. past tense of _take_   _____

13. not straight   _____

14. made of wood   _____

15. a place to hang things   _____

Notes for Home: Your child wrote words in which the vowel digraph _oo_ stands for the vowel sound in _wood_. **Home Activity:** Have your child write a phrase using each _oo_ word on the page.

Name _____

The vowel digraph *oo* stands for the vowel sound in *foot*.

Choose the word that has the same vowel sound as *foot*. Write the word to complete the sentence.

1. Janet hung her coat on the _____ in the closet.

   hoop   hook   hanger

2. The restaurant's food improved when the new _____ took over.

   cook   clock   chef

3. The author's first _____ made the best-seller list.

   bloom   novel   book

4. We _____ a walk through the nature preserve.

   troop   took   found

5. The girls waded across the _____.

   pool   brook   bloom

6. Do you think Liz _____ the instructions?

   understand   thought   understood

7. An icy drink tastes _____ on a hot summer day.

   cold   good   poor

8. My friends _____ in line to get concert tickets.

   stop   stoop   stood

9. We have a _____ floor in our kitchen.

   wood   tile   cool

10. My winter jacket has a _____.

    kangaroo   hat   hood

Notes for Home: Your child wrote words in which the vowel digraph *oo* stands for the vowel sound in *foot*. **Home Activity:** Have your child make two lists of rhyming words from the page.

Write the words from the box to complete the puzzle.

wooden	book	stood	cook	took
shook	hook	look	woodpecker	crook

Down

1. see
2. quivered
3. made of lumber
4. grasped; seized
7. dishonest person

Across

5. remained upright
6. small peg
7. chef
8. noisy bird
9. something to read

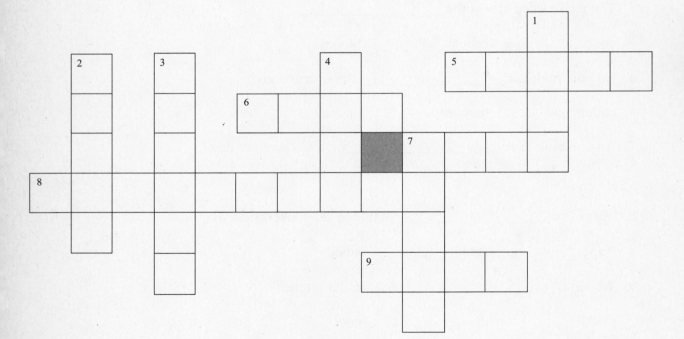

Notes for Home: Your child wrote words in which the vowel digraph *oo* stands for the vowel sound in *foot*. **Home Activity:** Have your child make up riddles for the words *brook, foot, hood,* and *wood.*

The vowel digraph *oo* stands for the vowel sound in these words.

m**oo**n   b**oo**t

Add the vowel digraph *oo* to each word in the box. Then write the words to answer the clues.

br____m	gr____m	st____l	m____se	g____se
sp____n	p____dle	cab____se	p____l	ch____se
l____se	n____dle	bamb____	f____l	racc____n

1. place to swim   _____

2. tool for eating   _____

3. something to sit on   _____

4. animal with a mask   _____

5. opposite of *bride*   _____

6. used for sweeping   _____

7. kind of dog   _____

8. opposite of *tight*   _____

9. animal with webbed feet _____

10. pick   _____

11. food for a panda   _____

12. silly person   _____

13. end of a train   _____

14. one pasta shape   _____

15. animal with antlers   _____

Notes for Home: Your child wrote words in which the vowel digraph *oo* stands for the vowel sound in *moon*. **Home Activity:** Have your child use rhyming words from the page to write a poem.

Name _____

The vowel digraph *oo* stands for the vowel sound in *moon*.

Choose the word that has the same vowel sound as *moon*. Write the word to complete the sentence.

1. The flowers began to _____ because they needed water.

   drip   droop   drown

2. The butterfly emerged from its _____.

   cocoon   coat   cook

3. The _____ of an owl pierced the silence of the evening.

   howl   hoot   hook

4. The class picnic began at _____.

   nine   noun   noon

5. I laughed out loud when I read the _____.

   carton   cartoon   cookbook

6. Can you give me a _____ over the fence?

   bound   boost   both

7. The _____ is Earth's only natural satellite.

   mouth   morning   moon

8. Will Rose _____ the movie we will see?

   chose   choose   choke

9. A _____ carries its baby in a pouch.

   kangaroo   crook   moth

10. The clown gave a bunch of _____ to the child.

    popcorn   boats   balloons

 Notes for Home: Your child wrote words in which the vowel digraph *oo* stands for the vowel sound in *moon*. **Home Activity:** Challenge your child to create a bumper sticker using *oo* words from the page.

Write the words in each sentence that have the same vowel sound as *moon*.

1. Every room in our school has a computer.

   _____

2. The cowboy looped the rope loosely over his saddle horn.

   _____

3. Noodles with vegetables are her favorite food.

   _____

4. Artists sold their crafts at booths from noon until 3 P.M.

   _____

5. It was too cool to swim in the pond today.

   _____

6. The carpenter used a special tool to make a groove in the wood.

   _____

7. My little brother has a loose tooth.

   _____

8. Will the troops get boots and uniforms?

   _____

9. After she shampoos her hair, it feels clean and smooth.

   _____

10. Use a spoon to scoop the ice cream into the bowl.

   _____

Notes for Home: Your child wrote words in which the vowel digraph *oo* stands for the vowel sound in *moon*. **Home Activity:** Ask your child to think of five other words with the same vowel sound and spelling as *moon* and use each one in a sentence.

The vowel digraph *oo* stands for the vowel sounds in these words.

sh**oo**t   st**oo**d

Say the first word in the row. Circle the word or words in the row that have the same vowel sound as the first word.

1. boot	moose	took	rooster
2. cookout	goose	hood	soothe
3. raccoon	drool	zoo	woodpecker
4. good	book	soon	rook
5. trooper	choose	spoof	crook
6. school	harpoon	hook	noose
7. wooden	brook	pool	foot
8. food	cocoon	nook	noon
9. bamboo	balloon	kangaroo	woodwork
10. took	boot	tool	look
11. proof	cool	croon	cook
12. tooth	tycoon	tool	took
13. hook	cookies	brook	cool
14. loom	pool	shampoo	stood
15. snooze	shook	smooth	spool

Notes for Home: Your child wrote words with the vowel digraph *oo*.
Home Activity: Have your child write sentences using one word with the same vowel sound as *shoot* and one word with the same vowel sound as *stood* in each sentence.

The vowel digraph *oo* stands for the vowel sounds in *too* and *book*.

Choose a word from the list that has the same vowel sound as the underlined word. Write the word to complete the sentence.

cookies	maroon	wooden	brood	good
raccoon	noon	hooks	stood	tooth
noodles	hood	typhoon	room	gloomy

1. Luis <u>took</u> a batch of freshly baked _____ to the party.

2. We _____ at the edge of the <u>brook</u>.

3. The _____ raided the garbage cans looking for <u>food</u>.

4. The <u>goose</u> led her _____ to the pond.

5. The <u>cook</u> hung the pots from _____ in the kitchen.

6. Don't <u>snoop</u> through the stuff in my _____!

7. Did you <u>choose</u> _____ or tacos for dinner?

8. The dentist used a special <u>tool</u> to pull my _____.

9. The <u>crook</u> wore a black _____ over his head.

10. <u>School</u> was let out at _____ because of the snowstorm.

11. The weather in April is often <u>cool</u> and _____.

12. I <u>mistook</u> the _____ duck for a real one!

13. The <u>balloons</u> were colored blue and _____.

14. The <u>booklet</u> had a _____ recipe for beef and bean stew.

15. Only a <u>fool</u> would go out in a _____.

Notes for Home: Your child wrote words with the vowel digraph *oo*.
Home Activity: Challenge your child to make lists of other words that have the same vowel sounds as *too* and *book*.

Replace the underlined word with a word that has the same vowel sound and makes sense in the sentence. Write the word.

cookbook	cool	lookout	trooper	woodpecker
pool	footsteps	rooster	kangaroos	crook
groom	spools	mood	gloomy	shook

1. The dog barked when it heard <u>woodwork</u>.   _____

2. Paul <u>took</u> hands with the president.   _____

3. The <u>goose</u> wore a black tuxedo to the wedding.   _____

4. It is too <u>smooth</u> to go swimming today.   _____

5. A <u>cook</u> uses its beak to drill into trees.   _____

6. The <u>raccoon</u> crowed each morning at dawn.   _____

7. The police surrounded the house and caught the <u>foot</u>.   _____

8. The tailor has several <u>stools</u> of thread in his sewing kit.   _____

9. The lifeguard watched the swimmers in the <u>room</u>.   _____

10. The state <u>groom</u> stopped the speeding driver.   _____

11. The rain made the day dark and <u>blooming</u>.   _____

12. The famous chef published a <u>fishhook</u>.   _____

13. The crowd was in a cheerful <u>proof</u>.   _____

14. In summer watchers keep a <u>football</u> for fires.   _____

15. <u>Balloons</u> have strong hind legs and tails.   _____

Notes for Home: Your child wrote words with the vowel digraph *oo*.
Home Activity: Have your child look through a newspaper to find other words with the vowel digraph *oo*. Ask your child to circle the *oo* words with the same vowel sound as *good* and to underline the *oo* words with the same vowel sound as *loose*.

Use words with the vowel digraph *oo* to complete the puzzle. The words you write across will have the same vowel sound as *moon*. The words you write down will have the same vowel sound as *wood*.

Down

1. stream

2. see

3. dishonest person

5. curved piece of metal

6. prepare food

Across

1. kind of footwear

2. used for weaving

4. masked animal

5. spear used for fishing

6. funny drawing

Notes for Home: Your child wrote words with the vowel digraph *oo*.
Home Activity: Help your child make a crossword puzzle using the words *balloon, bamboo, caboose, moon, shampoo, cookies, foot, good, took,* and *shook*.

Name _____

The vowel diphthongs *ou* and *ow* stand for the vowel sound in these words.

sound   **tow**n

Underline the letters that stand for the vowel sound in each word. Write the word next to its meaning.

frown	count	loud	gown	now
south	out	down	growl	brown
ground	crouch	mouth	round	crowd

1. name numbers in order   _____

2. dark color   _____

3. many people   _____

4. not then   _____

5. opposite of *smile*   _____

6. soil   _____

7. fancy dress   _____

8. part of a face   _____

9. stoop low   _____

10. opposite of *in*   _____

11. circular   _____

12. not quiet   _____

13. opposite of *north*   _____

14. a low, angry sound   _____

15. opposite of *up*   _____

Notes for Home: Your child wrote words with the vowel diphthongs *ou* and *ow*.
Home Activity: Have your child list four pairs of *ou* and *ow* words that rhyme.

The vowel diphthongs *ou* and *ow* stand for the vowel sound in *out* and *down*.

Underline the letters in each word that stand for the vowel sound you hear in *out*. Write the word that best completes each sentence.

1. The watchdog will _____ at strangers.

    shout   growl

2. Tulips are her favorite _____.

    flowers   fouls

3. A quick _____ will cool you off on a hot day.

    pound   shower

4. Throw a penny into the _____ for good luck.

    fountain   crowd

5. My brother fell asleep on the _____.

    towel   couch

6. Jay is _____ of his science project.

    proud   howl

7. There are sixteen _____ in a pound.

    ounces   owls

8. The laundry room is _____ in the basement.

    round   downstairs

9. Early in spring, the farmer will _____ the fields.

    plow   bounce

10. The cook added bean _____ to the salad.

    chowder   sprouts

Notes for Home: Your child wrote words with the vowel diphthongs *ou* and *ow*.
Home Activity: Have your child write sentences using the *ou* and *ow* words that were *not* written on the page.

Name _____   **Vowel Diphthongs *ou, ow***

The vowel diphthongs *ou* and *ow* stand for the vowel sound in *pound* and *frown*.

Underline the two words in each sentence with the vowel sound you hear in *pound*. Write each underlined word under the correct heading.

1. Charlie made clam chowder for the crowd at the party.
2. Is the new couch brown?
3. Rita's science report is about owls.
4. It's scary to encounter a growling dog.
5. Snow-covered mountains surround the village.
6. Cloudy days make me feel drowsy.
7. She was proud of the trout that she caught.
8. The cowboy rode slowly into town.
9. *Boat* has the same vowel sound as *road*.
10. After the storm, the power was out for a while.

/ow/ spelled *ou*	**/ow/ spelled *ow***
11. _____	21. _____
12. _____	22. _____
13. _____	23. _____
14. _____	24. _____
15. _____	25. _____
16. _____	26. _____
17. _____	27. _____
18. _____	28. _____
19. _____	29. _____
20. _____	30. _____

Notes for Home: Your child wrote words with the vowel diphthongs *ou* and *ow*.
Home Activity: Have your child write a poem using either *ou* or *ow* words.

Write the word that answers the riddle. Circle the letters that stand for the vowel sound you hear in *out*.

pout	crown	blouse	scout	south
eyebrow	clown	clouds	now	cowboy
trout	sundown	house	gown	thousand

1. What is something a king wears? _____

2. Which direction is opposite north? _____

3. Which person makes other people laugh? _____

4. What is a woman's shirt sometimes called? _____

5. What is located over the eye? _____

6. What is a freshwater fish? _____

7. Which person looks after cattle on a ranch? _____

8. Which person is sent ahead to get information? _____

9. What might a woman wear to a fancy party? _____

10. What word means "at this time"? _____

11. What is a place to live? _____

12. What is a large number? _____

13. What is another name for *sunset*? _____

14. Where does rain come from? _____

15. What is something an unhappy child does? _____

Notes for Home: Your child wrote words with the vowel diphthongs *ou* and *ow*.
Home Activity: Have your child write riddles for the following words: *hound, pouch, mouse, county, powder, flower, scowl.*

© Scott Foresman 4-6

Name _____

Replace the underlined word with a word that has the same vowel sound with the same spelling and makes sense in the sentence. Write the word.

brown	doubt	foul	allowed	loud
power	found	announced	county	proud
shower	mouse	powder	trowel	plow

1. Lee <u>cloud</u> his backpack in a corner of the closet. _____

2. Betty has long <u>down</u> hair. _____

3. It was impossible to talk over the <u>round</u> music. _____

4. A <u>noun</u> can hear well but has poor vision. _____

5. A <u>brow</u> cuts the soil and turns it over. _____

6. Congress has the <u>towel</u> to declare war. _____

7. Most people in the <u>fountain</u> voted for new roads. _____

8. He took a <u>crown</u> after exercising. _____

9. Are you <u>stout</u> to be an American citizen? _____

10. The batter hit a <u>south</u> ball to left field. _____

11. I <u>couch</u> whether they will be on time. _____

12. The store <u>amounted</u> it was having a sale. _____

13. Did you put chili <u>flower</u> in the soup? _____

14. She left the <u>scowl</u> in the flowerbed. _____

15. No dogs are <u>plowed</u> in the restaurant. _____

Notes for Home: Your child wrote words with the vowel diphthongs *ou* and *ow*.
Home Activity: Have your child write a phrase using each underlined word on the page.

Name _____

The vowel diphthongs *oi* and *oy* stand for the vowel sound in these words.

so**il**   **j**oy

In each word in the box, underline the letters that stand for the vowel sound you hear in *joy*. Then write the words next to their meanings.

join	avoid	boy	toy	disappoint
oyster	choice	loyal	boil	enjoy
voice	coin	voyage	ointment	spoil

1. opposite of *girl*   _____

2. selection   _____

3. penny, dime, or quarter   _____

4. bubble up, give off steam   _____

5. have fun with   _____

6. stay away from   _____

7. sound made through the mouth   _____

8. faithful   _____

9. make unfit or useless   _____

10. soothing skin cream   _____

11. an ocean animal   _____

12. plaything   _____

13. fail to please   _____

14. long trip   _____

15. bring together   _____

Notes for Home: Your child wrote words with the vowel diphthongs *oi* and *oy*.
Home Activity: Have your child write ten phrases using *oi* and *oy* words from the page.

The vowel diphthongs *oi* and *oy* stand for the vowel sound in *oil* and *joy*.

Write the word that completes the sentence and has the vowel sound you hear in *joy*.

1. The ankle is the _____ that connects the foot with the leg.

   bone   joint

2. Does your neighbor's loud music _____ you?

   annoy   bother

3. Pasta is Megan's _____ for dinner.

   food   choice

4. A _____ delivers our newspaper each morning.

   reporter   paperboy

5. He added fertilizer to the _____ to make the plants grow.

   ground   soil

6. Did you _____ your trip to San Francisco?

   enjoy   encounter

7. The king and queen lived in the _____ palace.

   royal   regal

8. Some household cleaners contain _____.

   perfume   poison

9. There was a _____ of rope in the bow of the boat.

   noose   coil

10. The hunter used a _____ to lure the animal into the trap.

    decoy   disguise

Notes for Home: Your child wrote words with the vowel diphthongs *oi* and *oy*.
Home Activity: Have your child look through a newspaper to find and highlight *oi* and *oy* words.

The vowel diphthongs *oi* and *oy* stand for the vowel sound in *soil* and *joy*.

Underline the word or words in each sentence that have the vowel sound you hear in *joy*. Then write each underlined word under the correct heading.

1. Dogs are loyal to their owners.

2. The spring rains brought needed moisture to the soil.

3. The crowd was too noisy and loud.

4. A high-pitched voice makes an annoying sound.

5. The boy toils in the fields with the farmer.

6. Joan enjoyed the journey home.

7. You won't be disappointed in the show.

8. Is Tom employed as a paperboy?

9. The boat moved to the right to avoid the rocks.

10. Will you join us on the voyage to the islands?

/oi/ spelled *oi*	**/oi/ spelled** *oy*
11. _____	19. _____
12. _____	20. _____
13. _____	21. _____
14. _____	22. _____
15. _____	23. _____
16. _____	24. _____
17. _____	25. _____
18. _____	

Notes for Home: Your child wrote words with the vowel diphthongs *oi* and *oy*.
Home Activity: Have your child choose three words on the page and make a list of words that rhyme with each one.

Circle the word or words that have the same vowel sound as the underlined word. Then write the letters that stand for that vowel sound.

1. The cook <u>spoiled</u> the soup by adding too much salt.

boil   boat   loiter   _____

2. He is lucky to have such <u>loyal</u> friends.

convoy   phone   foyer   _____

3. Pearls are formed inside the shell of an <u>oyster</u>.

onion   coy   annoy   _____

4. Dolores decided to <u>join</u> the debate team.

oil   couch   coil   _____

5. The skater was <u>disappointed</u> when she lost the competition.

rejoiced   moist   told   _____

6. The <u>Boy</u> Scouts sponsored their annual paper drive.

employ   bone   ahoy   _____

7. The nurse put <u>ointment</u> on the patient's cut.

paint   poison   noise   _____

8. The tornado <u>destroyed</u> several buildings in the business district.

boy   choose   decoy   _____

9. The yo-yo is a <u>toy</u> that appeals to people of all ages.

joy   tool   royal   _____

10. We will <u>avoid</u> the traffic by taking a detour.

door   coin   poise   _____

Notes for Home: Your child identified words with the vowel sound in *joy*.
Home Activity: Have your child choose a sentence from the page and write a story that begins with the sentence.

Write the word that answers the riddle. Circle the letters that stand for the vowel sound you hear in *joy*.

oily	coin	royal	noise	soybean
ahoy	enjoy	convoy	annoy	oyster
broil	avoid	point	loyal	join

1. What is a protein-rich food?   _____

2. What are loud sounds?   _____

3. What word means "bring together"?   _____

4. What is a sailor's cry?   _____

5. What word describes kings and queens?   _____

6. What word means "soaked with oil"?   _____

7. What word means "disturb or trouble"?   _____

8. What is a piece of metal money?   _____

9. What word means "stay away from"?   _____

10. What is a kind of shellfish?   _____

11. What word describes a way to cook?   _____

12. What word means "like, be happy with"?   _____

13. What word describes a good friend?   _____

14. What is a sharp end?   _____

15. What is a fleet of trucks that carries supplies? _____

Notes for Home: Your child wrote words with the vowel diphthongs *oi* and *oy*.
Home Activity: Have your child write riddles for the following words: *voice, ointment, poise, destroy, cowboy, joy.*

Name _____

In the consonant combinations *kn* and *gn*, two letters stand for only one sound. One letter is silent. Say these words.

        knee   The letter *k* is silent.

        si**gn**   The letter *g* is silent.

Write *kn* or *gn* to complete the word in each sentence. Then draw a line through the letter in the combination that you do not hear.

1. The sharp _____ife can cut the bread easily.

2. Dana's knees hurt from _____eeling in the garden to plant flowers.

3. Carlos wants to be a web page desi_____er.

4. Mei Lei learned to _____it a sweater in crafts class.

5. Oscar wrote the homework assi_____ment in his notebook.

6. The sailor tied two ropes together using a strong _____ot.

7. The baker will _____ead the dough with her hands.

8. The beaver used its strong teeth to _____aw through the log.

9. I _____ow I will remember where I put my keys if I just concentrate!

10. After the accident, the mechanic had to ali_____ the tires on the car.

11. Sir Lancelot was the bravest of the _____ights in Camelot.

12. The man flapped his hat at the _____ats swarming around his face.

13. Ravi tried to cram six books into his _____apsack.

14. I really thought I _____ew the answer to that question.

15. The politician hoped her campai_____ would help her win the election.

 Notes for Home: Your child completed words with the consonant combinations *kn* and *gn* in which one consonant is silent. **Home Activity:** Have your child spell each *kn* or *gn* word on the page using a hand signal such as a clap or a thumbs-down in place of the silent consonant in each word.

In the word *knee*, the *k* is silent.
In the word *sign*, the *g* is silent.

Circle *kn* or *gn* in each word. Then write the letter that you hear in the combination.

1. k n e e l e d _____   2. g n a t s _____

3. k n i g h t _____   4. d e s i g n _____

5. k n u c k l e s _____   6. r e i g n _____

7. a s s i g n s _____   8. k n e w _____

9. g n a r l e d _____   10. k n a p s a c k _____

• The letter that you hear in the consonant combinations in these words is _____.

Using the words above, write a word to complete each sentence.

11. The carpenter scraped his _____ on the rough board.

12. A graphic artist was hired to _____ a new catalog cover.

13. Rebecca packed her _____ for the long hike.

14. The young queen will _____ over the country for her lifetime.

15. Paco immediately raised his hand because he _____ the answer.

16. The branches of the old tree were twisted and _____.

17. Our teacher _____ thirty minutes of reading each night.

18. The tiny _____, like mosquitoes, swarmed around us at the beach.

19. Ava _____ down to talk to the small child.

20. In the story, the _____ fought a ferocious dragon.

Notes for Home: Your child wrote words with the consonant combinations *kn* and *gn* in which one consonant is silent. **Home Activity:** Spend some time with your child looking in the dictionary for words beginning with *kn* and *gn*. Discuss the words that you find.

Name _____

In the consonant combinations *wr* and *mb*, two letters stand for only one sound. One letter is silent. Say these words.

wren   The letter *w* is silent.
co**mb**   The letter *b* is silent.

Write *wr* or *mb* to complete the word in each phrase. Then draw a line through the letter in the combination that you do not hear.

1. cli_____ing a sheer rock face

2. a ram, a ewe, and a la_____

3. _____ist support at the computer keyboard

4. a baby noisily sucking her thu_____

5. nothing but cru_____s left from the cake

6. _____apped in colorful paper and ribbon

7. a _____eath of flowers and vines on the door

8. neat and legible hand_____iting

9. clogged pipes in the plu_____ing

10. _____inkled from being packed in a suitcase

Write each word above under the picture name that has the same consonant combination.

11. _____   16. _____

12. _____   17. _____

13. _____   18. _____

14. _____   19. _____

15. _____   20. _____

Notes for Home: Your child completed and sorted words with the consonant combinations *wr* and *mb* in which one consonant is silent. **Home Activity:** Have your child think of at least four objects whose names have the consonant combinations *wr* and *mb*. Ask your child which letter he or she hears and which letter is silent in each name.

In the word *wren*, the *w* is silent.
In the word *comb*, the *b* is silent.

Circle *wr* or *mb* in each word. Then write the letter that you hear in the combination.

1. w r i t e r _____

2. w r o n g _____

3. n u m b _____

4. w r e n c h _____

5. w r e a t h _____

6. l a m b _____

7. l i m b _____

8. w r i n g _____

9. w r i s t w a t c h _____

10. t o m b s t o n e _____

Using the words above, write each word next to its definition.

11. not right, incorrect _____

12. a person who is an author _____

13. a young sheep _____

14. a leg, an arm, a wing; a large tree branch _____

15. a timepiece worn on the arm just above the hand _____

16. to twist by force; to squeeze out _____

17. a stone that marks a grave _____

18. a tool to hold and turn nuts, bolts, and pipes _____

19. a ring of flowers or leaves twisted together _____

20. having lost the power to feel; deadened _____

Notes for Home: Your child wrote words with the consonant combinations *wr* and *mb* in which one consonant is silent. **Home Activity:** Take turns with your child trying to make up the longest sentence that makes sense using as many *mb* and *wr* words as you can. Start with a short sentence and add on words.

Name _____

In the consonant combinations *kn, gn, wr,* and *mb,* two letters stand for only one sound. One letter is silent.

knee   si**gn**   **wr**en   co**mb**

Circle the words in which *kn, gn, wr,* and *mb* stand for only one sound. Then write each circled word to answer a clue.

climbing	sickness	assign	knotted	gnaw
number	crumble	wrong	signature	numb
wrench	signal	darkness	symbol	dignity
dowry	known	crumbs	design	newborn

1. give someone a job to do   _____

2. tangled and snarled   _____

3. what a dog does to a bone   _____

4. not right   _____

5. too cold to feel anything   _____

6. going up a steep hill   _____

7. a tool used to tighten things   _____

8. bits or pieces of something   _____

9. familiar to everyone   _____

10. a plan or sketch used as a pattern   _____

Notes for Home: Your child wrote words with the consonant combinations *kn, gn, wr,* and *mb.* **Home Activity:** Ask your child to explain to you why he or she did not circle the other words in the box on the page.

© Scott Foresman 4-6

The consonant *c* can stand for two different sounds.

coat   *c* = /k/   **c**ity   *c* = /s/

Write each word in the list under the word in which *c* stands for the same sound.

celebrate	spicy	escalator	collar	discovered
compass	cents	cast	peaceful	sauce

coat   **city**

1. _____   6. _____

2. _____   7. _____

3. _____   8. _____

4. _____   9. _____

5. _____   10. _____

Use the words above to complete the sentences.

11. Tami's broken arm was in a _____ for eight weeks.

12. Hector always irons the _____ of his shirt last.

13. Rebecca paid eighty-five _____ for the fancy pencil.

14. The soldier used a _____ to find his way north.

15. Aunt Sue puts too much pepper in her spaghetti _____.

16. The baby looked _____ as he slept.

17. Keesha _____ a letter hidden in an old trunk.

18. We _____ New Year's Eve on December 31.

19. Kaj and I took the _____ to the second level of the mall.

20. Jalapeño peppers make the salsa very _____.

Notes for Home: Your child identified and wrote words in which the consonant *c* stands for /k/ or /s/. **Home Activity:** Write ten words in which *c* stands for /k/ or /s/ on index cards. Shuffle the cards. Have your child sort them into two piles according to the sound *c* stands for.

Name _____

When the consonant *c* is followed by the vowel *a, o,* or *u,* the *c* usually stands for /k/.

        cape   **c**one   **c**ube

When the consonant *c* is followed by the vowel *e* or *i,* the *c* usually stands for /s/.

        cent   **c**ity

Write the words in each phrase in which *c* stands for /k/ or /s/. Circle the sound *c* stands for in each word.

1. decided to eat in the cafeteria

   _____ /k/ /s/   _____ /k/ /s/

2. was excited to receive the surprise gift

   _____ /k/ /s/   _____ /k/ /s/

3. cooked oatmeal cereal for breakfast

   _____ /k/ /s/   _____ /k/ /s/

4. tried not to panic during the hurricane

   _____ /k/ /s/   _____ /k/ /s/

5. followed the curve around the corner

   _____ /k/ /s/   _____ /k/ /s/

6. add carrots and celery to the soup

   _____ /k/ /s/   _____ /k/ /s/

7. used a comb to curl the doll's hair

   _____ /k/ /s/   _____ /k/ /s/

8. danced to the music

   _____ /k/ /s/   _____ /k/ /s/

9. skidded on the icy surface

   _____ /k/ /s/   _____ /k/ /s/

10. planned the ceremony months in advance

    _____ /k/ /s/   _____ /k/ /s/

Notes for Home: Your child wrote words in which the consonant *c* stands for /k/ or /s/.
Home Activity: Challenge your child to think of a word pair for a category. One word must
have *c* with /k/ and the other must have *c* with /s/. Example: for the category *animals, cow*
and *rhinoceros.*

Name _____

The consonant *g* can stand for two different sounds.

goat   **g** = /g/   gem   **g** = /j/

Write each word in the list under the word in which *g* stands for the same sound.

Giants   region   goal   age
gold   encourages   begins   August

goat   **gentle**

1. _____   5. _____

2. _____   6. _____

3. _____   7. _____

4. _____   8. _____

Use the words above to complete the sentences. You will not use all of the words.

9. Our school football season _____ in August.

10. The name of our team is the _____.

11. Our team colors are navy and _____.

12. We are in the 12 and under _____ division.

13. Our division is located in the Midwest _____.

14. The coach always _____ us to have fun and to do our best.

15. With only seconds left to play, our kicker kicks a field _____, and we win the game!

Notes for Home: Your child identified and wrote words in which the consonant *g* stands for /g/ or /j/. **Home Activity:** Take turns with your child naming and listing words in which *g* stands for /g/ or /j/. See how many words you can name in five minutes.

The consonant *g* can stand for /g/.

    gate   **g**et   **g**ift   **g**ot   **g**ust

When *g* is followed by *e, i,* or *y,* the *g* sometimes stands for /j/.

                gem   **g**iant   **g**ym

Write the words in each phrase in which *g* stands for /g/ or /j/. Circle the sound *g* stands for in each word.

1. saw a cougar and a giraffe at the zoo

   _____ /g/ /j/   _____ /g/ /j/

2. purchased ten gallons of gasoline

   _____ /g/ /j/   _____ /g/ /j/

3. did not argue with the manager

   _____ /g/ /j/   _____ /g/ /j/

4. closed the garden gate

   _____ /g/ /j/   _____ /g/ /j/

5. eager to begin our new project

   _____ /g/ /j/   _____ /g/ /j/

6. last page in the magazine

   _____ /g/ /j/   _____ /g/ /j/

7. gave me the telephone message

   _____ /g/ /j/   _____ /g/ /j/

8. gears in the engine

   _____ /g/ /j/   _____ /g/ /j/

9. juicy oranges and tangerines

   _____ /g/ /j/   _____ /g/ /j/

10. fried the eggs in margarine

   _____ /g/ /j/   _____ /g/ /j/

Notes for Home: Your child wrote words in which the consonant *g* stands for /g/ or /j/.
Home Activity: Challenge your child to name a word pair for a category. One word must have /g/ spelled *g* and the other word must have /j/ spelled *g*. Example: for the category *foods,* *eggs* and *margarine.*

Name _____

The consonant *c* stands for /k/ in *coat* and /s/ in *cent*.
The consonant *g* stands for /g/ in *goat* and /j/ in *gem*.

Radio station WRCK plays "Hard Rock Music All the Time." Radio station WSFT plays "Soft Sounds—All Day, All Night." Find the word in each song title in which *c* stands for /k/ or /s/ or *g* stands for /g/ or /j/. If the word has the "hard" *c* or *g* sound, write the word under WRCK. If the word has the "soft" *c* or *g* sound, write the word under WSFT.

"Spice Jam"   "Music in the Air"   "Because I Know"
"Call Me Today"   "Long-ago Rhythm"   "Our Generation"
"Train Engine Blues"   "The Electric Slide"   "High Energy Polka"
"Hamburger Hustle"   "Finally Said Good-bye"   "City Swing"
"Giant Bubble Blow-Out"   "Face the Rain"   "Octopus Hip Hop"
"The Last Dance"   "Beginner Steps"   "New Age Tune"
"Got You on My Mind"   "Gentle Breezes"

WRCK (*c* /k/ or *g* /g/)   **WSFT** (*c* /s/ or *g* /j/)

1. _____   11. _____

2. _____   12. _____

3. _____   13. _____

4. _____   14. _____

5. _____   15. _____

6. _____   16. _____

7. _____   17. _____

8. _____   18. _____

9. _____   19. _____

10. _____   20. _____

Notes for Home: Your child wrote words in which the consonants *c* and *g* stand for /k/ and /s/ or /g/ and /j/. **Home Activity:** Think of the titles of songs you and your child are familiar with. Together decide whether any words in the titles have hard or soft *c* or *g* sounds.

© Scott Foresman 4–6

65

The consonant *x* can stand for the sound you hear in *box* and the sound you hear in *exact*. Say *box* and listen to the ending sound. Say *exact* and listen to the beginning sound.

Underline the word that has the consonant *x* in each phrase. Circle *box* if the *x* in the word stands for the same sound as in *box*. Circle *exact* if the *x* stands for the same sound as in *exact*.

1. expiration date on milk	box	exact
2. oxygen necessary for breathing	box	exact
3. sixteen years of age	box	exact
4. used an axe to chop wood	box	exact
5. a new exhibit at the museum	box	exact
6. smooth texture of silk	box	exact
7. cannot exist without food and water	box	exact
8. played the saxophone in the jazz band	box	exact
9. exercise for one hour at the gym	box	exact
10. relax in the bathtub	box	exact
11. exhausted after running a marathon	box	exact
12. an expensive gold watch	box	exact
13. a medical examination	box	exact
14. a long excerpt from a book	box	exact
15. coaxing the puppy out of its cage	box	exact

Notes for Home: Your child identified sounds the consonant *x* stands for in words.
Home Activity: Have your child look for words with *x* in a newspaper article. Together say each word and decide whether the *x* stands for the sound in *box* or the sound in *exact*.

Name _____

The consonant *x* can stand for the sounds in these words.

box   exact   xylem

Write each word in the list under the word in which *x* stands for the same sound.

executive	exotic	xylophone	axis	xenophobia
exciting	Texas	excellent	exaggerate	example

box	**exact**	**xylem**
1. _____	5. _____	9. _____
2. _____	6. _____	10. _____
3. _____	7. _____	
4. _____	8. _____	

Use the words above to complete the sentences.

11. The giant panda is a(n) _____ of an endangered animal.

12. Austin is the state capital of _____.

13. Naomi plays the _____ in the orchestra.

14. Fishers often _____ about the fish that got away.

15. The earth spins on its _____.

16. The corporate vice-presidents had a(n) _____ meeting.

17. White orchids are _____ tropical flowers.

18. The roller coaster ride was so _____ I couldn't stop screaming.

19. A fear of foreigners or outsiders is called _____.

20. Dogs have a(n) _____ sense of smell.

Notes for Home: Your child wrote words in which the consonant *x* stands for three different sounds. **Home Activity:** Together explore the *x* section in a dictionary. Note how few words in English begin with *x* and what sounds *x* stands for at the beginning of words.

Name _____

In English, the consonant *q* is almost always followed by the vowel *u*. Together the letters *qu* stand for the beginning sound in *quit*.

Circle *qu* in each word in the box. Then write the words to complete the phrases.

quilt	quarter	quiz	quarrel	frequently
banquet	equator	quacking	aqua	aquarium
quiet	question	require	queen	acquitted

1. the loud _____ of the ducks

2. an angry _____

3. _____ of the crime

4. a _____ with five true-and-false items

5. king and _____

6. visit our grandparents _____

7. penny, nickel, dime, _____

8. _____ in the library

9. colorful tropical fish in the _____

10. ask a _____

11. sewing a patchwork _____

12. the _____ color of the ocean water

13. the _____ around the center of the earth

14. _____ a signature on the application

15. a wedding _____ for 250 guests

Notes for Home: Your child wrote words with *qu*. **Home Activity:** Have your child look for *qu* words in the sports section of a newspaper. Examples: *quarterback, quick, conquer, equipment.*

68

Name _____

The letters *qu* can stand for the sound you hear in *quiet* and the sound you hear in *unique*. Say *quiet* and listen to the beginning sound. Say *unique* and listen to the ending sound.

Underline the *qu* word in each sentence. Circle *quiet* if the *qu* in the word stands for the same sound as in *quiet*. Circle *unique* if the *qu* stands for the same sound as in *unique*.

1. Twelve and one dozen are equal amounts.   quiet   unique

2. Click on "quit" before you shut down the computer.   quiet   unique

3. After the picnic, I counted twenty mosquito bites.   quiet   unique

4. The earthquake measured 6.5 on the Richter scale.   quiet   unique

5. Use quotation marks to show spoken words.   quiet   unique

6. The slimy movie monster was truly grotesque.   quiet   unique

7. You are required to have a license to drive a car.   quiet   unique

8. The quarterback threw the football seventy yards.   quiet   unique

9. She carried a bouquet of red and white carnations.   quiet   unique

10. Michaela was awarded a plaque at the science fair.   quiet   unique

11. The movie marquee is changed every Friday.   quiet   unique

12. Jose eats frequently at his favorite restaurant.   quiet   unique

13. Mr. Okada loves to go antique shopping.   quiet   unique

14. The quartet can play both jazz and classical music.   quiet   unique

15. Everyone wore costumes to the masquerade.   quiet   unique

Notes for Home: Your child identified the sounds *qu* stands for in words.
Home Activity: Have your child make up a tongue twister using *qu* words. Example: *Quiet quarterbacks quickly acquire quotas.*

Unscramble the letters to make a word with *x* or *qu* that makes sense in the sentence. Write the letters of the word in the spaces.

1. I heard the duck **ckauq**.   __ __ __ __ __

2. Jaime knows **caxytle** what job he wants.   __ __ __ __ __ __ __

3. When ice melts, it becomes a **ludiqi**.   __ __ __ __ __ __

4. You can **quareic** a taste for oysters.   __ __ __ __ __ __ __

5. Isabel read a chapter in her science **tbkxoeot**.

   __ __ __ __ __ __ __ __

6. We will have our final **mexa** at the end of the semester.   __ __ __ __

7. The opposite of *minimum* is **uixmamm**.   __ __ __ __ __ __ __

8. *King* is not a **nuequi** name for a dog.   __ __ __ __ __ __

9. Columbus is a famous **plxereor**.   __ __ __ __ __ __ __ __

10. I have to **roquecn** my fear of geometry.   __ __ __ __ __ __ __

11. A **fripex** comes at the beginning of a word.   __ __ __ __ __ __

12. Dinosaurs **dixetse** on Earth sixty-five million years ago.

   __ __ __ __ __ __ __ __

13. The ambulance arrived very **ulcqyik**.   __ __ __ __ __ __ __

14. The **peserxs** bus goes downtown without making any other stops.

   __ __ __ __ __ __ __ __

15. The expensive furniture is made with **ltuaqiy** materials.

   __ __ __ __ __ __ __ __

Notes for Home: Your child wrote words with *x* and *qu*. **Home Activity:** Have your child think of other *x* and *qu* words to scramble. Have your child give you clues about the words while you try to unscramble them. Take turns as "scrambler" and "guesser."

© Scott Foresman 4-6

Sometimes two consonants stand for the beginning sounds in a word. The consonant blends *sc, sk, sm, sn, sp, st,* and *sw* stand for the beginning sounds in these words.

scare **sk**in **sm**ile **sn**ake **sp**in **st**ore **sw**im

Write the *s*-blend word that completes each sentence. Circle the *s*-blend in the word.

1. Sonia added sugar to her cereal to make it _____.

   spoil sweet spin stale

2. Luis used a _____ to soak up the water.

   spice sponge sweat sweep

3. The horses were kept in the _____ at the night.

   swept spaceship swing stable

4. Mario will be performing a solo in the _____ competition.

   snowstorm smock skirt skating

5. This suspense novel is about a government _____.

   spy snowball spot skill

6. We listened to music on George's new _____ system.

   steam steel stereo station

7. The _____ piled in drifts as high as six feet.

   skeleton snow snacks spine

8. Michelle quickly _____ the newspaper headlines.

   sketched skimmed stayed scooped

9. I stepped on the _____ to see my weight.

   scales smile stack sniff

10. We could see the _____ from the campfire.

    swish swim stork smoke

Notes for Home: Your child wrote words that begin with *s*-blends. **Home Activity:** Have your child examine a cereal box to find *s*-blend words and use a colored marker to circle the words on the box.

The consonant blends *sc, sk, sm, sn, sp, st,* and *sw* stand for the beginning sounds in *scar, skip, smile, snore, spin, store,* and *swan.*

Write *sc, sk, sm, sn, sp, st,* or *sw* to complete the word in each phrase.

1. _____art the race

2. _____ooth as silk

3. _____ell words correctly

4. a bedtime _____ory

5. shelter from the _____orm

6. _____eet maple syrup

7. _____im in the pool

8. knife, fork, and _____oon

9. _____ap your fingers

10. a _____ore of 4–2

11. a _____ain on the shirt

12. dry, rough _____in

13. the hissing _____ake

14. _____eed limit of 35

15. a _____ary movie

16. not large, but _____all

17. a long velvet _____irt

18. a _____oop of ice cream

19. twinkling _____ars

20. a _____ail's slow pace

 Notes for Home: Your child completed words with *s*-blends. **Home Activity:** Have your child use at least three *s*-blend words to describe an activity or event. For example, to describe a baseball game, he or she might use *score, steal,* and *swing.*

The consonant blends *br, cr, dr, fr, gr, pr,* and *tr* stand for the beginning sounds in these words.

brain   **cr**y   **dr**ive   **fr**ee   **gr**ay   **pr**ize   **tr**uck

Write *br, cr, dr, fr, gr, pr,* or *tr* to complete each word and make it match its definition.

1. a three-sided geometric figure; a pharmacy; thankful or appreciative

_____iangle   _____ugstore   _____ateful

2. used for building; cost; earth or dirt

_____icks   _____ice   _____ound

3. attractive or good-looking; icing; switch or exchange

_____etty   _____osting   _____ade

4. liberty; wet thoroughly; sudden, loud noise

_____eedom   _____ench   _____ash

5. hang down or sag; turned into ice; exact

_____oop   _____ozen   _____ecise

6. a broad smile; a link or connection; railroad cars and engine

_____in   _____idge   _____ain

7. sketch; forecast; short, not long

_____aw   _____edict   _____ief

8. fearless or courageous; burial place; have a strong desire, long for

_____ave   _____ave   _____ave

9. a threesome; scare, terrify; jail

_____io   _____ighten   _____ison

10. smash or crack; groan or squeak; slow down or stop

_____eak   _____eak   _____ake

Notes for Home: Your child completed words with *r*-blends. **Home Activity:** Think of a challenging *r*-blend word. Look it up in a dictionary and read the definition aloud. Have your child name the word. Take turns as the "giver" and the "guesser."

Name _____

The consonant blends *br, cr, dr, fr, gr, pr,* and *tr* stand for the beginning sounds in *brain, cry, drive, free, gray, prize,* and *truck.*

Underline the *r*-blend in each word in the box. Then write the word that completes each sentence.

fruits	brisk	tricycle	broccoli	printer
brocade	dryer	fractions	green	practices
trout	drank	crawl	gravy	bricks

1. Javier _____ the piano for one hour each day.

2. My favorite green vegetable is _____.

3. Apple, pears, oranges, and grapes are all _____.

4. A _____ wind swirled the fallen leaves.

5. Most children _____ before they are able to walk.

6. Moshanda learned to ride a _____ on her third birthday.

7. The marathon runner _____ water continually.

8. Mrs. Kim mixed yellow and blue paint to make _____.

9. Scott connected the new laser _____ to his computer.

10. We have a favorite spot to fish for _____.

11. Grandmother poured _____ over her mashed potatoes.

12. Mr. Abert needed four quarters for the _____ at the laundromat.

13. The mason laid the _____ according to the building plans.

14. 1 2/3, 5 7/8 and 10 4/5 are examples of mixed _____.

15. The drapes in the castle ballroom were made of heavy gold _____.

Notes for Home: Your child wrote words with *r*-blends. **Home Activity:** Have your child make a list of *r*-blend words that he or she finds in a magazine article.

74

© Scott Foresman 4-6

The consonant blends *bl, cl, fl, gl, pl,* and *sl* stand for the beginning sounds in these words.

blow   **cl**ue   **fl**aw   **gl**eam   **pl**ug   **sl**ip

Write *bl, cl, fl, gl, pl,* or *sl* to complete the word that goes with the definition.

1. _____ant   put seeds in the ground to grow

   _____ant   tilt, lean, or slope

2. _____ame   to hold someone responsible for doing wrong

   _____ame   glowing tongues of fire; to flare, burn, blaze

3. _____ock   a group of sheep

   _____ock   used to measure or show time

4. _____oat   held up by air or water

   _____oat   to brag, often in a spiteful way

5. _____ank   a space left to be filled in

   _____ank   a long, flat piece of timber

6. _____ue   a sticky substance used to hold things together

   _____ue   a primary color; the color of a clear sky in daylight

7. _____ot   a small, narrow opening often used in machines to take coins

   _____ot   scheme or secret plan; a small piece of ground; storyline

8. _____ow   taking a long time; not fast or quick

   _____ow   to move like a current or stream

9. _____oom   open into flowers, blossom

   _____oom   darkness; low spirits

10. _____aw   a sharp, hooked nail on an animal's foot

    _____aw   a slight defect or fault

Notes for Home: Your child completed words with *l*-blends. **Home Activity:** Together with your child make up your own rhyming *l*-blend word groups. Some possibilities are *-ight, -ink, -under, -ush, -ew, -ate, -ump, -ood, -utter, -ip, -ume,* and *-aze.*

The consonant blends *bl, cl, fl, gl, pl,* and *sl* stand for the beginning sounds in *blow, clue, flaw, gleam, plug,* and *slip.*

Circle the *l*-blend words used in the following five-day weather forecasts.

MONDAY	1. overcast, gloomy skies
TUESDAY	2. dark clouds with storm front moving in
WEDNESDAY	3. heavy rain; flash flood warnings for the entire coast; make travel plans accordingly
THURSDAY	4. record west winds; blustery all day
FRIDAY	5. skies clearing with slightly warmer temperatures

Use the *l*-blend words below to complete each daily weather forecast description. You will not use all the words.

flurries	blizzard	pleasant	slight	floods
plunge	clashing	glimpses	blistering	gloomy

MONDAY	6. sunny, mild, and _____
TUESDAY	7. overcast with brief _____ of sunshine
WEDNESDAY	8. temperatures will _____ to a record low
THURSDAY	9. light snow _____ throughout the day
FRIDAY	10. _____ conditions make driving hazardous

 Notes for Home: Your child wrote words with *l*-blends. **Home Activity:** Have your child find and circle *l*-blend words used on the weather page of a newspaper.

Sometimes three consonants stand for the beginning sounds in a word. The three-letter blends *chr, sch, scr, shr, spl, spr, squ, str,* and *thr* stand for the beginning sounds in words such as *school, scream, split, sprain, strike,* and *three.*

Write the word that completes each sentence. Underline the three-letter blend in each word.

1. The toddler _____ paint all over the walls.

    screen   splattered   throw   shred

2. Each actor got a copy of the movie's _____.

    scrawl   square   script   scribble

3. It is important to _____ the fertilizer in a thin, even layer.

    spread   shrink   strand   splice

4. Thea used _____ to tie the packages together.

    shrivel   string   strap   scraps

5. Doctor Chin _____ appointments every half hour.

    schedules   squeezes   sprinkles   scrambles

6. The sudden appearance of the monster made the audience _____.

    spring   throb   screen   shriek

7. Pablo drew a perfect _____ using a ruler as his guide.

    square   chronic   string   sprain

8. Sara carefully polished the _____ trim on the new car.

    spring   chrome   scrape   strong

9. We walked single file _____ the narrow passageway.

    threw   thrown   through   throw

10. The dates on the time line were arranged in _____ order.

    scholarly   chronological   scheduled   chromosome

Notes for Home: Your child wrote words with three-letter blends. **Home Activity:** Help your child look for three-letter blend words in the copy on packages and containers in the kitchen and bathroom.

The three-letter blends *chr, sch, scr, shr, spl, spr, squ, str,* and *thr* stand for the beginning sounds in words such as *school, scream, split, sprain, strike,* and *three.*

Write the word that completes each analogy. Circle the three-letter blend in the word.

scream	three	spring	school	squeal
string	chrome	squad	splint	stream
throat	shrub	shrug	strawberries	sprain

1. summer : winter :: fall : _____

2. students : _____ :: audience : theater

3. grapes : vine :: _____ : bush

4. door : slam :: brakes : _____

5. leg : cast :: finger : _____

6. brain : skull :: _____ : neck

7. eye : wink :: shoulders : _____

8. twist : ankle :: _____ : wrist

9. _____ : river :: path : road

10. actors : cast :: soldiers : _____

11. whisper : _____ :: flute : tuba

12. frosting : cake :: _____ : car

13. _____ : tree :: hill : mountain

14. _____ : nine :: four : sixteen

15. _____ : rope :: guppy : trout

Notes for Home: Your child wrote three-letter blend words to complete analogies.
Home Activity: Have your child make up analogies using words with three-letter blends.
Some analogy relationships are opposites, same uses, and part to whole.

© Scott Foresman 4–6

Sometimes two consonants stand for the ending sounds in a word. The consonant blends *ct, ld, lf, lk, lt, mp, nd, nt, pt, sk, sp,* and *st* stand for the ending sounds in words such as *hold, silk, stamp, sent, task,* and *last.*

Unscramble the letters to make a final consonant blend word to complete each phrase. Write the word and circle its final consonant blend.

1. got a _____ in my leg   **m a c p r**

2. a carved, wooden _____   **s m k a**

3. a _____ bracelet   **l g d o**

4. _____ and cookies   **k l i m**

5. boxes stacked on the closet _____   **f h s e l**

6. a _____ on the end table   **p m l a**

7. a _____ with a buckle   **t e l b**

8. _____, second, third   **r i s f t**

9. line up one _____ the other   **b h i d e n**

10. _____ weather for sailing   **t r e c f e p**

11. gave a birthday _____   **e p e t n r s**

12. _____ her promise   **p k t e**

13. _____ measurements of the room   **t x c a e**

14. stung by a red _____   **s p a w**

15. saw _____ in the mirror   **y e l m f s**

Notes for Home: Your child wrote words with final consonant blends.
Home Activity: Take turns with your child scrambling the letters of final consonant blend words and having the other person unscramble the letters.

The consonant blends *ct, ld, lf, lk, lt, mp, nd, nt, pt, sk, sp,* and *st* stand for the ending sounds in words such as *hold, silk, stamp, sent, task,* and *fast.*

Underline the final consonant blend in each word. Then write the words to complete the menu.

melt	buttermilk	hand	lump	meant
cold	breakfast	last	crisp	overslept

"THE **(1.)** _____ STOP DINER"

TODAY'S **(2.)** _____ SPECIALS

All your favorite cereals—hot or **(3.)** _____

Our famous oatmeal—"You'll never find a **(4.)** _____."

Blueberry or **(5.)** _____ pancakes

Bacon, served **(6.)** _____ and hot

Fresh sweet rolls, made by **(7.)** _____ in our kitchen

Double apple pancake—so big, it's **(8.)** _____ to be shared

Waffles with whipped cream—they **(9.)** _____ in your mouth!

Coffee, made strong for those who **(10.)** _____

Create your own menu. Describe five items you would serve. Use one final consonant blend word in each description.

Menu

11. _____

12. _____

13. _____

14. _____

15. _____

Notes for Home: Your child wrote words with final consonant blends.
Home Activity: Help your child create his or her own menu or add items to those your child has already written. Remember to use a final consonant blend word in each description.

When two consonants stand for one sound, they are called a digraph. The consonant digraph *ch* stands for the beginning sound in these words.

chop **ch**ess **ch**irp

Underline the consonant digraph *ch* in each word in the box. Then write the words that name the pictures.

chain	checkers	chimney	chin	cherries
chalk	cheese	chicken	chair	check

1. _____

2. _____

3. _____

4. _____

5. _____

6. _____

7. _____

8. _____

9. _____

10. _____

Notes for Home: Your child wrote words with the initial consonant digraph *ch*.
Home Activity: Take turns with your child naming other words that begin with *ch*.

The consonant digraph *sh* stands for the beginning sound in these words.

               shape   **sh**ould   **sh**ore

Circle the consonant digraph *sh* in each word in the box. Then write the words to complete the sentences.

shell	showed	shared	shower	shelter
shadow	shelf	sheets	short	shop

1. Oscar arranged the books neatly on the _____.

2. Hugo was too _____ to ride the roller coaster.

3. Juliette _____ the pizza with her friends.

4. The frightened turtle pulled its head into its _____.

5. Your _____ gets longer in the afternoon.

6. Randell put the new _____ on the bed.

7. Kyoko went to the mall to _____ for a gift.

8. Scott _____ his art project to the class.

9. After the race, Jessica took a long, hot _____.

10. The campers found _____ from the sudden storm.

Notes for Home: Your child wrote words with the initial consonant digraph *sh*.
Home Activity: Have fun with the classic tongue twister: *She sells seashells by the seashore.*
Have your child make up his or her own tongue twister with *sh* words.

Name _____

The consonant digraph *th* stands for the beginning sounds in these words.

them   **th**ank

Write the word that completes the phrase and has the beginning sound in *them* or *thank*.

1. ____ book of poems   this   one   _____

2. one ____ miles   hundred   thousand   _____

3. a ____ gift   thoughtful nice   _____

4. rode ____ bikes   their   our   _____

5. rain and ____   lightning   thunder   _____

6. put a box ____   there   here   _____

7. ____ on a rose   thorns   petals   _____

8. more ____ my sister   for   than   _____

9. ____ of hot soup   thermos   bowl   _____

10. fell with a ____   thud   crash   _____

11. ____ right answer   a   the   _____

12. now and ____   then   forever   _____

13. ____-four cents   twenty   thirty   _____

14. ____ red shoes   her   those   _____

15. broke my ____   thumb   toe   _____

Notes for Home: Your child wrote words in which the consonant digraph *th* stands for two different initial sounds. **Home Activity:** Have your child look up *them* and *thank* in a dictionary and note the phonetic respellings for the words. Have your child locate the pronunciation key and find the symbols and example words that explain the respellings.

The consonant digraph *wh* stands for the beginning sound in these words.

whale   **wh**ip   **wh**ile

Find and write the 15 words with initial consonant digraph *wh* in the newspaper article.

Science Fair Winner Chosen

   Darnell Wheatly, with the help of his white cat, Snowball, won the science fair on Friday. Darnell wanted to know if face whiskers helped cats sense whether or not they could fit through spaces of different sizes. Darnell used cat treats and three boxes. He put a treat inside the largest box where Snowball could find it easily. Darnell whispered, "Go get it." Snowball whizzed over to the box, quickly went in, and got the treat. Darnell then put a treat in the medium-sized box and whistled for his cat. Snowball whirled around and ran to the box. Then she slowed down, carefully went in, and got the treat. The last box was just smaller than Snowball's body. What would happen? When Snowball put her face near the box, she began to whine and whimper. Darnell knew why she would not try to go in. Snowball's whiskery "antennae" let her sense that the box was too small for her body.

1. _____   2. _____   3. _____

4. _____   5. _____   6. _____

7. _____   8. _____   9. _____

10. _____   11. _____   12. _____

13. _____   14. _____   15. _____

 Notes for Home: Your child wrote words with the initial consonant digraph *wh*. **Home Activity:** Have your child scan a newspaper article and circle words that begin with *wh*.

Name _____

The consonant digraphs *sh, th, ch,* and *wh* stand for the beginning sounds in *share, thumb, cheese,* and *while.*

Write the word that belongs in each group. Circle the letters that stand for the beginning sound.

chin	thunder	ship	cherries	white
whirl	chalk	whale	third	shells
thimble	shovel	chair	sheets	thousand

1. pencil, crayon, _____

2. ax, hoe, _____

3. rain, lightning, _____

4. raspberries, blueberries, _____

5. sand, seaweed, _____

6. dolphin, shark, _____

7. bench, stool, _____

8. blanket, pillowcase, _____

9. turn, spin, _____

10. first, second, _____

11. sailboat, canoe, _____

12. ten, hundred, _____

13. black, brown, _____

14. nose, mouth, _____

15. needle, thread, _____

Notes for Home: Your child wrote words with the initial consonant digraphs *ch, sh, th,* and *wh.* **Home Activity:** Have your child add *ch, sh, th,* and *wh* to these word forms to make as many words as possible: ___*in,* ___*en,* ___*ip.*

Two consonants can stand for the ending sound in a word. The consonant digraphs *ch, sh,* and *th* stand for the ending sounds in these words.

ben**ch**   wa**sh**   bo**th**

Write the digraph *ch, sh,* or *th* to complete the word in each phrase.

1. sandy bea_____

2. a wrea_____ on the door

3. a long, curving pa_____

4. fre_____ homemade bread

5. smoo_____, not bumpy

6. sat on the cou_____

7. pu_____, don't pull

8. soup and salad for lun_____

9. fla_____ of lightning

10. ate a grilled cheese sandwi_____

11. fell with a cra_____

12. like a mo_____ to the flame

13. the laun_____ of the space shuttle

14. ma_____ the potatoes

15. ma_____ homework

Notes for Home: Your child completed words with the final consonant digraphs *ch, sh,* and *th.* **Home Activity:** Divide a sheet of paper into three columns labeled *sh, ch,* and *th.* Challenge your child to write as many final *sh* words as he or she can in three minutes. Then do the same for *ch* and *th.*

© Scott Foresman 4–6

The consonant digraphs *ch, sh,* and *th* stand for the ending sounds in *coach, dish,* and *south.* The final /ch/ can also be spelled *tch.*

Underline the final consonant digraph in each word. Then complete each sentence with a word that has the same final digraph as the word in dark type.

push	north	wash	math	fish
length	cash	hatch	tenth	teach
branch	teeth	wish	catch	bench

1. I paid _____ for the new **hairbrush** I bought.

2. The **coach** will _____ the team a new play.

3. The opposite direction of **south** is _____.

4. Our best baseball player can hit, **pitch**, and _____.

5. We sat and ate our **lunch** on a park _____.

6. I will _____ and dry each **dish** carefully.

7. It was amazing to **watch** the baby chicks _____.

8. My _____ project and my English paper are **both** due today.

9. The plural of **tooth** is _____.

10. Miguel measured the _____ and **width** of the window.

11. We saw many _____ jump and **splash** in the water.

12. October is the _____ **month**.

13. Kim saw the **flash** of a shooting star and made a _____.

14. Roberto could not **reach** the highest _____ of the tree.

15. Marie had to _____ to get all the **trash** into the can.

Notes for Home: Your child wrote words with the final consonant digraphs *ch, sh,* and *th.*
Home Activity: Ask your child to write a sentence with a final digraph word. Have your child read the sentence aloud without saying the word. You try to guess the word.

The consonant digraphs *gh* and *ph* stand for the *f* sound in *laugh* and *elephant*. The consonants *f* and *ff* stand for the *f* sound in *find* and *cliff*.

Write *gh, ph, f,* or *ff* to complete the word in each phrase.

1. lau_____ at a joke

2. rou_____, not smooth

3. my niece and ne_____ew

4. a tele_____one call

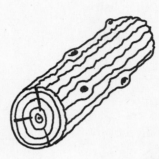

5. the lost and _____ound department

6. names in al_____abetical order

7. enou_____ money for bus fare

8. li_____eguard at the pool

9. main idea of the paragra_____

10. sneezing and cou_____ing

11. too much stu_____ in my backpack

12. tou_____ hide of an alligator

13. the first-place tro_____y

14. wa_____les and maple syrup

15. a high _____ence around the yard

Notes for Home: Your child completed words with the consonant digraphs *gh* and *ph* and the letters *f* or *ff*. **Home Activity:** Have your child make up elephant riddles using a *ph* or *gh* word in each answer. Example: Why did the elephant play the banjo? Because he didn't know how to play the saxophone!

The consonant digraphs *ng* and *nk* stand for the ending sounds in these words.

wro**ng**   si**nk**

Change the underlined word in the sentence to a word with the same final digraph that makes sense in the sentence. *Hint*: The two words will also rhyme.

1. Please <u>sang</u> your clothes in the closet.   _____

2. Bernice took her money to the <u>tank</u>.   _____

3. Xavier and his brother sleep in <u>chunk</u> beds.   _____

4. It took a <u>gong</u> time for Joseph to fall asleep.   _____

5. The <u>sing</u> rode with his knights to the castle.   _____

6. The skaters went round and round the <u>sink</u>.   _____

7. <u>Swing</u> an extra towel to the swimming pool.   _____

8. The baby monkey <u>rung</u> tightly to its mother.   _____

9. The <u>junk</u> lived in the woods.   _____

10. Latisha <u>gang</u> the bell several times.   _____

11. Reiko climbed the ladder one <u>sung</u> at a time.   _____

12. An elephant uses its <u>bunk</u> like a hand.   _____

13. Did I <u>sank</u> you for the present?   _____

14. The <u>wing</u> was a plain gold band.   _____

15. The flower is a soft shade of <u>wink</u>.   _____

Notes for Home: Your child wrote words with the final consonant digraphs *ng* and *nk*.
Home Activity: Have your child look through a favorite book for words ending in *ng* and *nk*.

Two consonants that stand for one sound are called a digraph. Digraphs, such as *sh, ch, th, wh, ph, gh, ng,* and *nk,* may appear at the beginning, in the middle, or at the end of words.

Complete each word with the digraph *sh, ch, th, wh, ph, gh, nk,* or *ng.*

Dear Grandmo_____er,

Greeti_____s from _____iladel_____ia, Pennsylvania, "the city of

bro_____erly love." The first _____ing I did was go to the Visitors'

Center and pick up a sightseeing pam_____let. I was in luck! A double-

decker tour bus was leavi_____ in two minutes. I saw famous historical

places every_____ere I looked. My favorite was _____e Liberty Bell.

(Yes, it is cracked!) For lun_____, I got the famous _____eesesteak

sandwi_____ from a vendor in Independence National Park. I will

_____ow you all of the _____otos I've taken wi_____ the new camera

you gave me (tha_____s again!) _____en I get back next week. The

wea_____er has been fine—warm with sun_____ine duri_____ the day

but _____illy at night. As you can tell, I've done more than enou_____

for one day. I'm havi_____ a great time. Wi_____ you were here.

Love,

Mike

Notes for Home: Your child completed words with consonant digraphs.
Home Activity: Have your child write a brief letter using at least five words with consonant digraphs.

© Scott Foresman 4–6

Name _____

The vowel *a* followed by the consonant *r* stands for the vowel sound in these words.

st**ar**   **car**pet

Underline the words that have the vowel sound you hear in *star*.

apart	stairs	collar	darkness	skirt
spare	harden	declare	carton	nearby
remark	bearing	large	hardly	depart
sparkle	corner	rare	deer	argue

Using the underlined words in the box, write the antonym for each word below.

1. small   _____

2. together   _____

3. arrive   _____

4. light   _____

5. soften   _____

Using the underlined words in the box, write the synonym for each word below.

6. glitter   _____

7. box   _____

8. scarcely   _____

9. quarrel   _____

10. comment   _____

Notes for Home: Your child wrote words in which *ar* stands for the vowel sound in *star*.
Home Activity: Have your child scan a newspaper article and draw a star by every word he or she finds that has the vowel sound in *star* spelled *ar*.

The letters *ar* stand for the vowel sound in *star* and *carpet*.

Write the words in each phrase in which *ar* stands for the vowel sound you hear in *star*.

1. got a rare bargain on a cardigan _____

2. partners who are never apart _____

3. beware of garbage in the harbor _____

4. tracked the departing airplane on radar _____

5. farmers preparing for the harvest _____

6. an article about a career in the army _____

7. fresh pears in a carton at the market _____

8. an artist carving a reindeer _____

9. startled by the blaring alarm _____

10. a barber with a cheerful remark _____

11. a hare in the garden in our yard _____

12. repairs needed on the large cargo ship _____

13. marvel at the clear harmony _____

14. stare at the sparklers in the darkness _____

15. careful to mark only in the margin _____

Notes for Home: Your child wrote words in which *ar* stands for the vowel sound in *star*. **Home Activity:** Take turns with your child writing phrases with at least one *ar* word and asking each other to identify that word.

The vowel *o* followed by the consonant *r* stands for the vowel sound in these words.

corn   **or**bit

Circle the words that have the vowel sound you hear in *corn*.

assorted	escort	forward	borrow	uniform
color	corner	worry	stormy	major
morning	effort	order	fortune	orchard

Write the circled words to complete the phrases.

1. depart at 8 o'clock in the _____

2. a dark and _____ night

3. comes in _____ colors and sizes

4. made a _____ in diamonds

5. gave the command "_____, march!"

6. many apple trees in an _____

7. the _____ of the room

8. a police officer's _____

9. words in alphabetical _____

10. _____ the official to the meeting

Notes for Home: Your child wrote words in which *or* stands for the vowel sound in *corn*.
Home Activity: Think of a clue for one of the *or* words on the page and have your child give an answer. Then have your child think of a clue for you.

The letters *or* stand for the vowel sound in *corn* and *orbit*.

Write the *or* words to complete the paragraph. Hint: Some words should be capitalized.

performing	absorbed	popcorn	orchard	chorus
forty	auditorium	chord	disorder	organ
hornets	important	unfortunately	normal	gorgeous

The **(1.)** _____ usually sings in places like the

(2.) _____. But today is not a **(3.)** _____

day. We are **(4.)** _____ in an unusual place—an apple

(5.) _____. Mrs. Juarez insists that it is a

(6.) _____ setting. And it is. The apple blossoms look like fluffy

white **(7.)** _____ on the trees and the ground.

(8.) _____, the blossoms attract **(9.)** _____.

This created some **(10.)** _____ among the

(11.) _____ of us! But then Mr. Abert played the opening

(12.) _____ on the **(13.)** _____.

We began to sing and soon we were **(14.)** _____ in the

music. The bugs didn't seem very **(15.)** _____ now. And

you know what? Mrs. Juarez was right.

Notes for Home: Your child wrote words in which *or* stands for the vowel sound in *corn*.
Home Activity: Have your child write a phrase or sentence using each *or* word in the box.

The vowels *e, i,* and *u* followed by the consonant *r* stand for the vowel sound in these words.

fer**n**   **bi**r**d**   **tu**r**n**

Underline the word in each sentence that has the vowel sound in *fern*. Then write each word under the correct heading.

1. The salty crackers made us very thirsty.

2. Concerned citizens wrote, called, and e-mailed their representatives.

3. The colors of Mardi Gras are gold, green, and purple.

4. The gymnast scored a perfect ten on the balance beam.

5. Hikers need thick socks and sturdy boots.

6. The children sat in a circle around the teacher.

7. I was nervous about making a speech in class.

8. The dancers were whirling around the room.

9. Adding *-ly* to *happy* makes the adjective into an adverb.

10. The purpose of the project is to construct better guardrails.

er as in *herd*	**ir** as in *bird*	**ur** as in *turn*
11. _____	15. _____	18. _____
12. _____	16. _____	19. _____
13. _____	17. _____	20. _____
14. _____		

© Scott Foresman 4–6

Notes for Home: Your child wrote words in which *er, ir,* and *ur* stand for the vowel sound in *fern, bird,* and *turn.* **Home Activity:** Have your child read a magazine article and highlight words in which *er, ir,* and *ur* stand for the vowel sound in *fern.*

The letters *er, ir,* and *ur* stand for the vowel sound in *fern, bird,* and *turn.*

Write the word that answers the clue and has the vowel sound you hear in *fern.*

1. illogical, impossible, and silly   _____

              ridiculous   absurd

2. a kind of tree whose bark peels off   _____

              birch   sycamore

3. a person who knows about a particular subject   _____

              expert   scholar

4. something perfectly round   _____

              sphere   circle

5. number that comes after twenty   _____

              forty   thirty

6. straight up and down   _____

              vertical   upright

7. something that generates heat   _____

              furnace   fireplace

8. on the outside   _____

              outward   external

9. a root of a plant eaten as a vegetable   _____

              carrot   turnip

10. too much of something   _____

              surplus   extra

Notes for Home: Your child wrote words in which *er, ir,* and *ur* stand for the vowel sound in *fern, bird,* and *turn.* **Home Activity:** Have your child sort the words on the page into categories of *er, ir,* and *ur* words.

The vowel-*r* patterns *are, air,* and *ear* stand for the vowel sound in these words.

care   ch**air**   b**ear**

The vowel-*r* patterns *ear* and *eer* stand for the vowel sound in these words.

near   d**eer**

Underline a word in each phrase with the vowel sound in *care* or *near*. Then write each word under the picture whose name that has the same vowel sound.

1. four sides of a square

2. the steering wheel of a car

3. appear suddenly

4. house in need of repair

5. fresh, yellow pears

6. share the last apple

7. a career as a lawyer

8. fearful of snakes

9. fell down the stairs

10. wearing jeans and a t-shirt

11. _____

12. _____

13. _____

14. _____

15. _____

16. _____

17. _____

18. _____

19. _____

20. _____

Notes for Home: Your child wrote words with *are, air, ear,* and *eer.* **Home Activity:** Have your child make lists of rhyming words with the patterns *are, air, ear,* and *eer.*

Name _____

The vowel-*r* patterns *are, air,* and *ear* stand for the vowel sound in *dare, pair,* and *bear.*

The vowel-*r* patterns *ear* and *eer* stand for the vowel sound in *near* and *steer.*

Circle the words in the box that have the vowel sounds you hear in *dare* and *near.* Then combine each circled word with a word below to make a compound word. Write the compound word.

better	marine	wear	greedy	chair
stair	care	merge	cheer	ear
deer	fair	year	target	scare

1. ____grounds   _____

2. ____free   _____

3. arm____   _____

4. ____book   _____

5. rein____   _____

6. ____ring   _____

7. ____case   _____

8. under____   _____

9. ____leader   _____

10. ____crow   _____

Notes for Home: Your child wrote words with *are, air, ear,* and *eer.* **Home Activity:** Have your child use each circled word in a sentence with another word that has the same pattern for the same vowel sound. Example: The *year* is *nearly* at an end.

The vowel-*r* patterns *ore* and *our* stand for the vowel sound in these words.

t*ore*   **f*our***

Circle the words that have the vowel sound in *tore*. Then write each word in the group where it belongs.

course	sore	mourn	explorer
rope	source	shout	brought
chore	house	store	court
protect	ignore	harbor	before

1. shop, market, _____

2. earlier, previously, _____

3. grieve, weep, _____

4. beginning, origin, _____

5. overlook, disregard, _____

6. pioneer, trailblazer, _____

7. tender, painful, _____

8. route, path, _____

9. job, task, _____

10. field, track, rink, _____

Notes for Home: Your child wrote words with *ore* and *our*. **Home Activity:** Have your child write sentences using one *ore* word and one *our* word in each sentence.

The vowel-*r* patterns *ore* and *our* stand for the vowel sound in *core* and *four*.

Write the words to complete the sentences. Circle the letters that stand for the vowel sound you hear in *core*.

wore	pouring	ashore	source	foretell
court	snore	course	encore	adores
explore	gourd	ignore	bored	mourned

1. What is the _____ of your information on fossils?

2. Ted made a birdhouse out of a dried, hollowed-out _____.

3. Katje _____ a dress from her native Netherlands.

4. After six months at sea, the sailors couldn't wait to go _____.

5. Try to _____ the noise from the party.

6. The children _____ their dog after it died.

7. Who could _____ that the weather would be so bad?

8. The long, dull speech _____ the listeners.

9. The cat wants to _____ every closet and cupboard in the house.

10. The floods caused the river to change its _____.

11. The ball hit the sideline on the left side of the _____.

12. Because it is all hers, Corinna _____ her new room.

13. The water is _____ out of a hole in the bottle.

14. His _____ could be heard three rooms away!

15. The audience called the singer to come back and sing an _____.

Notes for Home: Your child wrote words with *ore* and *our*. **Home Activity:** Have your child write rhymes using the word pairs *four/pour, course/source, store/chore,* and *more/score*.

© Scott Foresman 4-6

Name _____

The number of syllables in a word is the same as the number of vowel sounds in the word.

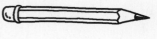 **pencil**
Number of vowel sounds: 2   (short *e* sound and schwa sound)
Number of syllables: 2

Say each word. Circle 1, 2, or 3 to show how many vowel sounds you hear in the word. Circle 1, 2, or 3 to show how many syllables the word has.

	Number of Vowel Sounds			**Number of Syllables**		
1. school	1	2	3	1	2	3
2. whisper	1	2	3	1	2	3
3. yesterday	1	2	3	1	2	3
4. city	1	2	3	1	2	3
5. grandmother	1	2	3	1	2	3
6. until	1	2	3	1	2	3
7. admit	1	2	3	1	2	3
8. dollars	1	2	3	1	2	3
9. hidden	1	2	3	1	2	3
10. holiday	1	2	3	1	2	3
11. concentrate	1	2	3	1	2	3
12. reach	1	2	3	1	2	3
13. computer	1	2	3	1	2	3
14. excitement	1	2	3	1	2	3
15. straight	1	2	3	1	2	3

 Notes for Home: Your child identified the number of vowel sounds and syllables in words.
Home Activity: Have your child list the names of favorite foods and identify the number of syllables in each word.

Name _____ **Multisyllabic Words**

Number of syllables in a word = number of vowel sounds in the word

	Number of Vowel Sounds	Number of Syllables
drill	1	1
foun/tain	2	2
mag/net/ic	3	3
fas/ci/na/tion	4	4

Say each word. Write the number of vowel sounds you hear. Write the number of syllables the word has.

	Number of Vowel Sounds	**Number of Syllables**
1. workbook	_____	_____
2. stronger	_____	_____
3. seven	_____	_____
4. interrupted	_____	_____
5. following	_____	_____
6. scratch	_____	_____
7. umbrella	_____	_____
8. complete	_____	_____
9. office	_____	_____
10. flicker	_____	_____
11. women	_____	_____
12. destination	_____	_____
13. overlap	_____	_____
14. surface	_____	_____
15. musical	_____	_____

Notes for Home: Your child identified the number of vowel sounds and syllables in words.
Home Activity: Have your child make a list of frequently used words with one, two, three, or four syllables.

Number of syllables in a word = number of vowel sounds in the word.

Circle the words with the same number of syllables as the underlined word. Write one of the circled words to complete the sentence.

1. <u>Remind</u> Tony to close the _____ quietly.

   cabinet   window   door   letter

2. The <u>rabbit</u> ate the carrots growing in the _____.

   park   kitchen   garden   balcony

3. Thanksgiving is a <u>holiday</u> in _____.

   January   July   November   October

4. The weather forecaster <u>predicts</u> a _____.

   hurricane   blizzard   danger   tornado

5. Ana's <u>favorite</u> food is _____.

   spaghetti   pizza   umbrella   yogurt

6. The new art <u>museum</u> is very _____.

   pretty   dangerous   beautiful   spacious

7. Pioneer <u>women</u> wore _____.

   gloves   bonnets   jewelry   helmets

8. Did you put a _____ in the <u>salad</u>?

   tomato   pencil   cucumber   radish

9. <u>Silver</u> is a precious _____.

   ore   mineral   buckle   metal

10. A _____ is a <u>desert</u> plant.

   cactus   marigold   rose   tulip

Notes for Home: Your child identified the number of syllables in words.
Home Activity: Have your child count the number of syllables in each word that was *not* circled on the page.

Adding affixes to words adds syllables to the words.

            pack   un/pack   power   pow/er/ful   heat   re/heat/a/ble

Write the number of syllables in the base word. Then add the affix and write the new word and the number of syllables in that word.

1. pleasant   _____

       Add *un-*.   _____   _____

       Now add *-ly*.   _____   _____

2. grace   _____

       Add *dis-*.   _____   _____

       Now add *-ful*.   _____   _____

3. help   _____

       Add *-less*.   _____   _____

       Now add *-ness*.   _____   _____

4. fill   _____

       Add *re-*.   _____   _____

       Now add *-able*.   _____   _____

5. treat   _____

       Add *mis-*.   _____   _____

       Now add *-ment*.   _____   _____

Notes for Home: Your child added affixes and endings to words and counted the number of syllables in the words. **Home Activity:** Point out words with affixes and endings in a newspaper article and have your child tell you the number of syllables in the words.

Name _____

Adding an ending to a word may or may not add a syllable. Say these words.

count	count/ed	walk	walked	call	call/ing
talk	talks	cry	cries		
star	stars	bench	bench/es		

Add the ending to each word in the list. Say the word. Write *Yes* if adding the ending adds a syllable. Write *No* if adding the ending does not add a syllable.

-ed

1. decide _____

2. gather _____

3. watch _____

4. guard _____

5. relate _____

6. challenge _____

7. protest _____

8. realize _____

-s

9. petal _____

10. messenger _____

11. clue _____

12. insect _____

-es

13. batch _____

14. radish _____

15. multiply _____

16. worry _____

-ing

17. shop _____

18. deny _____

19. depend _____

20. release _____

Notes for Home: Your child added endings to words and counted the number of syllables in the words. **Home Activity:** Together with your child study the words on the page and see what conclusions you can draw about when endings add syllables to words.

The schwa sound is a vowel sound that is heard in unaccented syllables. The letters *a, e, i, o,* and *u* can spell the schwa sound. This symbol (ə) represents the schwa sound.

above   **e**ffect   ca**b**in   lem**o**n   cact**u**s

Circle the letter that stands for the schwa sound in each word.

1. minus   a   e   i   o   u   2. robin   a   e   i   o   u

3. dollar   a   e   i   o   u   4. second   a   e   i   o   u

5. walrus   a   e   i   o   u   6. human   a   e   i   o   u

7. fossil   a   e   i   o   u   8. color   a   e   i   o   u

9. seven   a   e   i   o   u   10. zebra   a   e   i   o   u

11. moment   a   e   i   o   u   12. pencil   a   e   i   o   u

13. bottom   a   e   i   o   u   14. wagon   a   e   i   o   u

15. system   a   e   i   o   u   16. about   a   e   i   o   u

17. circus   a   e   i   o   u   18. barrel   a   e   i   o   u

19. shiver   a   e   i   o   u   20. gremlin   a   e   i   o   u

21. forum   a   e   i   o   u   22. sentence   a   e   i   o   u

23. origin   a   e   i   o   u   24. bonus   a   e   i   o   u

25. mirror   a   e   i   o   u

Notes for Home: Your child identified the letters that stand for the schwa sound in words.
Home Activity: Have your child look through newspaper ads to find bargains whose names have the schwa sound and make a shopping list of the words.

Name _____

The letters *a, e, i, o,* and *u* can spell the schwa sound.

above **e**ffect cab**i**n lem**o**n cact**u**s

Circle the letter that stands for the schwa sound in the first word. Then circle other words in the row in which the same letter stands for the schwa sound.

1. finger	water	clever	deepest
2. margin	timing	family	muffin
3. ahead	breakfast	panda	face
4. cotton	boat	honor	bacon
5. jewel	hammer	peak	eleven
6. apron	solo	bottom	weapon
7. goblin	fossil	picnic	carnival
8. bonus	focus	walrus	phone
9. zebra	last	beggar	loyal
10. minus	campus	useless	dreadful
11. salad	sales	allow	tuna
12. carol	today	pilot	stole
13. success	submit	recess	citrus
14. cabinet	mimic	pupil	minimum
15. severe	chicken	hundred	return

Notes for Home: Your child identified words in which the same letters stand for the schwa sound. **Home Activity:** Have your child create a bumper sticker using words that have the schwa sound, such as *loyal, dollar, panda, better, wisdom,* and *fortune.*

Underline the word in each pair that has the schwa sound. Write the underlined word that answers each clue. Then circle the letter that stands for the schwa sound.

quarter	dime	eleven	thirteen
shack	cabin	zebra	rhino
spider	monkey	team	family
minus	reduce	closet	dresser
inside	bottom	soup	salad

1. It's a small house made of logs.   _____

2. It's the opposite of *top*.   _____

3. It's worth twenty-five cents.   _____

4. This is a striped animal.   _____

5. This is part of a meal.   _____

6. This is a place for clothes.   _____

7. It means "less."   _____

8. It's often made up of parents and children.   _____

9. It spins a web.   _____

10. It's a number greater than ten.   _____

Notes for Home: Your child identified and wrote words that have the schwa sound.
Home Activity: Have your child read a story and find words that he or she thinks have the schwa sound and then look them up in a dictionary.

Only words of more than one syllable can have the schwa sound. Some words have the schwa sound in the first syllable.

bal/loon

Write a word from the box to complete each sentence. Underline the letter that stands for the schwa sound.

| canoe | machine | hazard | compete | about |
| distance | command | police | performed | mistake |

1. I took your jacket by _____.

2. He paddled a _____ down the river.

3. The _____ patrolled the crime scene.

4. The washing _____ needs to be repaired.

5. The _____ to the park is longer than I thought.

6. This book is _____ the travels of Marco Polo.

7. The athletes will _____ for the gold medal.

8. The doctor _____ an operation.

9. The general will _____ the troops.

10. Oily rags are a fire _____.

Notes for Home: Your child wrote words with the schwa sound and identified the letters that stand for the schwa sound. **Home Activity:** Have your child choose five words that have the schwa sound and write questions using the words.

Name _____

Replace the underlined word in each sentence with a word from the box in which the same letter stands for the schwa sound. Then write that letter.

mammal	giraffe	cocoon	table	dinner
suggests	collar	lantern	ribbon	column

1. Angela refinished her dining room <u>bundle</u> and chairs.

   _____   _____

2. The miner carried a <u>chapter</u> into the cave.

   _____   _____

3. The gift was tied with brightly colored <u>wagon</u>.

   _____   _____

4. Kim <u>suspends</u> that we go swimming.

   _____   _____

5. I made tacos and salad for <u>diver</u> last night.

   _____   _____

6. He was missing a button on the <u>plural</u> of his shirt.

   _____   _____

7. The cheetah is the fastest <u>marshal</u> on Earth.

   _____   _____

8. A <u>chorus</u> of smoke rose from the fire.

   _____   _____

9. A <u>divide</u> is an animal with a long neck.

   _____   _____

10. A caterpillar forms a <u>complaint</u>.

   _____   _____

Notes for Home: Your child identified letters that stand for the schwa sound.
Home Activity: Have your child write a paragraph about an adventure using words that have the schwa sound.

© Scott Foresman 4–6

Name _____

The plurals of most words are formed by adding -*s*.

horse   horse**s**

Write the word that names each picture.

1.

_____   _____

2.

_____   _____

3.

_____   _____

4.

_____   _____

5.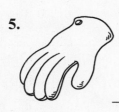

_____   _____

 Notes for Home: Your child formed the plurals of words by adding -*s*.
Home Activity: Have your child choose five household objects and write the plural forms of their names.

111

Name _____

To form the plurals of most words, -s is added.

desk + s = desk**s**

Write the plural form of each word.

1. wagon _____   2. gift _____

3. athlete _____   4. paper _____

5. shadow _____   6. turtle _____

7. dancer _____   8. cave _____

9. magnet _____   10. football _____

11. oven _____   12. lecture _____

13. jewel _____   14. plumber _____

15. crowd _____   16. instruction _____

17. chair _____   18. narrator _____

19. needle _____   20. journal _____

Notes for Home: Your child formed the plurals of words by adding -s.
Home Activity: Have your child write sentences using the words on this page.

The plurals of words that end in *x, s, ss, ch,* or *sh* are formed by adding *-es.*

box   box**es**   watch   watch**es**

Write the word that names the picture.

1.

_____   _____

2.

_____   _____

3.

_____   _____

4.

_____   _____

5.

_____   _____

© Scott Foresman 4-6

 Notes for Home: Your child formed the plurals of words ending in *x, s, ss, ch,* or *sh* by adding *-es.* **Home Activity:** Have your child choose five words from the page and write a clue for each word.

Name _____

To form the plural of a word ending with a consonant and *y*, the *y* is changed to *i*, and *-es* is added.

par**ty**   par**ties**

Write the plural form of a word in the box to complete each sentence.

factory	memory	mystery	grocery	cavity
charity	country	ceremony	hobby	baby

1. I have many good _____ of my trip to Alaska.

2. The two _____ splashed in the wading pool.

3. All cultures have _____ to mark important occasions.

4. I was dismayed when the dentist said I had two _____.

5. Several _____ opened in the new industrial park.

6. Her _____ are stamp collecting and rock climbing.

7. My favorite books are _____ set in foreign places.

8. The leaders of the two _____ signed the trade agreement.

9. Anya carried four bags of _____ into the kitchen.

10. Several _____ joined together for a fund-raising campaign.

 Notes for Home: Your child formed the plurals of words ending in a consonant and *y* by changing *y* to *i* and adding *-es*. **Home Activity:** Have your child write questions using the plural forms of words on the page.

© Scott Foresman 4–6

Name _____

Write the plural form of each word in the box in the correct list.

party	girl	vase	glass	picture
daisy	country	nurse	box	sandwich
wagon	diary	gas	brush	enemy

Add -s   **Add -es**

1. _____   6. _____

2. _____   7. _____

3. _____   8. _____

4. _____   9. _____

5. _____   10. _____

Change _y_ to _i_ and add -es

11. _____

12. _____

13. _____

14. _____

15. _____

Notes for Home: Your child formed the plurals of words by adding -s and -es.
Home Activity: Have your child write riddles for five plural words on the page.

Name _____

Write the plural form of a word from the list to answer each clue.

garden	string	knee	ranch	album
pencil	fox	marsh	dictionary	emergency
address	melody	battery	chorus	speech

1. These are wild animals.   _____

2. These are joints between the upper and lower legs.   _____

3. You pluck these on a guitar to make sounds.   _____

4. These go on the front of envelopes.   _____

5. These are several groups of singers.   _____

6. Flowers and vegetables grow in these.   _____

7. You look up words in these.   _____

8. These are wetlands.   _____

9. Cattle are raised on these.   _____

10. These call for a cool head and quick action.   _____

11. Politicians make a lot of these.   _____

12. You put pictures in these.   _____

13. Lots of toys need these.   _____

14. Songs have these.   _____

15. These are writing tools.   _____

Notes for Home: Your child has formed the plurals of words by adding -*s* and -*es*.
Home Activity: Have your child make lists of things found in the city and the country and write the plural of each word.

The plurals of words that end in a vowel and *o* are formed by adding -*s*.

radio**s**

The plurals of some words ending in a consonant and *o* are formed by adding -*s;* others by adding -*es*. Some words add either -*s* or -*es*.

cello**s**   potato**es**   banjo**s** or banjo**es**

Add -*s* or -*es* to each word to make the plural form of the word.

1. piano   _____

2. hero   _____

3. tornado   _____

4. patio   _____

5. soprano   _____

6. volcano   _____

7. video   _____

8. ratio   _____

9. tomato   _____

10. stereo   _____

Notes for Home: Your child formed the plurals of words ending in *o* by adding -*s* and- *es*.
Home Activity: Have your child check the spelling of each of the plural words on the page in a dictionary.

Name _____

The ending -*s* is added to a word ending in a vowel and *o* to form the plural.

The ending -*s* or -*es* is added to a word ending in a consonant and *o* to form the plural.

Write the plural forms of the words to complete the puzzle.

echo	soprano	photo	alto	patio
torpedo	radio	hero	piano	video

Across
2. women's lowest singing voices
3. large metal tubes containing explosives
8. brave people
9. things you can watch on a television
10. women's highest singing voices

Down
1. musical instruments with keys
4. places for outdoor dining
5. repeated sounds
6. pictures taken with a camera
7. machines that pick up or send sound

Notes for Home: Your child formed the plurals of words ending in *o* by adding -*s* or -*es*.
Home Activity: Have your child choose five words from the page and write a sentence for each one.

To form the plurals of some words ending in *f* or *fe*, the *f* or *fe* is changed to *v*, and *-es* is added. To form the plurals of words ending in *ff*, the ending *-s* is added.

half   hal**ves**   mu**ff**   muff**s**

Choose a word from the box and write the plural form to complete each sentence.

> calf   wife   loaf   sheriff   life
> cliff   leaf   knife   thief   shelf

1. Be very careful when handling sharp _____.

2. The travelers were robbed by a band of _____.

3. Ben raked four bags of _____.

4. A cat is said to have nine _____.

5. The farmer put the _____ in the pasture.

6. The heavy books made the _____ sag in the middle.

7. The trail led us to the edge of some sheer _____.

8. Women who are married are called _____.

9. Many _____ came to the law-enforcement convention.

10. The baker took the _____ of bread out of the oven.

Notes for Home: Your child formed the plurals of words ending in *ff, f,* or *fe*.
Home Activity: Have your child form the plurals of *elf, wolf,* and *cuff* and then write a sentence using each word.

Some words form their plurals in a special way.

goose—geese	mouse—mice	ox—oxen
woman—women	man—men	child—children

Some words have the same form for both singular and plural.

deer   sheep   moose   salmon

Write the answer to each clue to complete the puzzle.

Across
3. large animals that live in the woods, bigger than deer
7. domestic cattle used for farm work
8. large fish
10. young girls and boys

Down
1. woolly animals
2. large birds, like ducks
4. adult males
5. adult females
6. graceful animals that live in the woods
9. small rodents

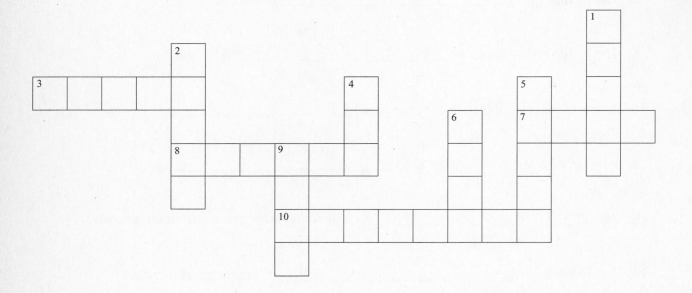

Notes for Home: Your child used the plurals of irregular words to complete a puzzle.
Home Activity: Have your child write two sentences using the words from the page that have the same form for both plural and singular.

Name _____

Compound words are made by combining two smaller words.

doghouse = dog + house

Write the two words that make up each compound word.

1. myself = _____ + _____

2. everything = _____ + _____

3. clothesline = _____ + _____

4. thumbtack = _____ + _____

5. sunshine = _____ + _____

6. footprints = _____ + _____

7. blindfold = _____ + _____

8. drawbridge = _____ + _____

9. stepladder = _____ + _____

10. spellbound = _____ + _____

11. watermelon = _____ + _____

12. password = _____ + _____

13. oatmeal = _____ + _____

14. wristwatch = _____ + _____

15. cloudburst = _____ + _____

Notes for Home: Your child identified words that make up compound words.
Home Activity: Have your child make a list of frequently used compound words and then identify the two words that make up each compound word.

Name _____

A compound word is made up of two smaller words.

rain + coat = raincoat

Choose a word to finish the compound word in the sentence. Write the word.

1. She put the letter in the mail_____.

   box   back   spot

2. Miguel wrote his assignment in his note_____.

   house   book   place

3. I stacked the logs in the fire_____.

   stand   snake   place

4. Tall sun_____ grew in the garden.

   cases   flowers   glasses

5. The rattle_____ was ready to strike.

   flake   drop   snake

6. The volley_____ team was undefeated.

   ball   wall   line

7. Val planted zinnias in the flower_____.

   coats   pots   books

8. Put the silver_____ on the table.

   line   writing   ware

9. I carry my books in a back_____.

   pack   ground   home

10. We ate dinner at a road_____ inn.

   shore   side   by

 Notes for Home: Your child put words together to make compound words.
Home Activity: Have your child write the following words on cards and sort them to make
compound words: *birth, text, house, horse, hand, day, writing, work, book, back.*

Name _____

A compound word is formed by putting two smaller words together.

every + thing = everything

Draw a line from a word in Column A to a word in Column B to make a compound word. Write the compound words.

Column A	Column B
1. out	ball
2. wild	by
3. base	side
4. arm	teller
5. any	born
6. sea	chair
7. through	flowers
8. new	shell
9. story	out
10. near	thing

11. _____ **12.** _____

13. _____ **14.** _____

15. _____ **16.** _____

17. _____ **18.** _____

19. _____ **20.** _____

© Scott Foresman 4-6

Notes for Home: Your child put words together to make and write compound words. **Home Activity:** Have your child make compound words by adding words to *sand, earth, light,* and *day.*

Some compound words are written as one word. Other compound words are written as two words.

everybody   all right

Write a compound word from the box to complete each sentence.

| high school | peanut butter | downstairs | remote control | first aid |
| wristwatch | spacecraft | no one | pen pal | flashlight |

1. He ate a _____ and jelly sandwich.

2. The championship game was played in the _____ gym.

3. It's a good idea to know _____ if you are going camping.

4. Does your _____ have a second hand?

5. We saw _____ we knew at the carnival.

6. Betty received a letter from her _____ in Scotland.

7. The _____ orbited the moon.

8. The children went _____ to play.

9. Use the _____ to change the television channel.

10. Keep a _____ handy in case of emergency.

Notes for Home: Your child wrote one- and two-word compound words to complete sentences. **Home Activity:** Encourage your child to keep a list of compound words that are written as two words.

Compound words may be written as one word or two words.

lifeguard   life raft

Choose two words to make a compound word that matches each clue. Check a dictionary to see whether each compound word is one word or two. Write the compound word.

birth	ground	high	snow	bird
flakes	way	day	bathing	camp
back	window	port	room	box
suit	living	car	bone	watcher

1. the spine in a body   _____

2. garment worn for swimming   _____

3. shelter for an automobile   _____

4. room for general family use   _____

5. the day you were born   _____

6. container for plants on a windowsill _____

7. person who observes wild birds   _____

8. a public road   _____

9. falls from the sky in winter   _____

10. a place where you sleep in a tent   _____

Notes for Home: Your child wrote one- and two-word compound words.
Home Activity: Have your child choose five words from the page and write a sentence for each one.

A contraction is a short way of writing two words. An apostrophe (') is used in place of the letter or letters omitted in the contraction. Sometimes the spelling will change.

we are → we're   will not → won't

she is → she's

Write the contraction for each pair of words.

1. he has   _____

2. we will   _____

3. they are   _____

4. would not   _____

5. must not   _____

6. I am   _____

7. they will   _____

8. did not   _____

9. are not   _____

10. where is   _____

11. she would   _____

12. you have   _____

13. I have   _____

14. that is   _____

15. let us   _____

Notes for Home: Your child formed contractions from pairs of words.
Home Activity: Have your child look through a newspaper and highlight words that could be written as contractions.

© Scott Foresman 4–6

An apostrophe (') takes the place of the letter or letters omitted in a contraction.

| let us | let(u)s | let's |

Write the two words from which each contraction was formed.

1. doesn't   _____   _____

2. hasn't   _____   _____

3. you've   _____   _____

4. I'll   _____   _____

5. we've   _____   _____

6. here's   _____   _____

7. haven't   _____   _____

8. she'll   _____   _____

9. we're   _____   _____

10. won't   _____   _____

11. it's   _____   _____

12. who's   _____   _____

13. shouldn't   _____   _____

14. wouldn't   _____   _____

15. isn't   _____   _____

Notes for Home: Your child identified the words from which contractions are formed.
Home Activity: Have your child look through a newspaper or magazine, find contractions, and identify the two words used to form each contraction.

Name _____

A contraction is a short way to write two words.   I will   I'll

Write a contraction for the underlined words in each sentence.

1. <u>We will</u> make pizza for lunch.

   _____

2. He <u>could not</u> have painted the house without your help.

   _____

3. <u>Who is</u> going to the concert this evening?

   _____

4. <u>We are</u> planning a trip to Mexico this summer.

   _____

5. Our dog <u>does not</u> like to be bathed.

   _____

6. <u>She would</u> like a camera for her birthday.

   _____

7. <u>You will</u> have to study for the math test tonight.

   _____

8. <u>They are</u> planting a garden in the yard.

   _____

9. <u>It is</u> the first day of spring.

   _____

10. <u>That is</u> the funniest thing I've ever heard!

   _____

Notes for Home: Your child combined words to form contractions. **Home Activity:** Have your child make a set of cards that can be combined to make contractions using the following words: *he, she, I, you, they, is, are, will, have, had.*

Sometimes two words can be combined to form a contraction.

Who is going to make dinner?   **Who's** going to make dinner?

Circle the words in each sentence that can be combined to make a contraction. Write the contraction.

1. He will represent the class at the student council meeting.

   _____

2. I did not invite my friend for lunch.

   _____

3. You have visited many countries over the summer.

   _____

4. It is a good day for skiing.

   _____

5. I hope they will like the movie.

   _____

6. She has read many new books.

   _____

7. I knew you would like the museum.

   _____

8. We could not find Dad's car keys.

   _____

9. They are going to soccer practice after school.

   _____

10. I would like to learn to play the guitar.

    _____

Notes for Home: Your child identified words that can be combined to form contractions.
Home Activity: Have your child read a story and look for words that can be combined to form contractions.

Underline the two contractions in each sentence. Write the words from which the contractions are formed.

1. You haven't told me when she'll be arriving.

   _____ _____   _____ _____

2. I don't understand why there's no answer.

   _____ _____   _____ _____

3. I'll meet you at the restaurant, and we'll have dinner together.

   _____ _____   _____ _____

4. Wouldn't you like to know who's going to give the keynote speech?

   _____ _____   _____ _____

5. They're going to the art museum while I'm at the planetarium.

   _____ _____   _____ _____

6. Although she'd like to be on the team, she hasn't been coming to practice.

   _____ _____   _____ _____

7. You're working on your report, aren't you?

   _____ _____   _____ _____

8. He won't tell me where he's hidden the key.

   _____ _____   _____ _____

9. Here's what he said: he'll pick you up at the airport.

   _____ _____   _____ _____

10. He's in the band, and she's on the tennis team.

    _____ _____   _____ _____

Notes for Home: Your child identified the words that make up contractions.
Home Activity: Have your child write a short dialogue without using any contractions and then rewrite it using contractions whenever possible.

Sometimes a base word doesn't change when *-ed* or *-ing* is added.

shout   shout**ed**   shout**ing**

If a base word ends in *e*, the *e* is dropped before *-ed* or *-ing* is added.

chase   chas**ed**   chas**ing**

Add the ending to each word and write the new word.

1. invite (-ing) _____

2. paint (-ed) _____

3. stay (-ed) _____

4. turn (-ed) _____

5. try (-ing) _____

6. live (-ed) _____

7. graze (-ing) _____

8. read (-ing) _____

9. flicker (-ed) _____

10. follow (-ing) _____

11. cover (-ed) _____

12. enter (-ed) _____

13. come (-ing) _____

14. write (-ing) _____

15. illustrate (-ed) _____

16. hear (-ing) _____

17. arrive (-ing) _____

18. receive (-ing) _____

19. skate (-ed) _____

20. jump (-ing) _____

© Scott Foresman 4-6

Notes for Home: Your child added *-ed* and *-ing* to base words. **Home Activity:** Ask your child to choose five words from the page and write a sentence using each word.

Name _____

The ending -es is added to words that end in *ch, sh, s, x,* or *z.*

pinch   pinch**es**

Add -es to the words in the box and write the new words to complete the sentences.

dash	wish	teach	fix	march
buzz	relax	finish	guess	miss

1. My sister _____ she had a kitten.

2. Dad _____ high school math.

3. She _____ that it will be evening before our company arrives.

4. After exercising, I find a warm bath really _____ me.

5. Jesse usually _____ his homework before dinnertime.

6. The bee _____ around the flowers.

7. After three weeks at camp, Kerry _____ her family.

8. The runner _____ for the finish line.

9. The school band _____ in parades several times a year.

10. A handy person _____ things around the house.

Notes for Home: Your child added -es to words ending in *ch, sh, s, x,* or *z.*
Home Activity: Ask your child to choose a sentence from the page and write a story that begins with the sentence.

Name _____

Add the ending to each word in the set. Write the new words.

Add *-es*

1. stretch _____

2. watch _____

3. push _____

4. dress _____

5. wax _____

Add *-ed*

6. tax _____

7. pour _____

8. replace _____

9. start _____

10. describe _____

Add *-ing*

11. type _____

12. send _____

13. finish _____

14. light _____

15. compete _____

Notes for Home: Your child added *-es, -ed,* and *-ing* to base words.
Home Activity: Have your child write phrases using ten words from this page.

© Scott Foresman 4-6

133

Add *-es, -ed,* or *-ing* to the base word to make a word that completes the sentence. Write the new word.

hatch   **1.** The chick is _____ from the egg.

saddle   **2.** She wanted to ride, so she _____ her horse.

reach   **3.** He is thirsty, so he _____ for a glass.

laugh   **4.** Are you _____ at the clown's antics?

save   **5.** Cara has _____ enough money for a new CD player.

graze   **6.** The cattle are _____ on the prairie.

patch   **7.** Tim _____ the holes in the wall yesterday.

skate   **8.** Have you _____ on the frozen pond?

wave   **9.** The candidate _____ at the people, who cheered loudly.

serve   **10.** Luke is _____ pizza to his friends.

rush   **11.** Because she is late, Hanna _____ through breakfast.

limit   **12.** I am _____ my phone calls to five minutes each.

stress   **13.** Mrs. Yan always _____ the need for patience.

remove   **14.** I had a hard time _____ the label from the disk.

borrow   **15.** Kevin _____ that book several weeks ago.

Notes for Home: Your child added *-es, -ed,* and *-ing* to base words.
Home Activity: Have your child add a different ending to each word on the page.

Name _____

The ending -er is used to compare two things. The ending -est is used to compare more than two things.

long   long**er** than that one   long**est** of them all

Add -er or -est to the base word. Write the new word to complete the phrase.

high   1. _____ of all the mountains

bright   2. _____ than a star

sweet   3. _____ apple of all

low   4. _____ branch on the tree

warm   5. _____ than yesterday

tall   6. _____ than his brother

cold   7. _____ month of the year

loud   8. _____ than a whisper

quick   9. _____ route to school

small   10. _____ than a basketball

smooth   11. _____ than a silk scarf

cool   12. _____ day since last spring

short   13. _____ of the two ponies

kind   14. _____ than she was before

fast   15. _____ runner on the team

Notes for Home: Your child added -er and -est to base words. **Home Activity:** Have your child write -er and -est words comparing things he or she might see at a carnival.

© Scott Foresman 4-6

Name _____

The endings -er and -est are used to compare things. If a base word ends in e, the e is dropped before -er or -est is added.

safe   saf**er** than the other one   saf**est** of all

Add -er or -est to the base word. Write the new word to complete the phrase.

large   1. _____ elephant in the whole herd

pale   2. _____ shade of pink I've ever seen

close   3. _____ park to our school

white   4. _____ than a snowflake

cute   5. _____ puppy in the litter

wise   6. _____ than an owl

blue   7. _____ than the sky

late   8. _____ than an hour ago

fine   9. _____ meal I've ever eaten

brave   10. _____ soldier in the army

nice   11. _____ than our old house

pure   12. _____ than other brands of soap

severe   13. _____ sentence allowed by law

rude   14. _____ than any salesclerk should be

lame   15. _____ excuse I have ever heard

Notes for Home: Your child added -er and -est to words ending in e.
Home Activity: Have your child use -er and -est words to compare TV shows, books, or movies.

The endings *-er* and *-est* are used to compare two or more things.

  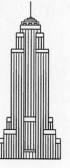

a tall building   a tall**er** building than the first one   the tall**est** building of the three

Add *-er* or *-est* to the base word. Write the new word to complete the sentence.

fast   **1.** Is a leopard _____ than a rhinoceros?

late   **2.** John turned in his homework _____ than I did.

close   **3.** Is the police station _____ to the post office or library?

old   **4.** My sister is _____ than my brother.

bright   **5.** The North Star is the _____ star in the sky.

warm   **6.** The weather in May is _____ than that in March.

cute   **7.** The striped kitten is the _____ of all.

small   **8.** Is a lemon _____ than a grapefruit?

loud   **9.** A bugle makes a _____ sound than a flute.

sharp   **10.** The carving knife is the _____ knife we have.

Notes for Home: Your child added *-er* and *-est* to base words. **Home Activity:** Have your child write questions using the *-er* and *-est* words on the page.

When -es, -ed, -er, or -est is added to a base word ending in y, the y is changed to i before the ending is added. When -ing is added, the y remains.

If the base word is an adjective, add -er and -est and write both words. If the base word is a verb, add -es, -ed, and -ing and write all three words.

1. early _____

2. worry _____

3. lazy _____

4. deny _____

5. merry _____

6. carry _____

7. pretty _____

8. try _____

9. silly _____

10. hurry _____

11. apply _____

12. happy _____

13. study _____

14. funny _____

15. easy _____

Notes for Home: Your child added endings to base words that end in y.
Home Activity: Have your child use words with endings from the page in oral sentences.

When *-ed, -ing, -er,* or *-est* is added to a word with a short vowel sound and a single final consonant, the consonant is doubled before the ending is added.

big	big**ger**	big**gest**
hug	hug**ged**	hug**ging**

Add *-er* and *-est* to each base word.

Add -er   **Add -est**

1. sad   _____   _____

2. hot   _____   _____

3. red   _____   _____

4. fat   _____   _____

5. wet   _____   _____

Add *-ed* or *-ing* to a word from the box to complete each sentence. Write the new word.

> slip   brag   tap   hug   stop

6. After three days, the rain has finally _____.

7. Brian is always _____ about his bike.

8. Ahmed _____ on a patch of ice.

9. Grandma picked up the baby and _____ her.

10. I wish Connie would stop _____ her pencil!

Notes for Home: Your child added endings to base words. **Home Activity:** Have your child make a list of other words in which the final consonant is doubled before endings are added.

Add the ending to each word in the list. Write the new word.

Add -es

1. copy _____

2. fly _____

3. supply _____

4. spy _____

5. scurry _____

Add -ed

6. reply _____

7. marry _____

8. clip _____

9. fry _____

10. trot _____

Add -ing

11. shop _____

12. plot _____

13. cry _____

14. trap _____

15. plan _____

Add -er

16. empty _____

17. sad _____

18. busy _____

19. thin _____

20. healthy _____

Add -est

21. scary _____

22. lonely _____

23. wet _____

24. red _____

25. easy _____

Notes for Home: Your child added endings to base words. **Home Activity:** Take turns with your child writing a phrase with each word on the page.

© Scott Foresman 4-6

Name _____

Possessive nouns show who or what owns something. To make a singular noun possessive, an apostrophe (') and an *s* are added to the word.

the wheels of the car   the car**'s** wheels

Write a possessive noun to complete each phrase.

1. the glasses of my grandmother   my _____ glasses

2. the helmet of the soldier   the _____ helmet

3. the streets of the city   the _____ streets

4. the principal of the school   the _____ principal

5. the rays of the sun   the _____ rays

6. the news of the year   the _____ news

7. the toys of the child   the _____ toys

8. the troops of the commander   the _____ troops

9. the purse of her mother   her _____ purse

10. the oceans of Earth   _____ oceans

11. the scarf of Manuel   _____ scarf

12. the desk of the teacher   the _____ desk

13. the backpack of Emiko   _____ backpack

14. the roof of the building   the _____ roof

15. the trip of our friend   our _____ trip

Notes for Home: Your child added *'s* to singular nouns to make their possessive forms.
Home Activity: Have your child write the name of each family member, add *'s,* and then write the name of an item to show ownership.

© Scott Foresman 4–6

Name _____

To make the possessive form of a plural noun that ends in *s*, an apostrophe (') is added to the word.

the desks of the students   the students' desks

Write a possessive noun to complete each phrase.

1. the jackets of the girls   the _____ jackets

2. the collars of the dogs   the _____ collars

3. the branches of the trees   the _____ branches

4. the books of the teachers   the _____ books

5. the caves of the bears   the _____ caves

6. the racquets of the players   the _____ racquets

7. the pictures of the artists   the _____ pictures

8. the brushes of the painters   the _____ brushes

9. the eggs of the hens   the _____ eggs

10. the boots of the hikers   the _____ boots

11. the yards of the houses   the _____ yards

12. the ropes of the climbers   the _____ ropes

13. the sales of the stores   the _____ sales

14. the jokes of the boys   the _____ jokes

15. the tails of the cats   the _____ tails

Notes for Home: Your child added an apostrophe to plural nouns ending in *s* to make their possessive forms. **Home Activity:** Have your child write five phrases from the page as sentences.

To make the possessive form of a plural noun that does not end in *s*, an apostrophe (') and an *s* are added to the word.

the bikes of the women   the women**'s** bikes

Add *'s* to each word.

1. feet   _____

2. men   _____

3. teeth   _____

4. children   _____

5. mice   _____

6. geese   _____

7. oxen   _____

Write a possessive noun to complete each phrase.

8. the kites of the children   the _____ kites

9. the hats of the men   the _____ hats

10. the beaks of the geese   the _____ beaks

11. the roots of the teeth   the _____ roots

12. the yokes of the oxen   the _____ yokes

13. the feet of the mice   the _____ feet

14. the cheers of the people   the _____ cheers

15. the laughter of the women   the _____ laughter

Notes for Home: Your child added *'s* to plural nouns that do not end in *s* to make their possessive forms. **Home Activity:** Have your child write sentences using the possessive nouns in items 1–7.

© Scott Foresman 4-6

Singular nouns — 's   girl**'s**
Plural nouns ending in *s* — '   dogs**'**
Plural nouns not ending in *s* — 's   teeth**'s**

Circle the correct possessive form of the noun to complete the sentence.

1. The (cities', city's) connecting road made it easy to travel between them.

2. The (children', children's) bicycles were in the garage.

3. The tour (guides', guide's) colorful uniforms stood out in a crowd.

4. One (boy's, boys') notebook was missing.

5. The mechanic repaired the (airplanes', airplane's) engine.

6. The (campers', camper's) tents were pitched around the fire.

7. The (womens', women's) group meets on Thursday evening.

8. The (foxes', fox's) tail was large and bushy.

9. The (beekeeper's, beekeepers') hat was covered with netting.

10. The three lab (assistants', assistant's) reports were very accurate.

11. The (student's, students') scores on the test ranged from 83 to 99.

12. The (jobs', job's) salary was higher than she had expected.

13. The map showed Allen where the (men's, mens') locker room was.

14. Mr. Kronksy used heavy tape to secure the (boxes', box's) lids.

15. Rosa tried to ignore the (geese', geese's) loud honking.

Notes for Home: Your child identified the correct possessive noun in sentences.
Home Activity: Have your child write sentences using any correct possessive nouns *not* circled on the page.

© Scott Foresman 4-6

Name _____

Add an apostrophe and *s* or an apostrophe to make the correct possessive form of each noun.
Then write the words to complete the sentences.

1. elephants _____

2. men _____

3. tourist _____

4. table _____

5. guests _____

6. people _____

7. schools _____

8. dress _____

9. mice _____

10. Edison _____

11. Samantha really liked the _____ color.

12. The wooden staircase had been damaged by the _____ gnawing.

13. The _____ legs were made of oak.

14. Last year the _____ ski team won the gold medal.

15. Each month the _____ principals meet to share information.

16. Did you know that all _____ tusks are ivory?

17. The politician worked hard to gain the _____ support.

18. The light bulb and phonograph are among _____ inventions.

19. The _____ lost camera was found in the airport.

20. All of the _____ coats were hanging in the closet.

Notes for Home: Your child wrote possessive forms of nouns to complete sentences.
Home Activity: Have your child make a list of things found in a school and then write words
that show ownership of each item.

A base word is a word to which other word parts, or affixes, may be added to make new words. Affixes may be endings, prefixes, or suffixes.

wash	**wash + ed**	**re + wash**
base word	base word + ending	prefix + base word

Divide each word into its base word and affix.

	Base Word		**Affix**
1. careful	_____	+	_____
2. building	_____	+	_____
3. quickly	_____	+	_____
4. enjoyment	_____	+	_____
5. darkness	_____	+	_____
6. thoughtless	_____	+	_____
7. laughable	_____	+	_____
8. freedom	_____	+	_____

	Affix		**Base Word**
9. recall	_____	+	_____
10. disagree	_____	+	_____
11. pretest	_____	+	_____
12. misunderstood	_____	+	_____
13. unpaid	_____	+	_____
14. impolite	_____	+	_____
15. nonsense	_____	+	_____

Notes for Home: Your child divided words into base words and affixes.
Home Activity: Have your child look in a newspaper to find at least six words made up of a base word and affix and write the base word and affix for each word.

Affixes are word parts that have meaning. They may be added to the beginning or end of the base word.

Draw a line from each affix in Column A to a base word in Column B. Then write the new word.

A	B	New Word
1. -ly	hope	_____
2. -dom	soft	_____
3. -or	king	_____
4. -less	act	_____
5. re-	possible	_____
6. non-	heat	_____
7. im-	like	_____
8. dis-	sense	_____
9. -ment	teach	_____
10. -er	slow	_____
11. -ful	assign	_____
12. -est	hope	_____
13. sub-	legal	_____
14. im-	way	_____
15. il-	patient	_____

Notes for Home: Your child combined base words and affixes to make new words.
Home Activity: On a sheet of paper, write four affixes at the top of four columns. Challenge your child to list as many words with that affix as possible given one minute for each column.

© Scott Foresman 4–6

Name _____

When the affix or affixes are removed, only the base word remains.

Write the affix or affixes in each word. Then write the base word.

	Affix(es)	**Base Word**
1. kindness	_____	_____
2. faster	_____	_____
3. pretested	_____	_____
4. smallest	_____	_____
5. helpful	_____	_____
6. recalled	_____	_____
7. crying	_____	_____
8. childish	_____	_____
9. unacceptable	_____	_____
10. freedom	_____	_____
11. midnight	_____	_____
12. illegal	_____	_____
13. effortless	_____	_____
14. insincerely	_____	_____
15. healthy	_____	_____

Notes for Home: Your child identified base words and affixes in words.
Home Activity: Have your child build as many new words as possible by adding affixes to these words: *pay, build, teach, polite, deep.*

Name _____

Different affixes can be added to a base word to give the word different meanings.

paint   **re**paint   paint**ing**   **un**painted   paint**er**

Choose an affix to add to the base word to form a new word that completes the sentence. Write the new word.

write   **1.** Please _____ your rough draft.

        sub-   re-   non-

play   **2.** The puppies were very _____.

        -est   -ing   -ful

loud   **3.** Morris raised the volume to the _____ setting.

        -est   -ment   -ly

sense   **4.** I could not understand the baby's _____ words.

        pre-   mis-   non-

spell   **5.** Many people _____ the word *receive*.

        mis-   il-   dis-

match   **6.** Monique sorted the socks into _____ pairs.

        -ful   -ing   -ish

heat   **7.** The baking directions said to first _____ the oven.

        pre-   inter-   sub-

effort   **8.** Mia made the difficult dive seem _____.

        -less   -ish   -ing

buckled   **9.** The passengers _____ their seat belts after takeoff.

        non-   dis-   un-

act   **10.** The young _____ auditioned for the play.

        -ion   -or   -ing

Notes for Home: Your child formed and wrote words by adding affixes to base words. **Home Activity:** Have your child look for words with affixes in printed directions. Talk together about how the meaning of the directions would change if the affixes in the words were changed.

Name _____

A base word can have an affix at the beginning or at the end. A base word can have more than one affix.

Start at *First Base*. Draw a line between the affix(es) and the base word. Write the base word. Follow the numbers to *Second Base, Third Base,* and *Home Plate* until you have written all the base words.

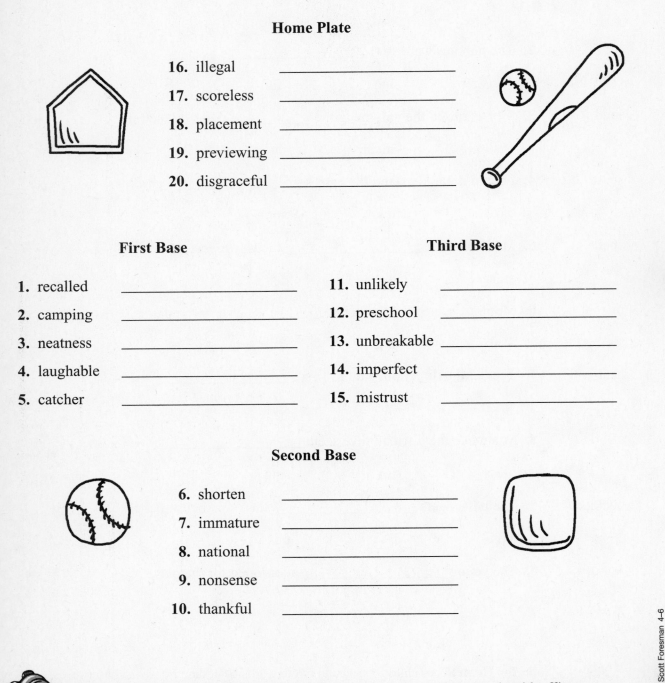

Home Plate

16. illegal _____
17. scoreless _____
18. placement _____
19. previewing _____
20. disgraceful _____

First Base

1. recalled _____
2. camping _____
3. neatness _____
4. laughable _____
5. catcher _____

Third Base

11. unlikely _____
12. preschool _____
13. unbreakable _____
14. imperfect _____
15. mistrust _____

Second Base

6. shorten _____
7. immature _____
8. national _____
9. nonsense _____
10. thankful _____

Notes for Home: Your child identified and wrote the base words in words with affixes.
Home Activity: Have your child scan a newspaper article and underline the base words in ten or more words with affixes in the article.

© Scott Foresman 4-6

Name _____

A prefix is a word part added to the beginning of a word that changes the word's meaning. The prefix *re-* means "again."

re + paint = **re**paint   to paint again

Add *re-* to make new words. Then write the words to complete the sentences.

_____cycles   _____fill   _____new   _____read   _____told

_____elected   _____heat   _____organized   _____set   _____united

_____enter   _____loaded   _____place   _____tie   _____view

1. Tanya stopped skating to _____ her laces.

2. Our mayor was _____ for a second term.

3. I had to _____ the glass that I dropped and broke.

4. The critic gave that movie a good _____.

5. Our community _____ paper, plastic, and aluminum.

6. Grandma _____ the story of her coming to America.

7. Last Sunday, I cleaned out and _____ my closet.

8. I quickly read the notice; then I _____ it more slowly.

9. The colonists' rifles had to be _____ after every shot.

10. After a long separation, Kate was _____ with her cousin.

11. Joseph will _____ the leftovers in the microwave.

12. The price of a bucket of popcorn includes one free _____.

13. We needed to show our ticket stub to _____ the theater.

14. Jasmine _____ the alarm on her clock radio.

15. Emilio needed to _____ the overdue library book.

Notes for Home: Your child added the prefix *re-* to base words and wrote those words in sentences. **Home Activity:** Have your child find ten action words (verbs) in a magazine or newspaper article. Add *re-* to the words and talk about how this changes the meaning of the article.

Name _____

The prefix *mis-* means "bad," "wrong," or "incorrect."

mis + use = **mis**use   to use in the wrong way

Welcome to the first annual Miss **Mis-** Contest! Read the statement by each of our ten "contestants." Then write the *mis-* word that best describes that contestant.

Contestant #1: "I use an eraser to correct these."

I am Miss _____.   Mistakes   Miscount   Mislead

Contestant #2: "I bought a CD at the music store without checking for a sale price."

I am Miss _____.   Misapply   Misfit   Misspent

Contestant #3: "I can't find my homework!"

I am Miss _____.   Misuse   Mistrust   Misplace

Contestant #4: "Sometimes I say words incorrectly."

I am Miss _____.   Misjudge   Mispronounce   Misspell

Contestant #5: "I ran out of gas because I didn't figure the mileage correctly."

I am Miss _____.   Misapply   Miscalculate   Misfit

Contestant #6: "I'm a 12-year-old actress but was given the role of a grandmother."

I am Miss _____.   Miscast   Mistrust   Misjudge

Contestant #7: "I get lost a lot because I can't read and follow directions."

I am Miss _____.   Mistrusted   Misread   Miscount

Contestant #8: "I like wearing a striped shirt with a plaid skirt and polka dot socks."

I am Miss _____.   Misused   Misjudged   Mismatched

Contestant #9: "Magazines and newspapers never print exactly what I say."

I am Miss _____.   Misquoted   Mistrust   Misbehave

Contestant #10: "I was given the wrong information about the store's return policy."

I am Miss _____.   Misinformed   Misfire   Mishandle

Notes for Home: Your child wrote words with the prefix *mis-*. **Home Activity:** Help your child make up "contestant" descriptions using *mis-* words that were not used on the page.

Name _____

The prefix *un-* means "not" or "opposite of."

un + happy = **un**happy   not happy, opposite of *happy*

Write the word with *un-* that matches each meaning. Then write the words to complete the sentences.

1. not true   _____

2. not paid   _____

3. not equal   _____

4. not pleasant   _____

5. opposite of *lock* _____

6. not safe   _____

7. opposite of *pack* _____

8. not usual   _____

9. opposite of *load* _____

10. not fair   _____

11. The overdue bill was _____.

12. Use the key to _____ the door.

13. Let's _____ our suitcases later.

14. Going out of turn is _____.

15. A pint and a quart are _____ amounts.

16. Riding without using a seat belt is _____.

17. A skunk's odor is very _____.

18. A lie is _____.

19. Snow in May is _____.

20. She will _____ the boxes from the truck.

Notes for Home: Your child wrote words with the prefix *un-*. **Home Activity:** Have your child think of "un-" advertising slogans based on the opposite qualities of items or products. For example: Dogs—the "uncats"—great pets that don't choke on fur balls!

The prefixes *non-* and *un-* mean "not."

non + profit = **non**profit   not for profit   un + happy = **un**happy   not happy

Add *non-* or *un-* to make new words. Then write the words to complete the sentences.

_____sure	_____tidy	_____lucky	_____tied	_____fat
_____sense	_____stop	_____comfortable	_____seen	_____fiction
_____known	_____familiar	_____flammable	_____violence	_____solved

1. Renaldo _____ the ribbon before opening the gift.

2. The lumpy mattress was very _____.

3. The true identity of the suspect is _____ at this time.

4. Skim milk is used to make _____ yogurt.

5. I promised to clean up my _____ room.

6. The hidden camera was _____ by the shoppers.

7. Reginald was _____ of the correct answer.

8. The toddler spoke only _____ words.

9. Joe felt _____ after he lost his wallet and got a flat tire.

10. After years of investigation, the mystery is still _____.

11. Biographies are _____ books.

12. The express train runs _____ from here to downtown.

13. Children's pajamas are made of _____ materials.

14. Pablo was _____ with his new school.

15. Dr. Martin Luther King, Jr. believed in _____.

Notes for Home: Your child wrote words with the prefixes *un-* and *non-*.
Home Activity: Take turns with your child naming words with *non-* and *un-* and writing them in two lists.

© Scott Foresman 4–6

Name _____

The prefix _pre-_ means "before."

pre + approved = **pre**approved   approved before

The prefix _dis-_ means "not" or "opposite of."

dis + similar = **dis**similiar   not similar, opposite of _similar_

Add _dis-_ or _pre-_ to each base word to make a word that makes sense in the sentence.

1. _____agreed   The coach _____ with the referee.

2. _____test   Our teacher gave us a _____.

3. _____continued   Terrell _____ his magazine subscription.

4. _____approves   Al _____ of watching too much TV.

5. _____view   We saw a sneak _____ of the movie.

6. _____comfort   The icy winds added to our _____.

7. _____organized   My desk drawer is very _____.

8. _____teen   Twelve is the last year you are a _____.

9. _____honest   Stealing is _____.

10. _____school   Ana went to _____ before kindergarten.

11. _____paid   Mrs. Panek _____ her rent for two months.

12. _____qualified   Felice was _____ after misspelling a word.

13. _____appeared   The setting sun _____ from the sky.

14. _____heat   First _____ the oven to 350°.

15. _____connected   Sometimes I am _____ from the Internet.

Notes for Home: Your child wrote words with the prefixes _pre-_ and _dis-_.
Home Activity: Have your child draw pictures to illustrate the meanings of two or more _dis-_ or _pre-_ words from the page.

© Scott Foresman 4-6

Name _____

The prefix *sub-* means "under," "nearly," or "again."

        sub + title = **sub**title   a title under the main title

The prefix *en-* means "to make or cause to be."

        en + circle = **en**circle   make a circle around

The prefix *mis-* means "bad," "wrong," or "incorrect."

        mis + use = **mis**use   use incorrectly

Draw a line to connect the prefix to the correct base word. Write the new word next to its definition.

1. mis-   way   **A.** railroad under the ground   _____

    sub-   joy   **B.** be happy with   _____

    en-   read   **C.** see words incorrectly   _____

2. sub-   behave   **A.** act badly   _____

    mis-   close   **B.** put a wall around   _____

    en-   marine   **C.** underwater ship   _____

3. mis-   large   **A.** make bigger   _____

    sub-   spell   **B.** use the wrong letters   _____

    en-   divide   **C.** break apart again   _____

4. mis-   danger   **A.** put in a harmful position   _____

    en-   inform   **B.** give incorrect information   _____

    sub-   urban   **C.** near the city   _____

5. mis-   total   **A.** nearly the final amount   _____

    sub-   tangle   **B.** get twisted; caught in   _____

    en-   trust   **C.** doubt, not be sure of   _____

Notes for Home: Your child wrote words with the prefixes *sub-, en-,* and *mis-*.
Home Activity: Have your child look for advertisements in magazines or newspapers that use words with *sub-, en-,* or *mis-*. Have your child create his or her own ad using one or more words with those prefixes.

© Scott Foresman 4–6

The prefixes *in-* and *im-* mean "not" or "within."

im + possible = **im**possible   not possible

in + field = **in**field   within the field

Add *in-* or *im-* to each base word. Then write two of the new words to complete the sentences. Hint: The prefix *im-* is added to base words that begin with *b, m,* or *p.*

1. _____patient   _____correct   _____complete   _____polite

   Not saying "thank you" is considered _____.

   The jigsaw puzzle is still _____.

2. _____side   _____proper   _____land   _____valid

   3/2 and 18/5 are examples of _____ fractions.

   The _____ of the coat was lined with wool.

3. _____prisoned   _____movable   _____expensive   _____active

   The thief was _____ for five years.

   The camera was _____ because it was on sale.

4. _____direct   _____sincere   _____mature   _____definite

   Mia was _____ about the exact time to meet.

   The babysitter could not control the _____ child.

5. _____efficient   _____passable   _____perfect   _____convenient

   Meeting you an hour earlier is _____ for me.

   The huge snowdrifts made the roads _____.

Notes for Home: Your child wrote words with the prefixes *in-* and *im-*.
Home Activity: Have your child illustrate one word with *im-* and one with *in-*. Then have your child draw companion illustrations of these words without the prefixes.

The prefixes *in-*, *im-*, *il-*, and *ir-* mean "not." The prefix *im-* is added to base words that begin with *b*, *m*, or *p*. The prefix *il-* is added to base words that begin with *l*. The prefix *ir-* is added to base words that begin with *r*.

Add *in-*, *im-*, *il-*, or *ir-* to the word in dark type. Write the new word to complete the sentence.

1. not **literate**   A person who cannot read is _____.

2. not **mature**   An eight-year-old child is _____.

3. not **visible**   Air is _____.

4. not **pure**   Polluted water is _____.

5. not **responsible**   Forgetting homework is _____.

6. not **legible**   Careless handwriting is _____.

7. not **exact**   Measuring without a ruler is _____.

8. not **flexible**   Hard rubber is very _____.

9. not **reversible**   The judge's ruling was _____.

10. not **legal**   Shoplifting is _____.

11. not **practical**   Not saving money is _____.

12. not **edible**   Spoiled meat is _____.

13. not **resistible**   Fresh baked brownies are _____.

14. not **movable**   The heavy box of books is _____.

15. not **personal**   The brief note was _____.

Notes for Home: Your child wrote words with the prefixes *in-*, *im-*, *il-*, and *ir-*.
Home Activity: Have your child write sentences for several of the words with prefixes on the page.

Name _____

The prefix *semi-* means "half," "partly," or "twice." **semi**annual
The prefix *mid-* means "of, in, or near the middle of." **mid**term
The prefix *inter-* means "between" or "together at the same time." **inter**act

Add *semi-, mid-,* or *inter-* to the base word to make a word that tells about the picture.

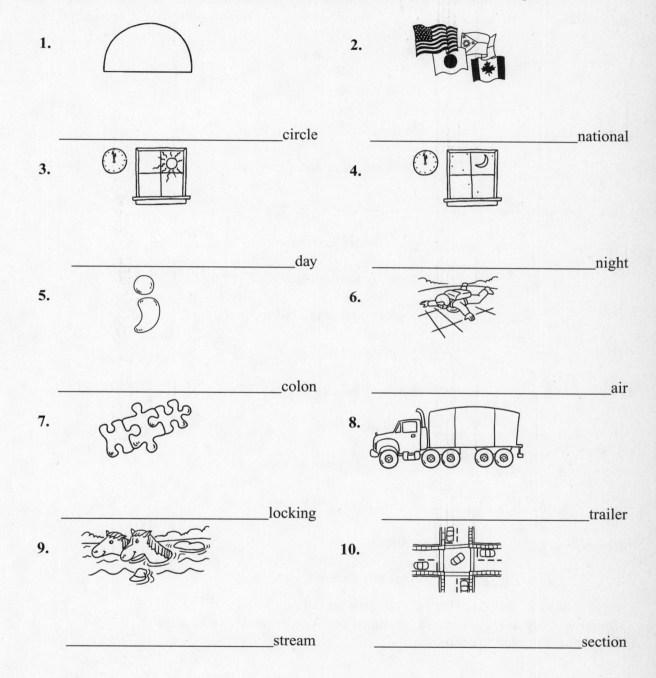

1.

_____circle

2.

_____national

3.

_____day

4.

_____night

5.

_____colon

6.

_____air

7.

_____locking

8.

_____trailer

9.

_____stream

10.

_____section

Notes for Home: Your child completed words with the prefixes *semi-, mid-,* and *inter-*.
Home Activity: Have your child sketch or describe pictures that could be used to illustrate
the words *semisolid, midsummer,* and *interstate.*

159

The prefixes *semi-*, *mid-*, and *inter-* when added to a word change the word's meaning.

Write the words to match the definitions. Write one letter in each space.

interchangeable	midsummer	Midwest	semisolid	interwoven
Internet	midtown	semiannual	semisweet	midweek
interstate	midway	semifinal	semitropical	semimonthly

1. _ _ _ _ _ [ ] _ _   the central United States

2. _ _ _ [ ] _ _ _ _   network between computer information sites

3. [ ] _ _ _ _ _   halfway; in the middle

4. _ _ _ [ ] _ _ _ _ _   between bitter and sweet

5. _ _ _ _ _ _ _ _ _ _ _ [ ] _ _   switchable

6. _ _ _ _ _ _ _ _ [ ] _   twice each month

7. _ _ _ _ [ ] _ _ _ _   halfway through July

8. _ [ ] _ _ _ _ _ _ _   a game before the last or final game

9. _ _ _ _ _ [ ] _ _ _   between states

10. _ _ _ [ ] _ _ _   central part of the city or town

11. _ [ ] _ _ _ _ _ _ _   twice a year

12. _ _ _ _ _ [ ] _ _ _   mixed or woven together

13. _ _ _ _ [ ] _ _ _ _ _   almost tropical

14. _ _ _ [ ] _ _ _   Wednesday

15. _ _ _ _ _ [ ] _ _ _   partially frozen water

Write the letters in the boxes in order on the lines below.
Question: Why did the chef add two drops of ink to the newlyweds' dinner?
Answer: He wanted to make

_ _ _ _ _ _ _ _ _ _ _ _ _ _ _ _ **for** _ _ _ !

Notes for Home: Your child wrote words with the prefixes *semi-*, *mid-*, and *inter-*.
Home Activity: Work with your child to make up your own riddles using words that begin with *semi-*, *mid-*, or *inter-* as part of the question or answer.

Name _____

A suffix is a word part added to the end of a word that changes the word's meaning.

The suffix *-ful* means "full of." hope + ful = hope**ful** full of hope
The suffix *-less* means "without." hope + less = hope**less** without hope

Add *-ful* and *-less* to the base word. Write the two new words to complete the sentences.

1. hope Sighting land made the sailors feel _____.

Being lost at sea had made them feel _____.

2. thought It was _____ of you to remember my birthday.

How _____ of you to forget my birthday!

3. color The all white room seemed _____.

The _____ room was painted red and purple.

4. rest Sitting in rush hour traffic makes me _____.

Lying on a beach is very _____.

5. help The climbers were _____without a rope.

The tour guide offered _____ suggestions.

6. use First aid training is very _____.

Without batteries, the flashlight was _____.

7. care Be _____ with that hot water!

Hurrying will result in _____ work.

8. thank Cleaning the bathroom is a _____ task.

I am _____ I wasn't hurt in the accident.

9. fear The _____ child hid under the covers.

The _____ firefighter ran into the burning building.

10. harm He explained how to approach a _____ snake

and how to avoid a _____ one.

Notes for Home: Your child wrote words with the suffixes *-ful* and *-less*.
Home Activity: Have your child list other base words that have opposite meanings when the suffixes *-ful* and *-less* are added. Examples: *meaning, power, joy.*

The suffix *-or* or *-er* means a person or thing that does something.

| instruct + or = instruct**or** | person who instructs |
| mix + er = mix**er** | thing that mixes |

Add *-er* or *-or* to the word in dark type to make a word that describes the picture. You will need to drop letters before adding a suffix. Use a dictionary to check the spellings of *-er* and *-or* words.

1. person who **sings**

_____

2. person who **dances**

_____

3. machine that **blends**

_____

4. person who **drives**

_____

5. person who **acts**

_____

6. person who **farms**

_____

7. person who **sails**

_____

8. person who is elected to the **Senate**

_____

9. person who serves on a **jury**

_____

10. machine that **prints**

_____

Notes for Home: Your child wrote words with the suffix *-er* or *-or*.
Home Activity: Have your child find occupations or items listed in the Yellow Pages® business directory that end in *-or* or *-er*.

Name _____

The suffix -y added to a word makes the word an adjective.

snow + y = snowy   It is a snowy day.

The suffix -ly added to a word makes the word an adjective or an adverb.

dangerous + ly = dangerous**ly**   He is driving dangerously.

Add -y or -ly to each word. Then write the words to complete the sentences.

patient_____   friend_____   mess_____   slow_____   dirt_____

wind_____   loud_____   water_____   sweat_____   time_____

1. Michael organized his _____ desk.

2. The turtle crawled _____ across the room.

3. Paul loaded the _____ clothes into the washer.

4. The fans cheered _____ for their team.

5. We were hot and _____ after an hour of exercising.

6. Terasita waited _____ for the store to open.

7. Shaking hands is a _____ gesture.

8. The tasteless soup was thin and _____.

9. The _____ warning of the alarm kept me from being late.

10. Meeko likes to fly kites on _____ days.

Notes for Home: Your child wrote words with the suffixes -y and -ly.
Home Activity: Have your child look through a magazine or newspaper article, find three words with the suffix -y and three words with the suffix -ly, and identify the base word in each one.

The suffixes *-ment, -ness, -ation, -ion,* and *-dom* added to words make the words nouns.

argue + ment = argu**ment**   collect + ion = collec**tion**

Combine a base word from the box with the suffix given to make a word that fits in the definition. You may need to drop a letter before adding the suffix.

imagine	invite	free	king	elect
state	quick	pollute	arrange	wise
bore	examine	educate	agree	ill

1. a test; _____ **(-ation)**

2. an understanding; a contract; _____ **(-ment)**

3. a request to come to a party or event; _____ **(-ation)**

4. position or a certain order; _____ **(-ment)**

5. state of being fast or swift; _____ **(-ness)**

6. schooling; learning; training; _____ **(-ion)**

7. country ruled by a king or queen; _____ **(-dom)**

8. making choices by voting; _____ **(-ion)**

9. disease; an unhealthy condition; _____ **(-ness)**

10. dirty air, water, and land; _____ **(-ion)**

11. thinking and acting as you want; _____ **(-dom)**

12. something said; a type of sentence; _____ **(-ment)**

13. knowledge based on experience; _____ **(-dom)**

14. ability to picture ideas in your mind; _____ **(-ation)**

15. nothing to do; _____ **(-dom)**

Notes for Home: Your child wrote words with the suffixes *-ment, -ness, -ation, -ion,* and *-dom.* **Home Activity:** Challenge your child to think of another word with each of the suffixes *-ment, -ness, -ation, -ion,* and *-dom.*

The suffixes *-al, -ic, -ive, -ish, -ible,* and *-able* added to words make the words adjectives.

profession + al = profession**al**   sense + ible = sens**ible**

Add the base word and the suffix to make an adjective. You may need to change the spelling of the base word before you add the suffix. Then write the words to complete the phrases.

1. wash + able =   _____   2. artist + ic =   _____

3. self + ish =   _____   4. enjoy + able =   _____

5. nation + al =   _____   6. colony + al =   _____

7. flex + ible =   _____   8. base + ic =   _____

9. rely + able =   _____   10. support + ive =   _____

11. our _____ government

12. a _____ child who would not share

13. exercises to keep your body strong and _____

14. a _____ clock that keeps perfect time

15. a relaxing and _____ vacation

16. _____ fabric that shouldn't be dry cleaned

17. a young sculptor with _____ talent

18. a re-creation of a town in _____ America

19. being _____ when someone needs help

20. the _____ equipment needed for scuba diving

Notes for Home: Your child wrote words with the suffixes *-al, -ic, -ive, -ish, -ible,* and *-able.*
Home Activity: Have your child write one more word with each of the six suffixes on this page.

Name _____

Look at these words.

ham/mer   star/ry

Each word has two like consonants after the first vowel. The first vowel is between two consonants. This vowel usually stands for the short vowel sound unless it is followed by *r*.

Divide each word into syllables as you write the word. Put an X by each word with a short vowel sound in the first syllable.

1. letter _____ _____   2. rabbit _____ _____

3. yellow _____ _____   4. puppet _____ _____

5. worry _____ _____   6. horror _____ _____

7. tunnel _____ _____   8. ribbon _____ _____

9. butter _____ _____   10. jelly _____ _____

11. lettuce _____ _____   12. drummer _____ _____

13. pepper _____ _____   14. cotton _____ _____

15. hurry _____ _____   16. furry _____ _____

17. pillow _____ _____   18. current _____ _____

19. cabbage _____ _____   20. button _____ _____

Notes for Home: Your child divided words with two like consonants in the middle into syllables. **Home Activity:** Help your child make a list of other words with two like consonants in the middle.

Look at these words.

bas/ket   car/ton

Each word has two unlike consonants after the first vowel. The first vowel is between two consonants. This vowel usually stands for the short vowel sound unless it is followed by *r*.

ta/ble   ap/ple

Each word ends in a consonant + *le*. The first vowel can stand for the long or short vowel sound. Do not divide words between the consonant and *le*.

Divide each word into syllables as you write the word. Put an X by each word with a short vowel sound in the first syllable.

1. sister _____ _____   **2.** corner _____ _____

3. dentist _____ _____   **4.** mustard _____ _____

5. perfect _____ _____   **6.** uncle _____ _____

7. cattle _____ _____   **8.** service _____ _____

9. window _____ _____   **10.** custard _____ _____

11. pencil _____ _____   **12.** picture _____ _____

13. market _____ _____   **14.** puddle _____ _____

15. cable _____ _____   **16.** carpet _____ _____

17. public _____ _____   **18.** thirteen _____ _____

19. blanket _____ _____   **20.** bugle _____ _____

Notes for Home: Your child divided words with two unlike consonants in the middle or a consonant + *le* pattern into syllables. **Home Activity:** Help your child make up sentences for some of the two-syllable words on the page.

Use the words in the box to answer the questions. Write each syllable of the word on a line.

turkey	hammer	letter	rabbit	garbage
candle	tunnel	picture	circus	hornet
carpet	mittens	ladle	simmer	bargain

1. Where can you see a clown?   _____ / _____

2. What is a type of floor covering?   _____ / _____

3. What is something you write to a friend?   _____ / _____

4. What is another name for *trash?*   _____ / _____

5. What is something that has a low price?   _____ / _____

6. What gives off light?   _____ / _____

7. What means "to boil gently"?   _____ / _____

8. What is a tool that a carpenter uses?   _____ / _____

9. What might a train travel through?   _____ / _____

10. What is a large cup-shaped spoon?   _____ / _____

11. What animal says "gobble"?   _____ / _____

12. What do you wear to keep your hands warm?   _____ / _____

13. What animal hops around?   _____ / _____

14. What can you put in a frame and hang on a wall?   _____ / _____

15. What animal can sting?   _____ / _____

Notes for Home: Your child divided words with two like or unlike consonants in the middle or a consonant + *le* into syllables. **Home Activity:** Have your child look through a newspaper to find other words with two consonants in the middle.

Syllabication

Name _____

Complete each sentence with a two-syllable word. Circle the word. Then write the word and divide it into syllables.

1. We had _____ pie at dinner.

   peach   custard

   _____ / _____

2. The _____ lived in the woods.

   snake   rabbit

   _____ / _____

3. Dad washed the _____.

   floor   window

   _____ / _____

4. We put _____ books on the shelf.

   fifteen   three

   _____ / _____

5. The _____ sweater had a flower on it.

   green   yellow

   _____ / _____

6. The _____ shaker needed to be filled.

   pepper   salt

   _____ / _____

7. I spoke to the _____ about my cold.

   nurse   doctor

   _____ / _____

8. We put all the food in a _____ basket.

   picnic   green

   _____ / _____

9. The _____ was on the big porch.

   swing   hammock

   _____ / _____

10. The girl has two _____ in her hair.

   bows   ribbons

   _____ / _____

Notes for Home: Your child divided words with two like or unlike consonants in the middle into syllables. **Home Activity:** Choose four two-syllable words from the page and create a sentence using each word.

Name _____

Look at these words.

pi/lot   ro/bot

Each word has one consonant after the first vowel. The first vowel stands for the long vowel sound. The first syllable ends with that vowel.

Divide each two-syllable word into syllables as you write the word. If it has only one syllable, *do not* write the word.

1. flavor _____   2. final _____

3. hotel _____   4. razor _____

5. clock _____   6. spider _____

7. lazy _____   8. clover _____

9. legal _____   10. trunk _____

11. boat _____   12. major _____

13. paper _____   14. black _____

15. motor _____   16. bacon _____

17. cocoa _____   18. trick _____

19. stack _____   20. soda _____

Notes for Home: Your child divided words with a long vowel sound into syllables.
Home Activity: Have your child write phrases using ten words from the page.

Name _____

Look at these words.

sev/en   riv/er

Each word has one consonant after the first vowel. The first vowel stands for the short vowel sound. The words are divided after the consonant that follows this vowel.

Divide each two-syllable word into syllables as you write the word. If it has only one syllable, *do not* write the word.

1. melon _____

2. ever _____

3. travel _____

4. robin _____

5. think _____

6. crust _____

7. lemon _____

8. petal _____

9. never _____

10. damage _____

11. spill _____

12. palace _____

13. visit _____

14. blank _____

15. cabin _____

16. medal _____

17. model _____

18. wagon _____

19. crack _____

20. camel _____

© Scott Foresman 4-6

Notes for Home: Your child divided words with a short vowel sound into syllables.
Home Activity: Challenge your child to make a list of ten two-syllable words that have a short vowel sound and divide them into syllables.

Write a word from the box to complete each sentence. Then write each syllable of the word on a line.

finish	river	camel	limit	pilot
lilac	medal	solid	hotel	music

1. The _____ landed the airplane on the runway.

   _____ / _____

2. The _____ bush blooms every spring.

   _____ / _____

3. The firefighter was awarded a _____ for bravery.

   _____ / _____

4. The crowd applauded as the runner crossed the _____ line.

   _____ / _____

5. My brother listens to _____ when he studies.

   _____ / _____

6. A _____ can travel a long distance without food or water.

   _____ / _____

7. During the winter, the lake was frozen _____.

   _____ / _____

8. The driver was ticketed for exceeding the speed _____.

   _____ / _____

9. The _____ had over five hundred rooms.

   _____ / _____

10. A large amount of rain caused the _____ to overflow.

   _____ / _____

Notes for Home: Your child divided words into syllables based on the vowel sound in the first syllable. **Home Activity:** Have your child write a riddle for each word in the box.

© Scott Foresman 4-6

Complete each sentence with a two-syllable word that has a long vowel sound. Circle the word. Then write the word, dividing it into syllables.

1. We had _____, toast, and eggs for breakfast.

   bacon   melon

   _____ / _____

2. The _____ lived by the tall grass on the plateau.

   tiger   camel

   _____ / _____

3. The _____ crawled along the rocks.

   lizard   spider

   _____ / _____

4. I wanted to buy a _____ at the store.

   wagon   paper

   _____ / _____

5. The _____ in the movie was very pretty.

   music   palace

   _____ / _____

6. We got a new _____ for my bike.

   pedal   license

   _____ / _____

7. I heard the _____ tell about her career.

   pilot   doctor

   _____ / _____

8. The _____ was built on the side of a hill.

   hotel   cabin

   _____ / _____

9. The ad was in the _____ paper.

   city   local

   _____ / _____

10. The _____ was located near the center of town.

    station   river

    _____ / _____

Notes for Home: Your child divided words with long vowel sounds into syllables.
Home Activity: Challenge your child to make up movie titles using two-syllable words with long vowel sounds.

1. **Two-syllable words with two like or unlike consonants after the first vowel**

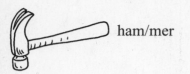 ham/mer

bas/ket

2. **Two-syllable words with one consonant after the first vowel**

 pi/lot

 sev/en

3. **Two-syllable words with a consonant +** *le*

ap/ple

ta/ble

On the first line, write the number of the rule that tells how to divide the word. Then write the word and divide it into syllables.

1. gallop _____ _____
2. copper _____ _____

3. cancel _____ _____
4. music _____ _____

5. minute _____ _____
6. siren _____ _____

7. litter _____ _____
8. cozy _____ _____

9. muscle _____ _____
10. crazy _____ _____

11. razor _____ _____
12. channel _____ _____

13. vanish _____ _____
14. maple _____ _____

15. pillow _____ _____
16. wisdom _____ _____

17. motor _____ _____
18. petal _____ _____

19. paddle _____ _____
20. locate _____ _____

 Notes for Home: Your child divided two-syllable words into syllables.
Home Activity: Have your child write the rules for dividing words on paper and write new words for each rule.

Choose a two-syllable word to replace the underlined one-syllable word. Write the word and divide it into syllables.

carton	jungle	river	carpet	apple
bonnet	music	lemon	bacon	hammer
robin	lantern	bugle	paddle	rabbit

1. The <u>sour</u> drops were in a fancy bag.   _____ / _____

2. Our new <u>rug</u> was a light brown color.   _____ / _____

3. I used the <u>oar</u> to move the canoe.   _____ / _____

4. The <u>tune</u> had a very fast rhythm.   _____ / _____

5. The soldier played a <u>horn</u>.   _____ / _____

6. The <u>stream</u> overflowed its banks.   _____ / _____

7. I ate a green <u>grape</u>.   _____ / _____

8. The <u>bird</u> pulled a worm out of the ground.   _____ / _____

9. The driver delivered a large <u>box</u>.   _____ / _____

10. The <u>hare</u> ran across the yard to the woods.   _____ / _____

11. The tiger wandered through the <u>grass</u>.   _____ / _____

12. The camper had a gas <u>light</u>.   _____ / _____

13. We had <u>pork</u> for breakfast with our eggs.   _____ / _____

14. This <u>tool</u> will help fix the broken door.   _____ / _____

15. The actress wore a green <u>hat</u> with feathers.   _____ / _____

Notes for Home: Your child divided two-syllable words into syllables.
Home Activity: Work with your child to write sentences with one-syllable words that can be changed to two-syllable words. Read the sentences to family members.

Two-syllable words that are divided between two consonants are usually accented on the first syllable.

ham´ mer   win´ dow

Divide each word into syllables as you write it. Then mark the accented syllable.

1. carrot   _____   **2.** yellow   _____

3. robber   _____   **4.** cabbage   _____

5. lantern   _____   **6.** narrow   _____

7. valley   _____   **8.** temper   _____

9. velvet   _____   **10.** bottom   _____

11. lumber   _____   **12.** letter   _____

13. practice   _____   **14.** elbow   _____

15. pepper   _____   **16.** pencil   _____

17. ladder   _____   **18.** walrus   _____

19. winter   _____   **20.** mitten   _____

Notes for Home: Your child divided words into syllables and marked the accented syllable.
Home Activity: Make a list of two-syllable words with two like or unlike consonants in the middle and ask your child to identify the accented syllable in each word.

Two-syllable words with one consonant after the first vowel are divided before or after the consonant and are usually accented on the first syllable. The first vowel can stand for the long or the short vowel sound.

pi´ lot   sev´ en

Divide each word into syllables as you write it. Then mark the accented syllable.

1. open _____

2. shovel _____

3. bacon _____

4. gravel _____

5. moment _____

6. humid _____

7. second _____

8. shiver _____

9. robot _____

10. radar _____

11. notice _____

12. unit _____

13. never _____

14. radish _____

15. music _____

16. pupil _____

17. bison _____

18. camel _____

19. tiger _____

20. robin _____

© Scott Foresman 4–6

Notes for Home: Your child divided words into syllables and marked the accented syllable.
Home Activity: Have your child write the words on the page in alphabetical order.

Two-syllable words with a prefix or suffix are usually accented on the base word.

play´ ing   un lock´   play´ ful

Divide each word into syllables as you write it. Then mark the accented syllable.

1. slower _____

2. nonfat _____

3. thankful _____

4. talking _____

5. friendly _____

6. careful _____

7. rewrite _____

8. crying _____

9. hardest _____

10. reread _____

11. untie _____

12. impure _____

13. distrust _____

14. nonstop _____

15. windy _____

16. unsure _____

17. misty _____

18. prepay _____

19. unfit _____

20. lucky _____

Notes for Home: Your child divided words into syllables and marked the accented syllable.
Home Activity: Have your child make a list of base words and add *un-*, *pre-*, *re-*, *dis-*, *-ing*, and *-ful* to make new words. Ask your child to divide each new word into syllables and mark the accented syllable.

© Scott Foresman 4–6

When an affix is added to a word that has more than one syllable, the accent often shifts to a syllable nearer to the affix.

mag′ net   →   mag net′ ic

Write each word in syllables and mark the accented syllable.

1. fantasy

_____

fantastic

_____

2. product

_____

production

_____

3. divide

_____

division

_____

4. real

_____

reality

_____

5. person

_____

personality

_____

6. memory

_____

memorial

_____

7. patriot

_____

patriotic.

_____

8. irrigate

_____

irrigation

_____

9. communicate

_____

communication

_____

10. equal

_____

equality

_____

Notes for Home: Your child identified the accented syllables in pairs of related words.
Home Activity: Have your child choose five pairs of related words and write sentences using each pair.

Mark the accent in each word. Write the longer word in each pair to complete the sentence.

1. The Alamo is a _____ site.

   history   historic

2. The _____ committee for the concert put up posters at school.

   public   publicity

3. The _____ party held its convention in Dallas, Texas.

   politics   political

4. Soccer is Ted's favorite after-school _____.

   active   activity

5. The _____ is a member of the community orchestra.

   music   musician

6. Machine parts were made by the _____ department.

   product   production

7. The _____ of the new library will be decided by the city council.

   locate   location

8. Terry's new suit required extensive _____.

   alter   alteration

9. The police conducted an _____ of the traffic accident.

   investigate   investigation

10. Planning the school carnival requires a great deal of _____.

    organize   organization

 Notes for Home: Your child identified the accented syllables in pairs of related words. **Home Activity:** Have your child write sentences for the shorter word in each pair on the page.

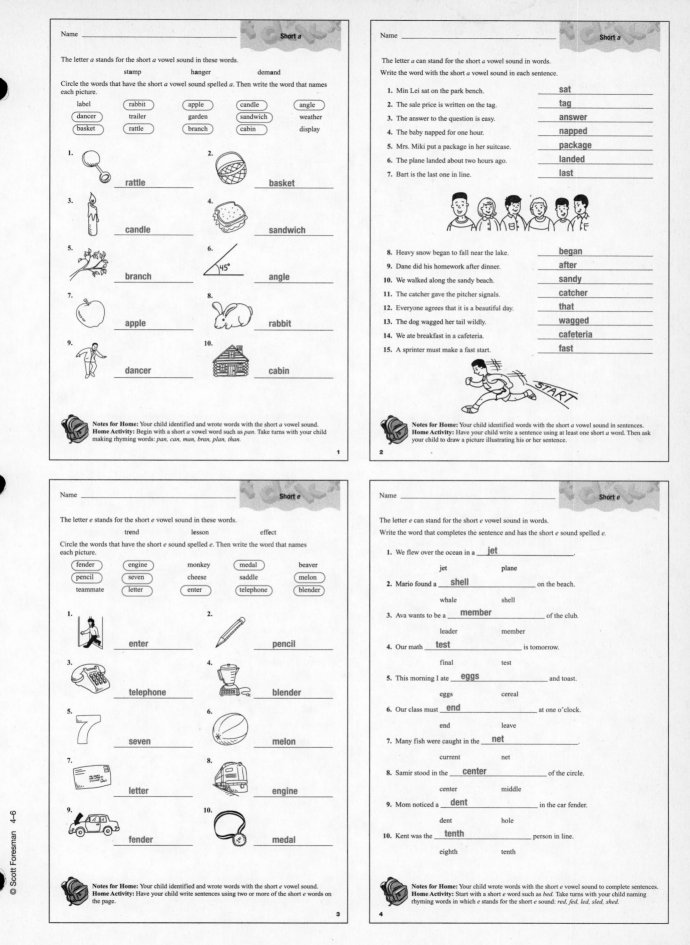

Worksheet 1 (Short a)

Name _____

Short a

The letter *a* stands for the short *a* vowel sound in these words.

stamp   hanger   demand

Circle the words that have the short *a* vowel sound spelled *a*. Then write the word that names each picture.

label	(rabbit)	(apple)	(candle)	(angle)
(dancer)	trailer	garden	(sandwich)	weather
(basket)	(rattle)	(branch)	cabin	display

1. rattle
2. basket
3. candle
4. sandwich
5. branch
6. angle 45°
7. apple
8. rabbit
9. dancer
10. cabin

Notes for Home: Your child identified and wrote words with the short *a* vowel sound.
Home Activity: Begin with a short *a* vowel word such as *pan*. Take turns with your child making rhyming words: *pan, can, man, bran, plan, than*.

1

Worksheet 2 (Short a)

Name _____

Short a

The letter *a* can stand for the short *a* vowel sound in words.

Write the word with the short *a* vowel sound in each sentence.

1. Min Lei sat on the park bench.   sat
2. The sale price is written on the tag.   tag
3. The answer to the question is easy.   answer
4. The baby napped for one hour.   napped
5. Mrs. Miki put a package in her suitcase.   package
6. The plane landed about two hours ago.   landed
7. Bart is the last one in line.   last

8. Heavy snow began to fall near the lake.   began
9. Dane did his homework after dinner.   after
10. We walked along the sandy beach.   sandy
11. The catcher gave the pitcher signals.   catcher
12. Everyone agrees that it is a beautiful day. that
13. The dog wagged her tail wildly.   wagged
14. We ate breakfast in a cafeteria.   cafeteria
15. A sprinter must make a fast start.   fast

Notes for Home: Your child identified words with the short *a* vowel sound in sentences.
Home Activity: Have your child write a sentence using at least one short *a* word. Then ask your child to draw a picture illustrating his or her sentence.

2

Worksheet 3 (Short e)

Name _____

Short e

The letter *e* stands for the short *e* vowel sound in these words.

trend   lesson   effect

Circle the words that have the short *e* sound spelled *e*. Then write the word that names each picture.

(fender)	(engine)	monkey	(medal)	beaver
(pencil)	(seven)	cheese	saddle	(melon)
teammate	(letter)	(enter)	(telephone)	(blender)

1. enter
2. pencil
3. telephone
4. blender
5. seven
6. melon
7. letter
8. engine
9. fender
10. medal

Notes for Home: Your child identified and wrote words with the short *e* vowel sound.
Home Activity: Have your child write sentences using two or more of the short *e* words on the page.

3

Worksheet 4 (Short e)

Name _____

Short e

The letter *e* can stand for the short *e* vowel sound in words.

Write the word that completes the sentence and has the short *e* sound spelled *e*.

1. We flew over the ocean in a ___jet___.
   jet   plane
2. Mario found a ___shell___ on the beach.
   whale   shell
3. Ava wants to be a ___member___ of the club.
   leader   member
4. Our math ___test___ is tomorrow.
   final   test
5. This morning I ate ___eggs___ and toast.
   eggs   cereal
6. Our class must ___end___ at one o'clock.
   end   leave
7. Many fish were caught in the ___net___.
   current   net
8. Samir stood in the ___center___ of the circle.
   center   middle
9. Mom noticed a ___dent___ in the car fender.
   dent   hole
10. Kent was the ___tenth___ person in line.
    eighth   tenth

Notes for Home: Your child wrote words with the short *e* vowel sound to complete sentences.
Home Activity: Start with a short *e* word such as *bed*. Take turns with your child naming rhyming words in which *e* stands for the short *e* sound: *red, fed, led, sled, shed*.

4

© Scott Foresman 4–6

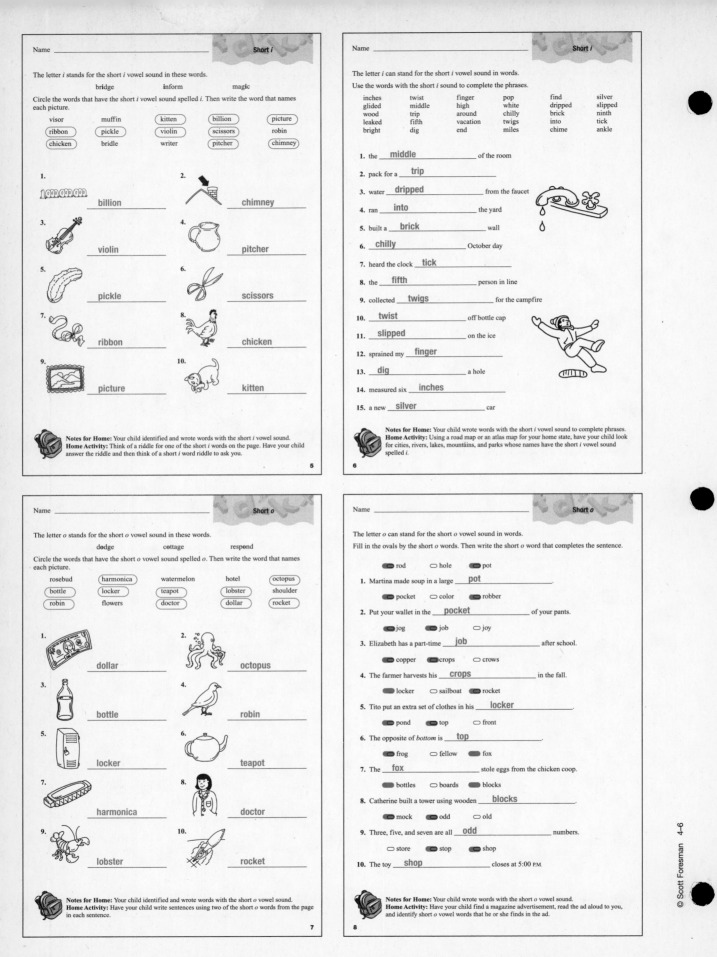

Name _____   Short *i*

The letter *i* stands for the short *i* vowel sound in these words.

bridge   inform   magic

Circle the words that have the short *i* vowel sound spelled *i*. Then write the word that names each picture.

visor   muffin   (kitten)   (billion)   (picture)
(ribbon)   (pickle)   (violin)   scissors   robin
(chicken) bridle   writer   (pitcher)   (chimney)

1.   billion
2.   chimney
3.   violin
4.   pitcher
5.   pickle
6.   scissors
7.   ribbon
8.   chicken
9.   picture
10.   kitten

Notes for Home: Your child identified and wrote words with the short *i* vowel sound.
Home Activity: Think of a riddle for one of the short *i* words on the page. Have your child answer the riddle and then think of a short *i* word riddle to ask you.

5

Name _____   Short *i*

The letter *i* can stand for the short *i* vowel sound in words.

Use the words with the short *i* sound to complete the phrases.

inches	twist	finger	pop	find	silver
glided	middle	high	white	dripped	slipped
wood	trip	around	chilly	brick	ninth
leaked	fifth	vacation	twigs	into	tick
bright	dig	end	miles	chime	ankle

1. the ___middle___ of the room
2. pack for a ___trip___
3. water ___dripped___ from the faucet
4. ran ___into___ the yard
5. built a ___brick___ wall
6. ___chilly___ October day
7. heard the clock ___tick___
8. the ___fifth___ person in line
9. collected ___twigs___ for the campfire
10. ___twist___ off bottle cap
11. ___slipped___ on the ice
12. sprained my ___finger___
13. ___dig___ a hole
14. measured six ___inches___
15. a new ___silver___ car

Notes for Home: Your child wrote words with the short *i* vowel sound to complete phrases.
Home Activity: Using a road map or an atlas map for your home state, have your child look for cities, rivers, lakes, mountains, and parks whose names have the short *i* vowel sound spelled *i*.

6

Name _____   Short *o*

The letter *o* stands for the short *o* vowel sound in these words.

dodge   cottage   respond

Circle the words that have the short *o* vowel sound spelled *o*. Then write the word that names each picture.

rosebud   (harmonica)   watermelon   hotel   (octopus)
(bottle)   (locker)   (teapot)   (lobster) shoulder
(robin)   flowers   (doctor)   (dollar)   (rocket)

1.   dollar
2.   octopus
3.   bottle
4.   robin
5.   locker
6.   teapot
7.   harmonica
8.   doctor
9.   lobster
10.   rocket

Notes for Home: Your child identified and wrote words with the short *o* vowel sound.
Home Activity: Have your child write sentences using two of the short *o* words from the page in each sentence.

7

Name _____   Short *o*

The letter *o* can stand for the short *o* vowel sound in words.

Fill in the ovals by the short *o* words. Then write the short *o* word that completes the sentence.

●rod   ○hole   ●pot
1. Martina made soup in a large ___pot___.

●pocket ○color   ●robber
2. Put your wallet in the ___pocket___ of your pants.

●jog   ●job   ○joy
3. Elizabeth has a part-time ___job___ after school.

●copper ●crops   ○crows
4. The farmer harvests his ___crops___ in the fall.

●locker ○sailboat ●rocket
5. Tito put an extra set of clothes in his ___locker___.

●pond   ●top   ○front
6. The opposite of *bottom* is ___top___.

●frog   ○fellow ●fox
7. The ___fox___ stole eggs from the chicken coop.

●bottles ○boards ●blocks
8. Catherine built a tower using wooden ___blocks___.

●mock   ●odd   ○old
9. Three, five, and seven are all ___odd___ numbers.

○store   ●stop   ●shop
10. The toy ___shop___ closes at 5:00 P.M.

Notes for Home: Your child wrote words with the short *o* vowel sound.
Home Activity: Have your child find a magazine advertisement, read the ad aloud to you, and identify short *o* vowel words that he or she finds in the ad.

8

© Scott Foresman 4–6

182   Answers

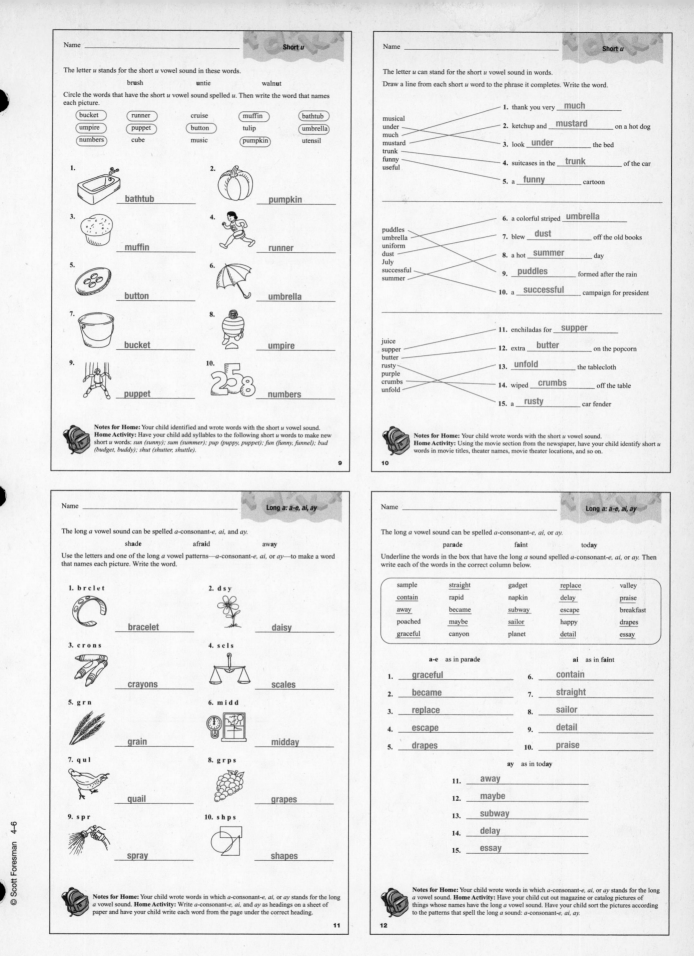

Page 9 — Short *u*

Name _____

Short *u*

The letter *u* stands for the short *u* vowel sound in these words.

brush   untie   walnut

Circle the words that have the short *u* vowel sound spelled *u*. Then write the word that names each picture.

(bucket) (runner) cruise (muffin) (bathtub)
(umpire) (puppet) (button) tulip (umbrella)
(numbers) cube music (pumpkin) utensil

1. bathtub
2. pumpkin
3. muffin
4. runner
5. button
6. umbrella
7. bucket
8. umpire
9. puppet
10. numbers

Notes for Home: Your child identified and wrote words with the short *u* vowel sound.
Home Activity: Have your child add syllables to the following short *u* words to make new short *u* words: *sun (sunny); sum (summer); pup (puppy, puppet); fun (funny, funnel); bud (budget, buddy); shut (shutter, shuttle).*

9

Page 10 — Short *u*

Name _____

Short *u*

The letter *u* can stand for the short *u* vowel sound in words.

Draw a line from each short *u* word to the phrase it completes. Write the word.

musical
under
much
mustard
trunk
funny
useful

1. thank you very **much**
2. ketchup and **mustard** on a hot dog
3. look **under** the bed
4. suitcases in the **trunk** of the car
5. a **funny** cartoon

puddles
umbrella
uniform
dust
July
successful
summer

6. a colorful striped **umbrella**
7. blew **dust** off the old books
8. a hot **summer** day
9. **puddles** formed after the rain
10. a **successful** campaign for president

juice
supper
butter
rusty
purple
crumbs
unfold

11. enchiladas for **supper**
12. extra **butter** on the popcorn
13. **unfold** the tablecloth
14. wiped **crumbs** off the table
15. a **rusty** car fender

Notes for Home: Your child wrote words with the short *u* vowel sound.
Home Activity: Using the movie section from the newspaper, have your child identify short *u* words in movie titles, theater names, movie theater locations, and so on.

10

Page 11 — Long *a*: *a-e, ai, ay*

Name _____

Long *a*: *a-e, ai, ay*

The long *a* vowel sound can be spelled *a-consonant-e*, *ai*, and *ay*.

shade   afraid   away

Use the letters and one of the long *a* vowel patterns—*a-consonant-e, ai,* or *ay*—to make a word that names each picture. Write the word.

1. b r c l e t — bracelet
2. d s y — daisy
3. c r o n s — crayons
4. s c l s — scales
5. g r n — grain
6. m i d d — midday
7. q u l — quail
8. g r p s — grapes
9. s p r — spray
10. s h p s — shapes

Notes for Home: Your child wrote words in which *a-consonant-e, ai,* or *ay* stands for the long *a* vowel sound. **Home Activity:** Write *a-consonant-e, ai,* and *ay* as headings on a sheet of paper and have your child write each word from the page under the correct heading.

11

Page 12 — Long *a*: *a-e, ai, ay*

Name _____

Long *a*: *a-e, ai, ay*

The long *a* vowel sound can be spelled *a-consonant-e, ai,* or *ay*.

parade   faint   today

Underline the words in the box that have the long *a* sound spelled *a-consonant-e, ai,* or *ay*. Then write each of the words in the correct column below.

sample	straight	gadget	replace	valley
contain	rapid	napkin	delay	praise
away	became	subway	escape	breakfast
poached	maybe	sailor	happy	drapes
graceful	canyon	planet	detail	essay

a-e as in parade
1. graceful
2. became
3. replace
4. escape
5. drapes

ai as in faint
6. contain
7. straight
8. sailor
9. detail
10. praise

ay as in today
11. away
12. maybe
13. subway
14. delay
15. essay

Notes for Home: Your child wrote words in which *a-consonant-e, ai,* or *ay* stands for the long *a* vowel sound. **Home Activity:** Have your child cut out magazine or catalog pictures of things whose names have the long *a* vowel sound. Have your child sort the pictures according to the patterns that spell the long *a* sound: *a-consonant-e, ai, ay.*

12

© Scott Foresman 4–6

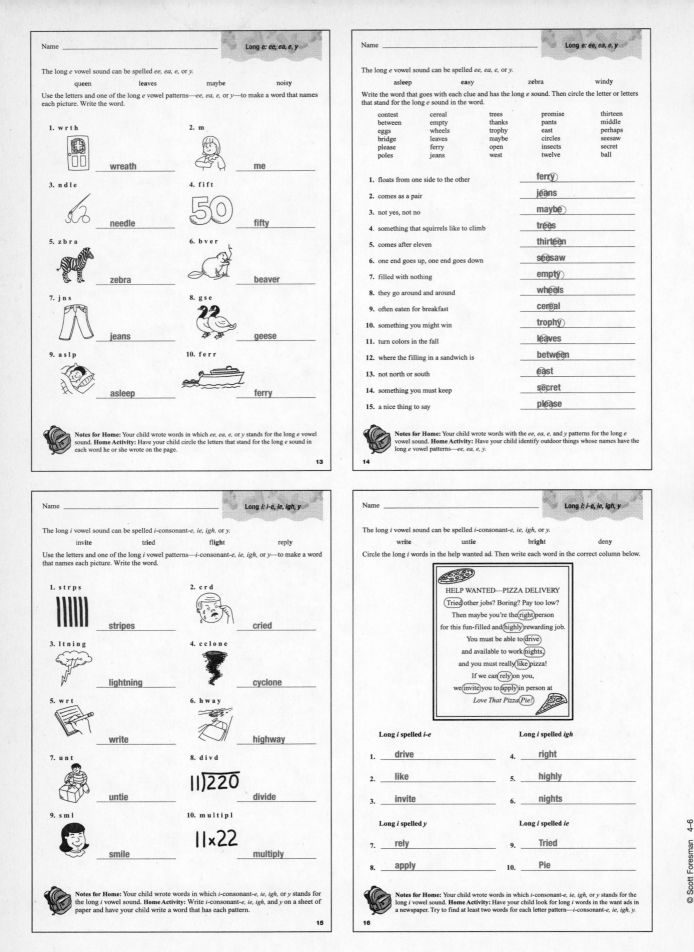

Top-left worksheet (page 13)

The long e vowel sound can be spelled *ee*, *ea*, *e*, or *y*.

| queen | leaves | maybe | noisy |

Use the letters and one of the long e vowel patterns—*ee*, *ea*, *e*, or *y*—to make a word that names each picture. Write the word.

1. w r t h   wreath
2. m   me
3. n d l e   needle
4. f i f t   fifty
5. z b r a   zebra
6. b v e r   beaver
7. j n s   jeans
8. g s e   geese
9. a s l p   asleep
10. f e r r   ferry

Notes for Home: Your child wrote words in which *ee*, *ea*, *e*, or *y* stands for the long e vowel sound. **Home Activity:** Have your child circle the letters that stand for the long e sound in each word he or she wrote on the page.

13

Top-right worksheet (page 14)

The long e vowel sound can be spelled *ee*, *ea*, *e*, or *y*.

| asleep | easy | zebra | windy |

Write the word that goes with each clue and has the long e sound. Then circle the letter or letters that stand for the long e sound in the word.

contest	cereal	trees	promise	thirteen
between	empty	thanks	pants	middle
eggs	wheels	trophy	east	perhaps
bridge	leaves	maybe	circles	seesaw
please	ferry	open	insects	secret
poles	jeans	west	twelve	ball

1. floats from one side to the other   ferry
2. comes as a pair   jeans
3. not yes, not no   maybe
4. something that squirrels like to climb   trees
5. comes after eleven   thirteen
6. one end goes up, one end goes down   seesaw
7. filled with nothing   empty
8. they go around and around   wheels
9. often eaten for breakfast   cereal
10. something you might win   trophy
11. turn colors in the fall   leaves
12. where the filling in a sandwich is   between
13. not north or south   east
14. something you must keep   secret
15. a nice thing to say   please

Notes for Home: Your child wrote words with the *ee*, *ea*, and *y* patterns for the long e vowel sound. **Home Activity:** Have your child identify outdoor things whose names have the long e vowel patterns—*ee*, *ea*, *e*, *y*.

14

Bottom-left worksheet (page 15)

The long i vowel sound can be spelled *i-consonant-e*, *ie*, *igh*, or *y*.

| invite | tried | flight | reply |

Use the letters and one of the long i vowel patterns—*i-consonant-e*, *ie*, *igh*, or *y*—to make a word that names each picture. Write the word.

1. s t r p s   stripes
2. c r d   cried
3. l t n i n g   lightning
4. c c l o n e   cyclone
5. w r t   write
6. h w a y   highway
7. u n t   untie
8. d i v d   11)220   divide
9. s m l   smile
10. m u l t i p l   11×22   multiply

Notes for Home: Your child wrote words in which *i-consonant-e*, *ie*, *igh*, or *y* stands for the long i vowel sound. **Home Activity:** Write *i-consonant-e*, *ie*, *igh*, and *y* on a sheet of paper and have your child write a word that has each pattern.

15

Bottom-right worksheet (page 16)

The long i vowel sound can be spelled *i-consonant-e*, *ie*, *igh*, or *y*.

| write | untie | bright | deny |

Circle the long i words in the help wanted ad. Then write each word in the correct column below.

HELP WANTED—PIZZA DELIVERY
Tried other jobs? Boring? Pay too low?
Then maybe you're the right person
for this fun-filled and highly rewarding job.
You must be able to drive
and available to work nights,
and you must really like pizza!
If we can rely on you,
we invite you to apply in person at
Love That Pizza Pie!

Long i spelled *i-e*
1. drive
2. like
3. invite

Long i spelled *igh*
4. right
5. highly
6. nights

Long i spelled *y*
7. rely
8. apply

Long i spelled *ie*
9. Tried
10. Pie

Notes for Home: Your child wrote words in which *i-consonant-e*, *ie*, *igh*, or *y* stands for the long i vowel sound. **Home Activity:** Have your child look for long i words in the want ads in a newspaper. Try to find at least two words for each letter pattern—*i-consonant-e*, *ie*, *igh*, *y*.

16

© Scott Foresman 4-6

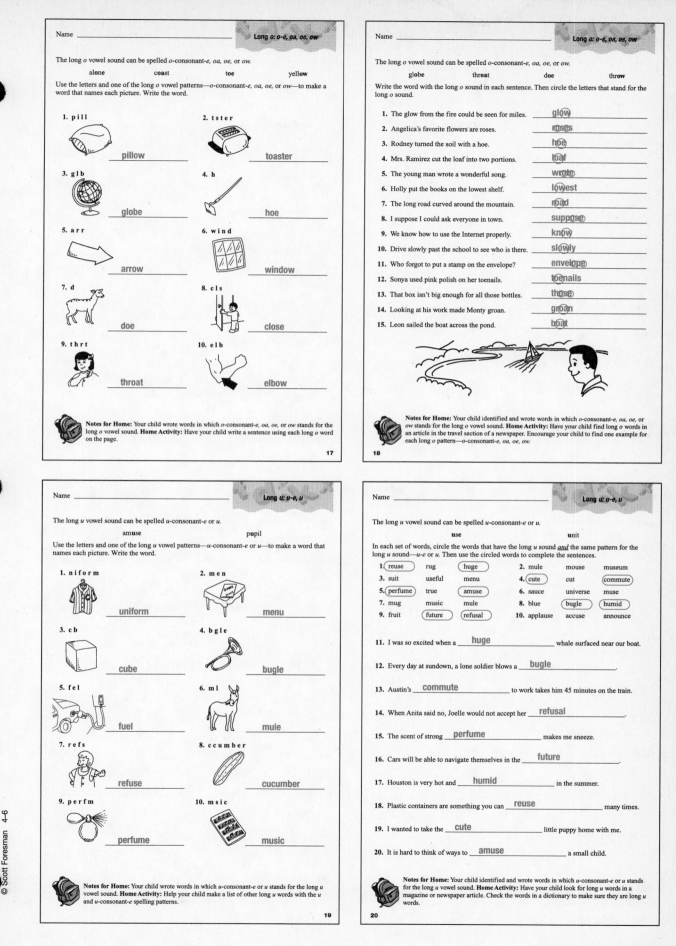

Worksheet 17 (top left)

Name _____   Long *o: o-e, oa, oe, ow*

The long *o* vowel sound can be spelled *o*-consonant-*e*, *oa*, *oe*, or *ow*.

  alone   coast   toe   yellow

Use the letters and one of the long *o* vowel patterns—*o*-consonant-*e*, *oa*, *oe*, or *ow*—to make a word that names each picture. Write the word.

1. p ill   pillow

2. t ster   toaster

3. g l b   globe

4. h   hoe

5. a r r   arrow

6. wind   window

7. d   doe

8. c l s   close

9. t h r t   throat

10. e l b   elbow

Notes for Home: Your child wrote words in which *o*-consonant-*e*, *oa*, *oe*, or *ow* stands for the long *o* vowel sound. **Home Activity:** Have your child write a sentence using each long *o* word on the page.

17

Worksheet 18 (top right)

Name _____   Long *o: o-e, oa, oe, ow*

The long *o* vowel sound can be spelled *o*-consonant-*e*, *oa*, *oe*, or *ow*.

  globe   throat   doe   throw

Write the word with the long *o* sound in each sentence. Then circle the letters that stand for the long *o* sound.

1. The glow from the fire could be seen for miles.   glow
2. Angelica's favorite flowers are roses.   roses
3. Rodney turned the soil with a hoe.   hoe
4. Mrs. Ramirez cut the loaf into two portions.   loaf
5. The young man wrote a wonderful song.   wrote
6. Holly put the books on the lowest shelf.   lowest
7. The long road curved around the mountain.   road
8. I suppose I could ask everyone in town.   suppose
9. We know how to use the Internet properly.   know
10. Drive slowly past the school to see who is there.   slowly
11. Who forgot to put a stamp on the envelope?   envelope
12. Sonya used pink polish on her toenails.   toenails
13. That box isn't big enough for all those bottles.   those
14. Looking at his work made Monty groan.   groan
15. Leon sailed the boat across the pond.   boat

Notes for Home: Your child identified and wrote words in which *o*-consonant-*e*, *oa*, *oe*, or *ow* stands for the long *o* vowel sound. **Home Activity:** Have your child find long *o* words in an article in the travel section of a newspaper. Encourage your child to find one example for each long *o* pattern—*o*-consonant-*e*, *oa*, *oe*, *ow*.

18

Worksheet 19 (bottom left)

Name _____   Long *u: u-e, u*

The long *u* vowel sound can be spelled *u*-consonant-*e* or *u*.

  amuse   pupil

Use the letters and one of the long *u* vowel patterns—*u*-consonant-*e* or *u*—to make a word that names each picture. Write the word.

1. n iform   uniform

2. m en   menu

3. c b   cube

4. b gle   bugle

5. f el   fuel

6. m l   mule

7. r efs   refuse

8. c cumber   cucumber

9. p erfm   perfume

10. m s ic   music

Notes for Home: Your child wrote words in which *u*-consonant-*e* or *u* stands for the long *u* vowel sound. **Home Activity:** Help your child make a list of other long *u* words with the *u* and *u*-consonant-*e* spelling patterns.

19

Worksheet 20 (bottom right)

Name _____   Long *u: u-e, u*

The long *u* vowel sound can be spelled *u*-consonant-*e* or *u*.

  use   unit

In each set of words, circle the words that have the long *u* sound *and* the same pattern for the long *u* sound—*u-e* or *u*. Then use the circled words to complete the sentences.

1. reuse	rug	huge	2. mule	mouse	museum
3. suit	useful	menu	4. cute	cut	commute
5. perfume	true	amuse	6. sauce	universe	muse
7. mug	music	mule	8. blue	bugle	humid
9. fruit	future	refusal	10. applause	accuse	announce

11. I was so excited when a ___huge___ whale surfaced near our boat.

12. Every day at sundown, a lone soldier blows a ___bugle___.

13. Austin's ___commute___ to work takes him 45 minutes on the train.

14. When Anita said no, Joelle would not accept her ___refusal___.

15. The scent of strong ___perfume___ makes me sneeze.

16. Cars will be able to navigate themselves in the ___future___.

17. Houston is very hot and ___humid___ in the summer.

18. Plastic containers are something you can ___reuse___ many times.

19. I wanted to take the ___cute___ little puppy home with me.

20. It is hard to think of ways to ___amuse___ a small child.

Notes for Home: Your child identified and wrote words in which *u*-consonant-*e* or *u* stands for the long *u* vowel sound. **Home Activity:** Have your child look for long *u* words in a magazine or newspaper article. Check the words in a dictionary to make sure they are long *u* words.

20

© Scott Foresman 4–6

Many words have this pattern of letters: consonant + vowel + consonant + e (CVCe). Usually the vowels in words with this pattern stand for the long vowel sounds.

CVCe	CVCe	CVCe	CVCe
f a c e	k i t e	n o t e	c u t e

Circle the word in each row that has the CVCe pattern. Then write the example word (*face, kite, note,* or *cute*) that has the same vowel sound as the circled word.

1. please	(vase)	best	face
2. bread	(time)	rock	kite
3. (mule)	limb	mouse	cute
4. hoe	hop	(hope)	note
5. need	(nose)	nail	note
6. (cage)	curl	coal	face
7. four	(file)	feet	kite
8. girl	goat	(gate)	face
9. (cube)	crab	crib	cute
10. even	leave	(five)	kite

Notes for Home: Your child identified words with the consonant-vowel-consonant-*e* (CVCe) pattern. **Home Activity:** Write these word forms on a sheet of paper: __*a__e*, __*i__e*, __*o__e*, __*u__e*. Have your child add consonants to make words with the CVCe pattern.

21

These words have the consonant + vowel + consonant + *e*, or CVCe, pattern.

    face   kite   note   cute

Write the CVCe word that names each picture. Then circle the letters that stand for the vowel sound.

1.	nose	a-e	i-e	(o-e)	u-e
2.	five	a-e	(i-e)	o-e	u-e
3.	cage	(a-e)	i-e	o-e	u-e
4.	mule	a-e	i-e	o-e	(u-e)
5.	robe	a-e	i-e	(o-e)	u-e
6.	bike	a-e	(i-e)	o-e	u-e
7.	pipe	a-e	(i-e)	o-e	u-e
8.	cube	a-e	i-e	o-e	(u-e)
9.	bone	a-e	i-e	(o-e)	u-e
10.	rake	(a-e)	i-e	o-e	u-e

Notes for Home: Your child wrote words with the CVCe spelling pattern. **Home Activity:** Have your child look through a newspaper article and highlight words that have the CVCe pattern.

22

These words have the consonant + vowel + consonant + *e*, or CVCe, pattern.

    take   kite   vote   cube

Find and write the CVCe word in each phrase.

1. wash your face	face
2. cute pink slippers	cute
3. found the right size	size
4. rode the horse	rode
5. choose a ripe pear	ripe
6. huge grizzly bear	huge
7. a single red rose	rose
8. dig a large hole	hole
9. bake an apple pie	bake
10. lost the final game	game
11. refuse to change seats	refuse
12. ripped the note in half	note
13. pleased to be alone	alone
14. invite a friend to stay	invite
15. follow the parade route	parade

Notes for Home: Your child identified and wrote words with the CVCe pattern. **Home Activity:** Have your child write words that rhyme with some of the CVCe words he or she wrote on the page.

23

Many words have this pattern of letters: vowel + consonant + consonant + vowel (VCCV). This pattern will help you divide the word into syllables.

VCCV	VCCV
p i c / t u r e	f o l / l o w

Underline the word with the VCCV pattern in each row. Then write the VCCV word and divide it into syllables.

1. soccer	shiver	soc/cer
2. book	chapter	chap/ter
3. after	above	af/ter
4. dollar	shape	dol/lar
5. sandwich	picnic	pic/nic
6. advice	heavy	ad/vice
7. wheat	harvest	har/vest
8. daytime	evening	day/time
9. butter	peanut	but/ter
10. atlas	thesaurus	at/las
11. compete	comedy	com/pete
12. pilot	doctor	doc/tor
13. summer	autumn	sum/mer
14. salad	dessert	des/sert
15. ceiling	carpet	car/pet

Notes for Home: Your child identified syllables using the VCCV pattern in words. **Home Activity:** Have your child find the VCCV pattern in the names of at least four sports or activities. Examples: tennis, basketball, swimming, soccer, stamp collecting.

24

Name _____ **Common Word Patterns (VCCV)**

These words have the vowel + consonant + consonant + vowel, or VCCV, pattern. This pattern will help you divide the words into syllables.

pic/ture   **fol/low**   **fif/teen**

Circle the words in the box that have the VCCV pattern.

patch	(rabbit)	classroom	(carpet)	(wonder)
debated	(problem)	situation	(morning)	cookie
(signal)	around	(winter)	closet	(pepper)
tomatoes	(button)	hamster	(under)	ready

Choose a circled word from above to complete each sentence. Write the word in syllables.

1. I was late for school this ___mor/ning___.

2. The ___rab/bit___ dug a burrow in our garden.

3. The traffic ___sig/nal___ changed from green to yellow.

4. I ___won/der___ why cats sleep so many hours a day.

5. Carol puts plenty of ___pep/per___ in the sauce.

6. Angelo looked ___un/der___ the bed for his missing shoe.

7. They chose a gold ___car/pet___ for the living room.

8. Erich goes cross-country skiing in the ___win/ter___.

9. Does anyone know the answer to the fifth math ___prob/lem___?

10. I noticed that I had lost a ___but/ton___ off my jacket.

Notes for Home: Your child identified and wrote words with the vowel + consonant + consonant + vowel (VCCV) pattern. **Home Activity:** Encourage your child to think of at least three household objects whose names contain the VCCV pattern. Examples: carpet, mirror, dresser, pillow.

25

Name _____ **Vowel Digraphs** *au, aw* /ò/

The vowel digraphs *au* and *aw* stand for the vowel sound in these words.

saucer   **hawk**

Underline the words in the box that have the vowel sound you hear in *saucer* and *hawk*. Then write each underlined word under the picture whose name has the same pattern for the vowel sound.

fault	awful	drawn	aware	author
cruise	amuse	beauty	shawl	barrel
crawl	pause	shared	assume	applaud
audio	faucet	straw	because	lawn
awake	lawyer	waffle	laundry	music

1. ___fault___   9. ___crawl___

2. ___audio___   10. ___awful___

3. ___pause___   11. ___lawyer___

4. ___faucet___   12. ___drawn___

5. ___because___   13. ___straw___

6. ___laundry___   14. ___shawl___

7. ___author___   15. ___lawn___

8. ___applaud___

Notes for Home: Your child wrote words with the vowel digraphs *au* and *aw*. **Home Activity:** Encourage your child to think of two more *au* and *aw* words and write them in sentences.

26

Name _____ **Vowel Digraphs** *al, all* /ò/

The vowel digraphs *al* and *all* stand for the vowel sound in these words.

almost   sm**all**

Fill in the oval by the word that completes each sentence and has the vowel sound in *small*. Write the word and circle the letters that stand for that vowel sound.

1. Iko used _____ to draw a picture.
   ● chalk   ○ charcoal
   ___ch(al)k___

2. Morris puts _____ on his scrambled eggs.
   ○ pepper   ● salt
   ___s(al)t___

3. I can't _____ the ingredients I need for the stew.
   ● recall   ○ remember
   ___rec(all)___

4. We _____ like ice cream for dessert.
   ● also   ○ both
   ___(al)so___

5. Michelle is several inches _____ than Stefan.
   ○ shorter   ● taller
   ___t(all)er___

6. On Saturdays Kara plays _____ with her friends.
   ○ soccer   ● baseball
   ___baseb(all)___

7. They _____ on the phone last night.
   ● talked   ○ spoke
   ___t(alk)ed___

8. Dayna _____ new kitchen cabinets.
   ○ built   ● installed
   ___inst(all)ed___

9. Grandpa _____ wears a hat to keep his head warm.
   ● always   ○ sometimes
   ___(alw)ays___

10. Our annual _____ averages only ten inches.
    ● rainfall ○ precipitation
    ___rainf(all)___

Notes for Home: Your child wrote words with the vowel digraphs *al* and *all*. **Home Activity:** Have your child make a list of other words with the vowel digraphs *al* and *all*.

27

Name _____ **Vowel Digraphs** *au, aw, al, all* /ò/

The vowel digraphs *au, aw, al,* and *all* stand for the vowel sound in these words.

author   **aw**ful   **al**most   sm**all**

Circle the words in the box that have the vowel sound you hear in *small*. Then combine each circled word with a word below to make a compound word. Write the compound word and circle the letters that stand for the vowel sound you hear in *small*.

(law)	blow	(ball)	(walk)	stand
tale	(draw)	(auto)	suit	(fall)
allow	(straw)	pull	(saw)	shallow
(slaw)	huge	chew	(sauce)	salad

1. water_____   ___water(fall)___

2. _____berry   ___str(aw)berry___

3. side_____   ___side(walk)___

4. _____graph   ___(auto)graph___

5. cole_____   ___cole(slaw)___

6. _____suit   ___(law)suit___

7. _____pan   ___(sauce)pan___

8. basket_____   ___basket(ball)___

9. _____bridge   ___(draw)bridge___

10. _____dust   ___(saw)dust___

Notes for Home: Your child wrote words with the vowel digraphs *au, aw, al,* and *all*. **Home Activity:** Have your child use each circled word in a sentence with another word that has the same pattern for the vowel sound.

28

The vowel digraph *ea* can stand for the short *e* vowel sound.

feather

Write the letters *ea* to complete each word. Then write each word in the group where it belongs.

1. br __ea__ d
2. sw __ea__ ter
3. h __ea__ d
4. br __ea__ kfast
5. tr __ea__ sure
6. dr __ea__ dful
7. thr __ea__ d
8. st __ea__ dy
9. m __ea__ sure
10. m __ea__ dow

11. dinner, lunch, __breakfast__
12. needle, scissors, __thread__
13. shirt, pants, __sweater__
14. muffins, rolls, __bread__
15. shoulders, neck, __head__
16. wealth, riches, __treasure__
17. weigh, estimate, __measure__
18. field, pasture, __meadow__
19. terrible, awful, __dreadful__
20. regular, even, __steady__

Notes for Home: Your child wrote words in which *ea* stands for the short *e* vowel sound.
Home Activity: Have your child write groups of related words for the *ea* words *tread, wealth,* and *pleasant.*

29

The vowel digraph *ea* can stand for the short *e* vowel sound.

bread   feather

Write the word that completes the phrase and has the short *e* sound spelled *ea*.

1. a coat made of __leather__

fleece
leather

2. wildflowers growing in the __meadow__

meadow
field

3. knitted a __sweater__

sweater
vest

4. spoke in a calm __steady__ voice

pleasing
steady

5. finally __ready__ to go

able
ready

6. eggs and toast for __breakfast__

breakfast
dinner

7. use a ruler to __measure__

measure
reach

8. a search for buried __treasure__

jewels
treasure

9. a mild __pleasant__ day

pleasant
peaceful

10. a very __heavy__ suitcase

heavy
empty

Notes for Home: Your child wrote words in which *ea* stands for the short *e* vowel sound.
Home Activity: In a five-minute time period, have your child list as many words as possible that rhyme with *head.*

30

The vowel digraphs *ie* and *ei* can stand for the long *e* sound.

piece   ceiling

Circle the word in each phrase in which *ie* or *ei* stands for the long *e* sound. Then write each circled word under the picture whose name has the same pattern for the long *e* sound.

1. not nice to (deceive) people
2. a (belief) in myself
3. a knight's sword and (shield)
4. a gleeful (shriek) of surprise
5. too (conceited) to see reality
6. need a (receipt) to return the present
7. (seized) the beagle's leash
8. a beautiful green (field)
9. the greedy leader of the (thieves)
10. a favorite (leisure) activity

11. __belief__
16. __deceive__
12. __shield__
17. __conceited__
13. __shriek__
18. __receipt__
14. __field__
19. __seized__
15. __thieves__
20. __leisure__

Notes for Home: Your child wrote words in which *ie* and *ei* stand for the long *e* vowel sound.
Home Activity: Have your child choose two or more *ie* or *ei* words from the page and write them together in a sentence.

31

The vowel digraphs *ie* and *ei* can stand for the long *e* sound.

field   ceiling

Underline the words in the box that have the long *e* sound spelled *ie* or *ei*. Then write the underlined words to complete the sentences.

brief	receive	seized	greed	relief
succeed	media	agree	receipt	these
speak	believes	legal	repeat	deceived
leisure	sweet	shield	niece	beige

1. A knight carried a sword and a __shield__ into battle.
2. My little sister __believes__ in the tooth fairy.
3. You need a __receipt__ to get a refund from the store.
4. Many people are __deceived__ by get-rich-quick schemes.
5. I visited my __niece__ and nephew in Chicago.
6. David __seized__ the barking dog by its collar.
7. Flo wrote a __brief__ one-paragraph summary of the story.
8. Did you __receive__ the letter I sent you last week?
9. My favorite __leisure__ activities are reading and tap dancing.
10. It was a __relief__ to see the train had not yet left.

Notes for Home: Your child wrote words in which *ie* and *ei* stand for the long *e* vowel sound.
Home Activity: Have your child sort the circled words on the page according to the vowel pattern that spells the long *e* sound.

32

© Scott Foresman 4-6

Panel 1 (top-left, page 33)

The vowel digraphs *ew*, *ui*, and *ue* stand for the vowel sound in these words.

grew   suit   clue

Circle the letters in each word that stand for the vowel sound you hear in *grew*. Then write the words to answer the clues.

cruise	flew	threw	chew	true
blue	drew	bruise	juice	fruit

1. color of the sky _____ blue
2. trip on a boat _____ cruise
3. something to drink _____ juice
4. apple or banana _____ fruit
5. not false _____ true
6. use your teeth for this _____ chew
7. injury to the body _____ bruise
8. what the artist did _____ drew
9. what the pitcher did to the ball _____ threw
10. what a bird did _____ flew

Notes for Home: Your child wrote words with the vowel digraphs *ew, ui,* and *ue*.
Home Activity: Have your child choose five words from the page and write a story using them.

33

Panel 2 (top-right, page 34)

The vowel digraphs *ew*, *ui*, and *ue* stand for the vowel sound in *threw, bruise,* and *glue.*

Underline the word or words in each book title that have the same vowel sound as *threw, bruise,* and *glue.* Write the word or words and circle the letters that stand for the vowel sound in *threw, bruise,* and *glue.*

1. Someone Stole the Queen's Jewelry
   Jewelry
2. Mr. Fix-It and His Magic Screwdrivers
   Screwdrivers
3. The Crew of the Haunted Cruise Ship
   Crew, Cruise
4. The Clue to the Missing Jewels
   Clue, Jewels
5. True Tales About Fabulous Fruit
   True, Fruit
6. The Night the Wind Blew the Lights Out
   Blew
7. The Knight Slew Seven Dragons
   Slew
8. Stewart Seton's Secret Stew
   Stewart, Stew
9. The Stranger in the Blue Suit
   Blue, Suit
10. The Man Drew a Line in the Sand
    Drew

Notes for Home: Your child wrote words with the vowel digraphs *ew, ui,* and *ue*.
Home Activity: Have your child write clues for five words on the page for you to answer. Then write clues for your child to answer.

34

Panel 3 (bottom-left, page 35)

Choose the word that has the same vowel sound as *threw, bruise,* and *true.* Write the word to complete the sentence.

1. Moss __grew__ under the shady tree.
   grew   ground   died
2. A diamond is a precious __jewel__.
   jelly   jewel   gem
3. Dave wore his new __suit__ to the graduation ceremony.
   sure   shirt   suit
4. The artist __drew__ a picture of the sunset.
   painted   drew   dream
5. We enjoyed our __cruise__ through the Panama Canal.
   cruise   coast   trip
6. The dog likes to __chew__ on old slippers.
   choke   chew   chow
7. Kelly __blew__ the candles out after dinner.
   blew   lit   put
8. Oranges are Oscar's favorite __fruit__.
   flavor   fruit   taste
9. Rosa used __glue__ to reattach the cup's handle.
   look   glue   paste
10. On a warm spring day the sky can be clear and __blue__.
    blue   bright   bluff

Notes for Home: Your child wrote words with the vowel digraphs *ew, ui,* and *ue*.
Home Activity: Challenge your child to think of five words that rhyme with words he or she wrote on the page.

35

Panel 4 (bottom-right, page 36)

The vowel digraph *oo* stands for the vowel sound in these words.

wood   soot

Add the vowel digraph *oo* to each word in the box. Then write the words to answer the clues.

l_oo_k	st_oo_d	h_oo_k	cr_oo_ked	c_oo_kies
c_oo_k	f_oo_t	b_oo_k	t_oo_k	sh_oo_k
g_oo_d	cr_oo_k	h_oo_d	w_oo_den	br_oo_k

1. opposite of *bad* _____ good
2. something to read _____ book
3. moved quickly up and down _____ shook
4. past tense of *stand* _____ stood
5. at the end of your leg _____ foot
6. head covering _____ hood
7. a small stream _____ brook
8. prepare food _____ cook
9. to see _____ look
10. sweet treats _____ cookies
11. a criminal _____ crook
12. past tense of *take* _____ took
13. not straight _____ crooked
14. made of wood _____ wooden
15. a place to hang things _____ hook

Notes for Home: Your child wrote words in which the vowel digraph *oo* stands for the vowel sound in *wood.* **Home Activity:** Have your child write a phrase using each *oo* word on the page.

36

© Scott Foresman 4–6

The vowel digraph *oo* stands for the vowel sound in *foot*.

Choose the word that has the same vowel sound as *foot*. Write the word to complete the sentence.

1. Janet hung her coat on the _____**hook**_____ in the closet.

   hoop   hook   hanger

2. The restaurant's food improved when the new _____**cook**_____ took over.

   cook   clock   chef

3. The author's first _____**book**_____ made the best-seller list.

   bloom   novel   book

4. We _____**took**_____ a walk through the nature preserve.

   troop   took   found

5. The girls waded across the _____**brook**_____.

   pool   brook   bloom

6. Do you think Liz _____**understood**_____ the instructions?

   understand   thought   understood

7. An icy drink tastes _____**good**_____ on a hot summer day.

   cold   good   poor

8. My friends _____**stood**_____ in line to get concert tickets.

   stop   stoop   stood

9. We have a _____**wood**_____ floor in our kitchen.

   wood   tile   cool

10. My winter jacket has a _____**hood**_____.

    kangaroo   hat   hood

Notes for Home: Your child wrote words in which the vowel digraph *oo* stands for the vowel sound in *foot*. **Home Activity:** Have your child make two lists of rhyming words from the page.

37

Write the words from the box to complete the puzzle.

| wooden | book | stood | cook | took |
| shook | hook | look | woodpecker | crook |

Down

1. see
2. quivered
3. made of lumber
4. grasped; seized
7. dishonest person

Across

5. remained upright
6. small peg
7. chef
8. noisy bird
9. something to read

Notes for Home: Your child wrote words in which the vowel digraph *oo* stands for the vowel sound in *foot*. **Home Activity:** Have your child make up riddles for the words *brook, foot, hood,* and *wood*.

38

The vowel digraph *oo* stands for the vowel sound in these words.

                    m**oo**n   b**oo**t

Add the vowel digraph *oo* to each word in the box. Then write the words to answer the clues.

br**oo**m	gr**oo**m	st**oo**l	m**oo**se	g**oo**se
sp**oo**n	p**oo**dle	cab**oo**se	p**oo**l	ch**oo**se
l**oo**se	n**oo**dle	bamb**oo**	f**oo**l	racc**oo**n

1. place to swim   **pool**

2. tool for eating   **spoon**

3. something to sit on   **stool**

4. animal with a mask   **raccoon**

5. opposite of *bride*   **groom**

6. used for sweeping   **broom**

7. kind of dog   **poodle**

8. opposite of *tight*   **loose**

9. animal with webbed feet   **goose**

10. pick   **choose**

11. food for a panda   **bamboo**

12. silly person   **fool**

13. end of a train   **caboose**

14. one pasta shape   **noodle**

15. animal with antlers   **moose**

Notes for Home: Your child wrote words in which the vowel digraph *oo* stands for the vowel sound in *moon*. **Home Activity:** Have your child use rhyming words from the page to write a poem.

39

The vowel digraph *oo* stands for the vowel sound in *moon*.

Choose the word that has the same vowel sound as *moon*. Write the word to complete the sentence.

1. The flowers began to _____**droop**_____ because they needed water.

   drip   droop   drown

2. The butterfly emerged from its _____**cocoon**_____.

   cocoon   coat   cook

3. The _____**hoot**_____ of an owl pierced the silence of the evening.

   howl   hoot   hook

4. The class picnic began at _____**noon**_____.

   nine   noun   noon

5. I laughed out loud when I read the _____**cartoon**_____.

   carton   cartoon   cookbook

6. Can you give me a _____**boost**_____ over the fence?

   bound   boost   both

7. The _____**moon**_____ is Earth's only natural satellite.

   mouth   morning   moon

8. Will Rose _____**choose**_____ the movie we will see?

   chose   choose   choke

9. A _____**kangaroo**_____ carries its baby in a pouch.

   kangaroo   crook   moth

10. The clown gave a bunch of _____**balloons**_____ to the child.

    popcorn   boats   balloons

Notes for Home: Your child wrote words in which the vowel digraph *oo* stands for the vowel sound in *moon*. **Home Activity:** Challenge your child to create a bumper sticker using *oo* words from the page.

40

© Scott Foresman 4–6

Write the words in each sentence that have the same vowel sound as *moon*.

1. Every room in our school has a computer.
   room, school

2. The cowboy looped the rope loosely over his saddle horn.
   looped, loosely

3. Noodles with vegetables are her favorite food.
   Noodles, food

4. Artists sold their crafts at booths from noon until 3 P.M.
   booths, noon

5. It was too cool to swim in the pond today.
   too, cool

6. The carpenter used a special tool to make a groove in the wood.
   tool, groove

7. My little brother has a loose tooth.
   loose, tooth

8. Will the troops get boots and uniforms?
   troops, boots

9. After she shampoos her hair, it feels clean and smooth.
   shampoos, smooth

10. Use a spoon to scoop the ice cream into the bowl.
    spoon, scoop

Notes for Home: Your child wrote words in which the vowel digraph *oo* stands for the vowel sound in *moon*. **Home Activity:** Ask your child to think of five other words with the same vowel sound and spelling as *moon* and use each one in a sentence.

41

The vowel digraph *oo* stands for the vowel sounds in these words.

     sh**oo**t   st**oo**d

Say the first word in the row. Circle the word or words in the row that have the same vowel sound as the first word.

1. boot — (moose) took (rooster)
2. cookout — goose (hood) soothe
3. raccoon — (drool) (zoo) woodpecker
4. good — (book) soon (rook)
5. trooper — (choose) (spoof) crook
6. school — (harpoon) hook (noose)
7. wooden — (brook) pool (foot)
8. food — (cocoon) nook (noon)
9. bamboo — (balloon) (kangaroo) woodwork
10. took — boot tool (look)
11. proof — (cool) (croon) cook
12. tooth — (tycoon) (tool) took
13. hook — (cookies) (brook) cool
14. loom — (pool) (shampoo) stood
15. snooze — shook (smooth) (spool)

Notes for Home: Your child wrote words with the vowel digraph *oo*. **Home Activity:** Have your child write sentences using one word with the same vowel sound as *shoot* and one word with the same vowel sound as *stood* in each sentence.

42

The vowel digraph *oo* stands for the vowel sounds in *too* and *book*.

Choose a word from the list that has the same vowel sound as the underlined word. Write the word to complete the sentence.

cookies   maroon   wooden   brood   good
raccoon   noon   hooks   stood   tooth
noodles   hood   tvphoon   room   gloomy

1. Luis <u>took</u> a batch of freshly baked **cookies** to the party.

2. We **stood** at the edge of the <u>brook</u>.

3. The **raccoon** raided the garbage cans looking for <u>food</u>.

4. The <u>goose</u> led her **brood** to the pond.

5. The <u>cook</u> hung the pots from **hooks** in the kitchen.

6. Don't <u>snoop</u> through the stuff in my **room**!

7. Did you <u>choose</u> **noodles** or tacos for dinner?

8. The dentist used a special <u>tool</u> to pull my **tooth**.

9. The <u>crook</u> wore a black **hood** over his head.

10. <u>School</u> was let out at **noon** because of the snowstorm.

11. The weather in April is often <u>cool</u> and **gloomy**.

12. I <u>mistook</u> the **wooden** duck for a real one!

13. The <u>balloons</u> were colored blue and **maroon**.

14. The <u>booklet</u> had a **good** recipe for beef and bean stew.

15. Only a <u>fool</u> would go out in a **typhoon**.

Notes for Home: Your child wrote words with the vowel digraph *oo*. **Home Activity:** Challenge your child to make lists of other words that have the same vowel sounds as *too* and *book*.

43

Replace the underlined word with a word that has the same vowel sound and makes sense in the sentence. Write the word.

cookbook   cool   lookout   trooper   woodpecker
pool   footsteps   rooster   kangaroos   crook
groom   spools   mood   gloomy   shook

1. The dog barked when it heard <u>woodwork</u>.   **footsteps**

2. Paul <u>took</u> hands with the president.   **shook**

3. The <u>goose</u> wore a black tuxedo to the wedding.   **groom**

4. It is too <u>smooth</u> to go swimming today.   **cool**

5. A <u>cook</u> uses its beak to drill into trees.   **woodpecker**

6. The <u>raccoon</u> crowed each morning at dawn.   **rooster**

7. The police surrounded the house and caught the <u>foot</u>.   **crook**

8. The tailor has several <u>stools</u> of thread in his sewing kit.   **spools**

9. The lifeguard watched the swimmers in the <u>room</u>.   **pool**

10. The state <u>groom</u> stopped the speeding driver.   **trooper**

11. The rain made the day dark and <u>blooming</u>.   **gloomy**

12. The famous chef published a <u>fishhook</u>.   **cookbook**

13. The crowd was in a cheerful <u>proof</u>.   **mood**

14. In summer watchers keep a <u>football</u> for fires.   **lookout**

15. <u>Balloons</u> have strong hind legs and tails.   **Kangaroos**

Notes for Home: Your child wrote words with the vowel digraph *oo*. **Home Activity:** Have your child look through a newspaper to find other words with the vowel digraph *oo*. Ask your child to circle the *oo* words with the same vowel sound as *good* and to underline the *oo* words with the same vowel sound as *loose*.

44

Answers **191**

Vowel Digraph *oo* /ü/, /ů/

Use words with the vowel digraph *oo* to complete the puzzle. The words you write across will have the same vowel sound as *moon*. The words you write down will have the same vowel sound as *wood*.

Down
1. stream
2. see
3. dishonest person
5. curved piece of metal
6. prepare food

Across
1. kind of footwear
2. used for weaving
4. masked animal
5. spear used for fishing
6. funny drawing

Crossword puzzle answers:
- 1 Across: B O O T
- BROOM (down from B)
- 2 Across: L O O M
- LOOK (down)
- 3 C, CROOK (down)
- 4 Across: R A C C O O N
- 5 Across: H A R P O O N
- HOOK (down)
- 6 Across: C A R T O O N
- COOK (down)

Notes for Home: Your child wrote words with the vowel digraph *oo*.
Home Activity: Help your child make a crossword puzzle using the words *balloon, bamboo, caboose, moon, shampoo, cookies, foot, good, took,* and *shook*.

45

Vowel Diphthongs *ou, ow*

The vowel diphthongs *ou* and *ow* stand for the vowel sound in these words.

sound   town

Underline the letters that stand for the vowel sound in each word. Write the word next to its meaning.

fr<u>ow</u>n	c<u>ou</u>nt	l<u>ou</u>d	g<u>ow</u>n	n<u>ow</u>
s<u>ou</u>th	<u>ou</u>t	d<u>ow</u>n	gr<u>ow</u>l	br<u>ow</u>n
gr<u>ou</u>nd	cr<u>ou</u>ch	m<u>ou</u>th	r<u>ou</u>nd	cr<u>ow</u>d

1. name numbers in order — count
2. dark color — brown
3. many people — crowd
4. not then — now
5. opposite of *smile* — frown
6. soil — ground
7. fancy dress — gown
8. part of a face — mouth
9. stoop low — crouch
10. opposite of *in* — out
11. circular — round
12. not quiet — loud
13. opposite of *north* — south
14. a low, angry sound — growl
15. opposite of *up* — down

Notes for Home: Your child wrote words with the vowel diphthongs *ou* and *ow*.
Home Activity: Have your child list four pairs of *ou* and *ow* words that rhyme.

46

Vowel Diphthongs *ou, ow*

The vowel diphthongs *ou* and *ow* stand for the vowel sound in *out* and *down*.

Underline the letters in each word that stand for the vowel sound you hear in *out*. Write the word that best completes each sentence.

1. The watchdog will **growl** at strangers.
   shout   gr<u>ow</u>l
2. Tulips are her favorite **flowers** .
   fl<u>ow</u>ers   fouls
3. A quick **shower** will cool you off on a hot day.
   pound   sh<u>ow</u>er
4. Throw a penny into the **fountain** for good luck.
   f<u>ou</u>ntain   crowd
5. My brother fell asleep on the **couch** .
   towel   c<u>ou</u>ch
6. Jay is **proud** of his science project.
   pr<u>ou</u>d   howl
7. There are sixteen **ounces** in a pound.
   <u>ou</u>nces   owls
8. The laundry room is **downstairs** in the basement.
   round   d<u>ow</u>nstairs
9. Early in spring, the farmer will **plow** the fields.
   pl<u>ow</u>   bounce
10. The cook added bean **sprouts** to the salad.
    chowder   spr<u>ou</u>ts

Notes for Home: Your child wrote words with the vowel diphthongs *ou* and *ow*.
Home Activity: Have your child write sentences using the *ou* and *ow* words that were *not* written on the page.

47

Vowel Diphthongs *ou, ow*

The vowel diphthongs *ou* and *ow* stand for the vowel sound in *pound* and *frown*.

Underline the two words in each sentence with the vowel sound you hear in *pound*. Write each underlined word under the correct heading.

1. Charlie made clam <u>chowder</u> for the <u>crowd</u> at the party.
2. Is the new <u>couch</u> <u>brown</u>?
3. Rita's science report is <u>about</u> <u>owls</u>.
4. It's scary to <u>encounter</u> a <u>growling</u> dog.
5. Snow-covered <u>mountains</u> <u>surround</u> the village.
6. <u>Cloudy</u> days make me feel <u>drowsy</u>.
7. She was <u>proud</u> of the <u>trout</u> that she caught.
8. The <u>cowboy</u> rode slowly into <u>town</u>.
9. *Boat* has the same <u>vowel</u> sound as *road*.
10. After the storm, the <u>power</u> was <u>out</u> for a while.

/ow/ spelled *ou*	/ow/ spelled *ow*
11. couch	21. chowder
12. about	22. crowd
13. encounter	23. brown
14. mountains	24. owls
15. surround	25. growling
16. Cloudy	26. drowsy
17. proud	27. cowboy
18. trout	28. town
19. sound	29. vowel
20. out	30. power

Notes for Home: Your child wrote words with the vowel diphthongs *ou* and *ow*.
Home Activity: Have your child write a poem using either *ou* or *ow* words.

48

---

192 Answers

Name _____

Vowel Diphthongs *ou, ow*

Write the word that answers the riddle. Circle the letters that stand for the vowel sound you hear in *out*.

pout	crown	blouse	scout	south
eyebrow	clown	clouds	now	cowboy
trout	sundown	house	gown	thousand

1. What is something a king wears? — **cr(ow)n**

2. Which direction is opposite north? — **s(ou)th**

3. Which person makes other people laugh? — **cl(ow)n**

4. What is a woman's shirt sometimes called? — **bl(ou)se**

5. What is located over the eye? — **eyebr(ow)**

6. What is a freshwater fish? — **tr(ou)t**

7. Which person looks after cattle on a ranch? — **c(ow)boy**

8. Which person is sent ahead to get information? — **sc(ou)t**

9. What might a woman wear to a fancy party? — **g(ow)n**

10. What word means "at this time"? — **n(ow)**

11. What is a place to live? — **h(ou)se**

12. What is a large number? — **th(ou)sand**

13. What is another name for *sunset*? — **sund(ow)n**

14. Where does rain come from? — **cl(ou)ds**

15. What is something an unhappy child does? — **p(ou)t**

Notes for Home: Your child wrote words with the vowel diphthongs *ou* and *ow*.
Home Activity: Have your child write riddles for the following words: *hound, pouch, mouse, county, powder, flower, scowl.*

49

50

Name _____

Vowel Diphthongs *ou, ow*

Replace the underlined word with a word that has the same vowel sound with the same spelling and makes sense in the sentence. Write the word.

brown	doubt	foul	allowed	loud
power	found	announced	county	proud
shower	mouse	powder	trowel	plow

1. Lee <u>cloud</u> his backpack in a corner of the closet. — **found**

2. Betty has long <u>down</u> hair. — **brown**

3. It was impossible to talk over the <u>round</u> music. — **loud**

4. A <u>noun</u> can hear well but has poor vision. — **mouse**

5. A <u>brow</u> cuts the soil and turns it over. — **plow**

6. Congress has the <u>towel</u> to declare war. — **power**

7. Most people in the <u>fountain</u> voted for new roads. — **county**

8. He took a <u>crown</u> after exercising. — **shower**

9. Are you <u>stout</u> to be an American citizen? — **proud**

10. The batter hit a <u>south</u> ball to left field. — **foul**

11. I <u>couch</u> whether they will be on time. — **doubt**

12. The store <u>amounted</u> it was having a sale. — **announced**

13. Did you put chili <u>flower</u> in the soup? — **powder**

14. She left the <u>scowl</u> in the flowerbed. — **trowel**

15. No dogs are <u>plowed</u> in the restaurant. — **allowed**

Notes for Home: Your child wrote words with the vowel diphthongs *ou* and *ow*.
Home Activity: Have your child write a phrase using each underlined word on the page.

Name _____

Vowel Diphthongs *oi, oy*

The vowel diphthongs *oi* and *oy* stand for the vowel sound in these words.

soil   joy

In each word in the box, underline the letters that stand for the vowel sound you hear in *joy*. Then write the words next to their meanings.

j<u>oi</u>n	av<u>oi</u>d	b<u>oy</u>	t<u>oy</u>	disapp<u>oi</u>nt
<u>oy</u>ster	ch<u>oi</u>ce	l<u>oy</u>al	b<u>oi</u>l	enj<u>oy</u>
v<u>oi</u>ce	c<u>oi</u>n	v<u>oy</u>age	<u>oi</u>ntment	sp<u>oi</u>l

1. opposite of *girl* — **boy**

2. selection — **choice**

3. penny, dime, or quarter — **coin**

4. bubble up, give off steam — **boil**

5. have fun with — **enjoy**

6. stay away from — **avoid**

7. sound made through the mouth — **voice**

8. faithful — **loyal**

9. make unfit or useless — **spoil**

10. soothing skin cream — **ointment**

11. an ocean animal — **oyster**

12. plaything — **toy**

13. fail to please — **disappoint**

14. long trip — **voyage**

15. bring together — **join**

Notes for Home: Your child wrote words with the vowel diphthongs *oi* and *oy*.
Home Activity: Have your child write ten phrases using *oi* and *oy* words from the page.

51

52

Name _____

Vowel Diphthongs *oi, oy*

The vowel diphthongs *oi* and *oy* stand for the vowel sound in *oil* and *joy*.

Write the word that completes the sentence and has the vowel sound you hear in *joy*.

1. The ankle is the **joint** _____ that connects the foot with the leg.
   bone   joint

2. Does your neighbor's loud music **annoy** _____ you?
   annoy   bother

3. Pasta is Megan's **choice** _____ for dinner.
   food   choice

4. A **paperboy** _____ delivers our newspaper each morning.
   reporter   paperboy

5. He added fertilizer to the **soil** _____ to make the plants grow.
   ground   soil

6. Did you **enjoy** _____ your trip to San Francisco?
   enjoy   encounter

7. The king and queen lived in the **royal** _____ palace.
   royal   regal

8. Some household cleaners contain **poison** _____.
   perfume   poison

9. There was a **coil** _____ of rope in the bow of the boat.
   noose   coil

10. The hunter used a **decoy** _____ to lure the animal into the trap.
    decoy   disguise

Notes for Home: Your child wrote words with the vowel diphthongs *oi* and *oy*.
Home Activity: Have your child look through a newspaper to find and highlight *oi* and *oy* words.

© Scott Foresman 4-6

Answers **193**

The vowel diphthongs *oi* and *oy* stand for the vowel sound in *soil* and *joy*.

Underline the word or words in each sentence that have the vowel sound you hear in *joy*. Then write each underlined word under the correct heading.

1. Dogs are loyal to their owners.
2. The spring rains brought needed moisture to the soil.
3. The crowd was too noisy and loud.
4. A high-pitched voice makes an annoying sound.
5. The boy toils in the fields with the farmer.
6. Joan enjoyed the journey home.
7. You won't be disappointed in the show.
8. Is Tom employed as a paperboy?
9. The boat moved to the right to avoid the rocks.
10. Will you join us on the voyage to the islands?

/oi/ spelled *oi*		/oi/ spelled *oy*	
11.	moisture	19.	loyal
12.	soil	20.	annoying
13.	noisy	21.	boy
14.	voice	22.	enjoyed
15.	toils	23.	employed
16.	disappointed	24.	paperboy
17.	avoid	25.	voyage
18.	join		

Notes for Home: Your child wrote words with the vowel diphthongs *oi* and *oy*.
Home Activity: Have your child choose three words on the page and make a list of words that rhyme with each one.

53

Circle the word or words that have the same vowel sound as the underlined word. Then write the letters that stand for that vowel sound.

1. The cook spoiled the soup by adding too much salt.
   (boil)   boat   (loiter)   oi
2. He is lucky to have such loyal friends.
   (convoy)   phone   (foyer)   oy
3. Pearls are formed inside the shell of an oyster.
   onion   (coy)   (annoy)   oy
4. Dolores decided to join the debate team.
   (oil)   couch   (coil)   oi
5. The skater was disappointed when she lost the competition.
   (rejoiced)   (moist)   told   oi
6. The Boy Scouts sponsored their annual paper drive.
   (employ)   bone   (ahoy)   oy
7. The nurse put ointment on the patient's cut.
   paint   (poison)   (noise)   oi
8. The tornado destroyed several buildings in the business district.
   (boy)   choose   (decoy)   oy
9. The yo-yo is a toy that appeals to people of all ages.
   (joy)   tool   (royal)   oy
10. We will avoid the traffic by taking a detour.
    door   (coin)   (poise)   oi

Notes for Home: Your child identified words with the vowel sound in *joy*.
Home Activity: Have your child choose a sentence from the page and write a story that begins with the sentence.

54

Write the word that answers the riddle. Circle the letters that stand for the vowel sound you hear in *joy*.

oily	coin	royal	noise	soybean
ahoy	enjoy	convoy	annoy	oyster
broil	avoid	point	loyal	join

1. What is a protein-rich food? soybean
2. What are loud sounds? noise
3. What word means "bring together"? join
4. What is a sailor's cry? ahoy
5. What word describes kings and queens? royal
6. What word means "soaked with oil"? oily
7. What word means "disturb or trouble"? annoy
8. What is a piece of metal money? coin
9. What word means "stay away from"? avoid
10. What is a kind of shellfish? oyster
11. What word describes a way to cook? broil
12. What word means "like, be happy with"? enjoy
13. What word describes a good friend? loyal
14. What is a sharp end? point
15. What is a fleet of trucks that carries supplies? convoy

Notes for Home: Your child wrote words with the vowel diphthongs *oi* and *oy*.
Home Activity: Have your child write riddles for the following words: *voice, ointment, poise, destroy, cowboy, joy.*

55

In the consonant combinations *kn* and *gn*, two letters stand for only one sound. One letter is silent. Say these words.

   knee   The letter *k* is silent.
   sign   The letter *g* is silent.

Write *kn* or *gn* to complete the word in each sentence. Then draw a line through the letter in the combination that you do not hear.

1. The sharp _kn_ife can cut the bread easily.
2. Dana's knees hurt from _kn_eeling in the garden to plant flowers.
3. Carlos wants to be a web page desi_gn_er.
4. Mei Lei learned to _kn_it a sweater in crafts class.
5. Oscar wrote the homework assi_gn_ment in his notebook.
6. The sailor tied two ropes together using a strong _kn_ot.
7. The baker will _kn_ead the dough with her hands.
8. The beaver used its strong teeth to _gn_aw through the log.
9. I _kn_ow I will remember where I put my keys if I just concentrate!
10. After the accident, the mechanic had to ali_gn_ the tires on the car.
11. Sir Lancelot was the bravest of the _kn_ights in Camelot.
12. The man flapped his hat at the _gn_ats swarming around his face.
13. Ravi tried to cram six books into his _kn_apsack.
14. I really thought I _kn_ew the answer to that question.
15. The politician hoped her campai_gn_ would help her win the election.

Notes for Home: Your child completed words with the consonant combinations *kn* and *gn* in which one consonant is silent. **Home Activity:** Have your child spell each *kn* or *gn* word on the page using a hand signal such as a clap or a thumbs-down in place of the silent consonant in each word.

56

© Scott Foresman 4–6

Page 57

In the word *knee*, the *k* is silent.
In the word *sign*, the *g* is silent.

Circle *kn* or *gn* in each word. Then write the letter that you hear in the combination.

1. (kn)eeled ___n___   2. (gn)ats ___n___
3. (kn)ight ___n___   4. desi(gn) ___n___
5. (kn)uckles ___n___   6. rei(gn) ___n___
7. assi(gn)s ___n___   8. (kn)ew ___n___
9. (gn)arled ___n___   10. (kn)apsack ___n___

• The letter that you hear in the consonant combinations in these words is ___n___ .

Using the words above, write a word to complete each sentence.

11. The carpenter scraped his ___knuckles___ on the rough board.

12. A graphic artist was hired to ___design___ a new catalog cover.

13. Rebecca packed her ___knapsack___ for the long hike.

14. The young queen will ___reign___ over the country for her lifetime.

15. Paco immediately raised his hand because he ___knew___ the answer.

16. The branches of the old tree were twisted and ___gnarled___ .

17. Our teacher ___assigns___ thirty minutes of reading each night.

18. The tiny ___gnats___ , like mosquitoes, swarmed around us at the beach.

19. Ava ___kneeled___ down to talk to the small child.

20. In the story, the ___knight___ fought a ferocious dragon.

Notes for Home: Your child wrote words with the consonant combinations *kn* and *gn* in which one consonant is silent. **Home Activity:** Spend some time with your child looking in the dictionary for words beginning with *kn* and *gn*. Discuss the words that you find.

57

Page 58

In the consonant combinations *wr* and *mb*, two letters stand for only one sound. One letter is silent. Say these words.

   wren   The letter *w* is silent.
   comb   The letter *b* is silent.

Write *wr* or *mb* to complete the word in each phrase. Then draw a line through the letter in the combination that you do not hear.

1. cli___mb___ing a sheer rock face

2. a ram, a ewe, and a la___mb___

3. ___wr___ist support at the computer keyboard

4. a baby noisily sucking her thu___mb___

5. nothing but cru___mb___s left from the cake

6. ___wr___apped in colorful paper and ribbon

7. a ___wr___eath of flowers and vines on the door

8. neat and legible hand___wr___iting

9. clogged pipes in the plu___mb___ing

10. ___wr___inkled from being packed in a suitcase

Write each word above under the picture name that has the same consonant combination.

11. ___wrist___   16. ___climbing___
12. ___wrapped___   17. ___lamb___
13. ___wreath___   18. ___thumb___
14. ___handwriting___   19. ___crumbs___
15. ___wrinkled___   20. ___plumbing___

Notes for Home: Your child completed and sorted words with the consonant combinations *wr* and *mb* in which one consonant is silent. **Home Activity:** Have your child think of at least four objects whose names have the consonant combinations *wr* and *mb*. Ask your child which letter he or she hears and which letter is silent in each name.

58

Page 59

In the word *wren*, the *w* is silent.
In the word *comb*, the *b* is silent.

Circle *wr* or *mb* in each word. Then write the letter that you hear in the combination.

1. (wr)iter ___r___   2. (wr)ong ___r___
3. nu(mb) ___m___   4. (wr)ench ___r___
5. (wr)eath ___r___   6. la(mb) ___m___
7. li(mb) ___m___   8. (wr)ing ___r___
9. (wr)istwatch ___r___   10. to(mb)stone ___m___

Using the words above, write each word next to its definition.

11. not right, incorrect ___wrong___

12. a person who is an author ___writer___

13. a young sheep ___lamb___

14. a leg, an arm, a wing; a large tree branch ___limb___

15. a timepiece worn on the arm just above the hand ___wristwatch___

16. to twist by force; to squeeze out ___wring___

17. a stone that marks a grave ___tombstone___

18. a tool to hold and turn nuts, bolts, and pipes ___wrench___

19. a ring of flowers or leaves twisted together ___wreath___

20. having lost the power to feel; deadened ___numb___

Notes for Home: Your child wrote words with the consonant combinations *wr* and *mb* in which one consonant is silent. **Home Activity:** Take turns with your child trying to make up the longest sentence that makes sense using as many *mb* and *wr* words as you can. Start with a short sentence and add on words.

59

Page 60

In the consonant combinations *kn*, *gn*, *wr*, and *mb*, two letters stand for only one sound. One letter is silent.

  knee   **sign**   **wren**   **comb**

Circle the words in which *kn*, *gn*, *wr*, and *mb* stand for only one sound. Then write each circled word to answer a clue.

(climbing)	sickness	(assign)	(knotted)	(gnaw)
number	crumble	(wrong)	signature	(numb)
(wrench)	signal	darkness	symbol	dignity
dowry	(known)	(crumbs)	(design)	newborn

1. give someone a job to do ___assign___

2. tangled and snarled ___knotted___

3. what a dog does to a bone ___gnaw___

4. not right ___wrong___

5. too cold to feel anything ___numb___

6. going up a steep hill ___climbing___

7. a tool used to tighten things ___wrench___

8. bits or pieces of something ___crumbs___

9. familiar to everyone ___known___

10. a plan or sketch used as a pattern ___design___

Notes for Home: Your child wrote words with the consonant combinations *kn*, *gn*, *wr*, and *mb*. **Home Activity:** Ask your child to explain to you why he or she did not circle the other words in the box on the page.

60

© Scott Foresman 4–6

The consonant *c* can stand for two different sounds.

coat   *c* = /k/   city   *c* = /s/

Write each word in the list under the word in which *c* stands for the same sound.

celebrate   spicy   escalator   collar   discovered
compass   cents   cast   peaceful   sauce

coat		city	
1. compass		6. celebrate	
2. escalator		7. spicy	
3. cast		8. cents	
4. collar		9. peaceful	
5. discovered		10. sauce	

Use the words above to complete the sentences.

11. Tami's broken arm was in a __cast__ for eight weeks.

12. Hector always irons the __collar__ of his shirt last.

13. Rebecca paid eighty-five __cents__ for the fancy pencil.

14. The soldier used a __compass__ to find his way north.

15. Aunt Sue puts too much pepper in her spaghetti __sauce__.

16. The baby looked __peaceful__ as he slept.

17. Keesha __discovered__ a letter hidden in an old trunk.

18. We __celebrate__ New Year's Eve on December 31.

19. Kaj and I took the __escalator__ to the second level of the mall.

20. Jalapeño peppers make the salsa very __spicy__.

Notes for Home: Your child identified and wrote words in which the consonant *c* stands for /k/ or /s/. **Home Activity:** Write ten words in which *c* stands for /k/ or /s/ on index cards. Shuffle the cards. Have your child sort them into two piles according to the sound *c* stands for.

61

When the consonant *c* is followed by the vowel *a, o,* or *u,* the *c* usually stands for /k/.

cape   cone   cube

When the consonant *c* is followed by the vowel *e* or *i,* the *c* usually stands for /s/.

cent   city

Write the words in each phrase in which *c* stands for /k/ or /s/. Circle the sound *c* stands for in each word.

1. decided to eat in the cafeteria
   __decided__ /k/ (/s/)   cafeteria (/k/) /s/

2. was excited to receive the surprise gift
   __excited__ /k/ (/s/)   receive /k/ (/s/)

3. cooked oatmeal cereal for breakfast
   __cooked__ (/k/) /s/   cereal /k/ (/s/)

4. tried not to panic during the hurricane
   __panic__ (/k/) /s/   hurricane (/k/) /s/

5. followed the curve around the corner
   __curve__ (/k/) /s/   corner (/k/) /s/

6. add carrots and celery to the soup
   __carrots__ (/k/) /s/   celery /k/ (/s/)

7. used a comb to curl the doll's hair
   __comb__ (/k/) /s/   curl (/k/) /s/

8. danced to the music
   __danced__ /k/ (/s/)   music (/k/) /s/

9. skidded on the icy surface
   __icy__ /k/ (/s/)   surface /k/ (/s/)

10. planned the ceremony months in advance
    __ceremony__ /k/ (/s/)   advance /k/ (/s/)

Notes for Home: Your child wrote words in which the consonant *c* stands for /k/ or /s/. **Home Activity:** Challenge your child to think of a word pair for a category. One word must have *c* with /k/ and the other must have *c* with /s/. Example: for the category *animals, cow* and *rhinoceros.*

62

The consonant *g* can stand for two different sounds.

goat   *g* = /g/   gem   *g* = /j/

Write each word in the list under the word in which *g* stands for the same sound.

Giants   region   goal   age
gold   encourages   begins   August

goat		gentle	
1. gold		5. Giants	
2. goal		6. region	
3. begins		7. encourages	
4. August		8. age	

Use the words above to complete the sentences. You will not use all of the words.

9. Our school football season __begins__ in August.

10. The name of our team is the __Giants__.

11. Our team colors are navy and __gold__.

12. We are in the 12 and under __age__ division.

13. Our division is located in the Midwest __region__.

14. The coach always __encourages__ us to have fun and to do our best.

15. With only seconds left to play, our kicker kicks a field __goal__, and we win the game!

Notes for Home: Your child identified and wrote words in which the consonant *g* stands for /g/ or /j/. **Home Activity:** Take turns with your child naming and listing words in which *g* stands for /g/ or /j/. See how many words you can name in five minutes.

63

The consonant *g* can stand for /g/.

gate   get   gift   got   gust

When *g* is followed by *e, i,* or *y,* the *g* sometimes stands for /j/.

gem   giant   gym

Write the words in each phrase in which *g* stands for /g/ or /j/. Circle the sound *g* stands for in each word.

1. saw a cougar and a giraffe at the zoo
   __cougar__ (/g/) /j/   giraffe /g/ (/j/)

2. purchased ten gallons of gasoline
   __gallons__ (/g/) /j/   gasoline (/g/) /j/

3. did not argue with the manager
   __argue__ (/g/) /j/   manager /g/ (/j/)

4. closed the garden gate
   __garden__ (/g/) /j/   gate (/g/) /j/

5. eager to begin our new project
   __eager__ (/g/) /j/   begin (/g/) /j/

6. last page in the magazine
   __page__ /g/ (/j/)   magazine (/g/) /j/

7. gave me the telephone message
   __gave__ (/g/) /j/   message /g/ (/j/)

8. gears in the engine
   __gears__ (/g/) /j/   engine /g/ (/j/)

9. juicy oranges and tangerines
   __oranges__ /g/ (/j/)   tangerines /g/ (/j/)

10. fried the eggs in margarine
    __eggs__ (/g/) /j/   margarine /g/ (/j/)

Notes for Home: Your child wrote words in which the consonant *g* stands for /g/ or /j/. **Home Activity:** Challenge your child to name a word pair for a category. One word must have /g/ spelled *g* and the other word must have /j/ spelled *g*. Example: for the category *foods, eggs* and *margarine.*

64

© Scott Foresman 4–6

Worksheet 65

Name _____

The consonant *c* stands for /k/ in *coat* and /s/ in *cent*.
The consonant *g* stands for /g/ in *goat* and /j/ in *gem*.

Radio station WRCK plays "Hard Rock Music All the Time." Radio station WSFT plays "Soft Sounds—All Day, All Night." Find the word in each song title in which *c* stands for /k/ or /s/ or *g* stands for /g/ or /j/. If the word has the "hard" *c* or *g* sound, write the word under WRCK. If the word has the "soft" *c* or *g* sound, write the word under WSFT.

"Spice Jam"   "Music in the Air"   "Because I Know"
"Call Me Today"   "Long-ago Rhythm"   "Our Generation"
"Train Engine Blues"   "The Electric Slide"   "High Energy Polka"
"Hamburger Hustle"   "Finally Said Good-bye"   "City Swing"
"Giant Bubble Blow-Out" "Face the Rain"   "Octopus Hip Hop"
"The Last Dance"   "Beginner Steps"   "New Age Tune"
"Got You on My Mind"   "Gentle Breezes"

WRCK (*c* /k/ or *g* /g/)

1. Call
2. Hamburger
3. Got
4. Music
5. Long-ago
6. Electric
7. Good-bye
8. Beginner
9. Because
10. Octopus

WSFT (*c* /s/ or *g* /j/)

11. Spice
12. Engine
13. Giant
14. Dance
15. Face
16. Gentle
17. Generation
18. Energy
19. City
20. Age

Notes for Home: Your child wrote words in which the consonants *c* and *g* stand for /k/ and /s/ or /g/ and /j/. **Home Activity:** Think of the titles of songs you and your child are familiar with. Together decide whether any words in the titles have hard or soft *c* or *g* sounds.

65

Worksheet 66

Name _____

The consonant *x* can stand for the sound you hear in *box* and the sound you hear in *exact*. Say *box* and listen to the ending sound. Say *exact* and listen to the beginning sound.

Underline the word that has the consonant *x* in each phrase. Circle *box* if the *x* in the word stands for the same sound as in *box*. Circle *exact* if the *x* stands for the same sound as in *exact*.

1. expiration date on milk — box — **exact**
2. oxygen necessary for breathing — **box** — exact
3. sixteen years of age — **box** — exact
4. used an axe to chop wood — **box** — exact
5. a new exhibit at the museum — box — **exact**
6. smooth texture of silk — **box** — exact
7. cannot exist without food and water — box — **exact**
8. played the saxophone in the jazz band — **box** — exact
9. exercise for one hour at the gym — **box** — exact
10. relax in the bathtub — **box** — exact
11. exhausted after running a marathon — box — **exact**
12. an expensive gold watch — **box** — exact
13. a medical examination — box — **exact**
14. a long excerpt from a book — **box** — exact
15. coaxing the puppy out of its cage — **box** — exact

Notes for Home: Your child identified sounds the consonant *x* stands for in words. **Home Activity:** Have your child look for words with *x* in a newspaper article. Together say each word and decide whether the *x* stands for the sound in *box* or the sound in *exact*.

66

Worksheet 67

Name _____

The consonant *x* can stand for the sounds in these words.

box   exact   xylem

Write each word in the list under the word in which *x* stands for the same sound.

executive   exotic   xylophone   axis   xenophobia
exciting   Texas   excellent   exaggerate   example

box
1. exciting
2. Texas
3. excellent
4. axis

exact
5. executive
6. exotic
7. exaggerate
8. example

xylem
9. xylophone
10. xenophobia

Use the words above to complete the sentences.

11. The giant panda is a(n) example of an endangered animal.
12. Austin is the state capital of Texas.
13. Naomi plays the xylophone in the orchestra.
14. Fishers often exaggerate about the fish that got away.
15. The earth spins on its axis.
16. The corporate vice-presidents had a(n) executive meeting.
17. White orchids are exotic tropical flowers.
18. The roller coaster ride was so exciting I couldn't stop screaming.
19. A fear of foreigners or outsiders is called xenophobia.
20. Dogs have a(n) excellent sense of smell.

Notes for Home: Your child wrote words in which the consonant *x* stands for three different sounds. **Home Activity:** Together explore the *x* section in a dictionary. Note how few words in English begin with *x* and what sounds *x* stands for at the beginning of words.

67

Worksheet 68

Name _____

In English, the consonant *q* is almost always followed by the vowel *u*. Together the letters *qu* stand for the beginning sound in *quit*.

Circle *qu* in each word in the box. Then write the words to complete the phrases.

quilt   quarter   quiz   quarrel   frequently
banquet   equator   quacking   aqua   aquarium
quiet   question   require   queen   acquitted

1. the loud quacking of the ducks
2. an angry quarrel
3. acquitted of the crime
4. a quiz with five true-and-false items
5. king and queen
6. visit our grandparents frequently
7. penny, nickel, dime, quarter
8. quiet in the library
9. colorful tropical fish in the aquarium
10. ask a question
11. sewing a patchwork quilt
12. the aqua color of the ocean water
13. the equator around the center of the earth
14. require a signature on the application
15. a wedding banquet for 250 guests

Notes for Home: Your child wrote words with *qu*. **Home Activity:** Have your child look for *qu* words in the sports section of a newspaper. Examples: *quarterback, quick, conquer, equipment*.

68

The letters *qu* can stand for the sound you hear in *quiet* and the sound you hear in *unique*. Say *quiet* and listen to the beginning sound. Say *unique* and listen to the ending sound.

Underline the *qu* word in each sentence. Circle *quiet* if the *qu* in the word stands for the same sound as in *quiet*. Circle *unique* if the *qu* stands for the same sound as in *unique*.

1. Twelve and one dozen are <u>equal</u> amounts. (quiet) unique
2. Click on "<u>quit</u>" before you shut down the computer. (quiet) unique
3. After the picnic, I counted twenty <u>mosquito</u> bites. quiet (unique)
4. The <u>earthquake</u> measured 6.5 on the Richter scale. (quiet) unique
5. Use <u>quotation</u> marks to show spoken words. (quiet) unique
6. The slimy movie monster was truly <u>grotesque</u>. quiet (unique)
7. You are <u>required</u> to have a license to drive a car. (quiet) unique
8. The <u>quarterback</u> threw the football seventy yards. (quiet) unique
9. She carried a <u>bouquet</u> of red and white carnations. quiet (unique)
10. Michaela was awarded a <u>plaque</u> at the science fair. quiet (unique)
11. The movie <u>marquee</u> is changed every Friday. quiet (unique)
12. Jose eats <u>frequently</u> at his favorite restaurant. (quiet) unique
13. Mr. Okada loves to go <u>antique</u> shopping. quiet (unique)
14. The <u>quartet</u> can play both jazz and classical music. (quiet) unique
15. Everyone wore costumes to the <u>masquerade</u>. quiet (unique)

Notes for Home: Your child identified the sounds *qu* stands for in words. **Home Activity:** Have your child make up a tongue twister using *qu* words. Example: *Quiet quarterbacks quickly acquire quotas.*

Unscramble the letters to make a word with *x* or *qu* that makes sense in the sentence. Write the letters of the word in the spaces.

1. I heard the duck **ckauq**. q u a c k
2. Jaime knows **caxytle** what job he wants. e x a c t l y
3. When ice melts, it becomes a **ludiqi**. l i q u i d
4. You can **quareic** a taste for oysters. a c q u i r e
5. Isabel read a chapter in her science **tbkxoeot**. t e x t b o o k
6. We will have our final **mexa** at the end of the semester. e x a m
7. The opposite of *minimum* is **uixmamm**. m a x i m u m
8. *King* is not a **nuequi** name for a dog. u n i q u e
9. Columbus is a famous **plxereor**. e x p l o r e r
10. I have to **roquecn** my fear of geometry. c o n q u e r
11. A **fripex** comes at the beginning of a word. p r e f i x
12. Dinosaurs **dixetse** on Earth sixty-five million years ago. e x i s t e d
13. The ambulance arrived very **ulcqyik**. q u i c k l y
14. The **peserxs** bus goes downtown without making any other stops. e x p r e s s
15. The expensive furniture is made with **ltuaqiy** materials. q u a l i t y

Notes for Home: Your child wrote words with *x* and *qu*. **Home Activity:** Have your child think of other *x* and *qu* words to scramble. Have your child give you clues about the words while you try to unscramble them. Take turns as "scrambler" and "guesser."

Sometimes two consonants stand for the beginning sounds in a word. The consonant blends *sc, sk, sm, sn, sp, st,* and *sw* stand for the beginning sounds in these words.

scare   skin   smile   snake   spin   store   swim

Write the *s*-blend word that completes each sentence. Circle the *s*-blend in the word.

1. Sonia added sugar to her cereal to make it ___(sw)eet___.
   spoil   sweet   spin   stale
2. Luis used a ___(sp)onge___ to soak up the water.
   spice   sponge   sweat   sweep
3. The horses were kept in the ___(st)able___ at the night.
   swept   spaceship   swing   stable
4. Mario will be performing a solo in the ___(sk)ating___ competition.
   snowstorm   smock   skirt   skating
5. This suspense novel is about a government ___(sp)y___.
   spy   snowball   spot   skill
6. We listened to music on George's new ___(st)ereo___ system.
   steam   steel   stereo   station
7. The ___(sn)ow___ piled in drifts as high as six feet.
   skeleton   snow   snacks   spine
8. Michelle quickly ___(sk)immed___ the newspaper headlines.
   sketched   skimmed   stayed   scooped
9. I stepped on the ___(sc)ales___ to see my weight.
   scales   smile   stack   sniff
10. We could see the ___(sm)oke___ from the campfire.
    swish   swim   stork   smoke

Notes for Home: Your child wrote words that begin with *s*-blends. **Home Activity:** Have your child examine a cereal box to find *s*-blend words and use a colored marker to circle the words on the box.

The consonant blends *sc, sk, sm, sn, sp, st,* and *sw* stand for the beginning sounds in *scar, skip, smile, snore, spin, store,* and *swan*.

Write *sc, sk, sm, sn, sp, st,* or *sw* to complete the word in each phrase.

1. __st__art the race
2. __sm__ooth as silk
3. __sp__ell words correctly
4. a bedtime __st__ory
5. shelter from the __st__orm
6. __sw__eet maple syrup
7. __sw__im in the pool
8. knife, fork, and __sp__oon
9. __sn__ap your fingers
10. a __sc__ore of 4–2
11. a __st__ain on the shirt
12. dry, rough __sk__in
13. the hissing __sn__ake
14. __sp__eed limit of 35
15. a __sc__ary movie
16. not large, but __sm__all
17. a long velvet __sk__irt
18. a __sc__oop of ice cream
19. twinkling __st__ars
20. a __sn__ail's slow pace

Notes for Home: Your child completed words with *s*-blends. **Home Activity:** Have your child use at least three *s*-blend words to describe an activity or event. For example, to describe a baseball game, he or she might use *score, steal,* and *swing.*

© Scott Foresman 4–6

The consonant blends *br, cr, dr, fr, gr, pr,* and *tr* stand for the beginning sounds in these words.

brain   **cr**y   **dr**ive   **fr**ee   **gr**ay   **pr**ize   **tr**uck

Write *br, cr, dr, fr, gr, pr,* or *tr* to complete each word and make it match its definition.

1. a three-sided geometric figure; a pharmacy; thankful or appreciative

   tr_iangle_   **dr**_ugstore_   **gr**_ateful_

2. used for building; cost; earth or dirt

   br_icks_   **pr**_ice_   **gr**_ound_

3. attractive or good-looking; icing; switch or exchange

   pr_etty_   **fr**_osting_   **tr**_ade_

4. liberty; wet thoroughly; sudden, loud noise

   fr_eedom_   **dr**_ench_   **cr**_ash_

5. hang down or sag; turned into ice; exact

   dr_oop_   **fr**_ozen_   **pr**_ecise_

6. a broad smile; a link or connection; railroad cars and engine

   gr_in_   **br**_idge_   **tr**_ain_

7. sketch; forecast; short, not long

   dr_aw_   **pr**_edict_   **br**_ief_

8. fearless or courageous; burial place; have a strong desire, long for

   br_ave_   **gr**_ave_   **cr**_ave_

9. a threesome; scare, terrify; jail

   tr_io_   **fr**_ighten_   **pr**_ison_

10. smash or crack; groan or squeak; slow down or stop

   br_eak_   **cr**_eak_   **br**_ake_

Notes for Home: Your child completed words with *r*-blends. **Home Activity:** Think of a challenging *r*-blend word. Look it up in a dictionary and read the definition aloud. Have your child name the word. Take turns as the "giver" and the "guesser."

73

The consonant blends *br, cr, dr, fr, gr, pr,* and *tr* stand for the beginning sounds in *brain, cry, drive, free, gray, prize,* and *truck.*

Underline the *r*-blend in each word in the box. Then write the word that completes each sentence.

fruits	brisk	tricycle	broccoli	printer
brocade	dryer	fractions	green	practices
trout	drank	crawl	gravy	bricks

1. Javier __practices__ the piano for one hour each day.

2. My favorite green vegetable is __broccoli__.

3. Apple, pears, oranges, and grapes are all __fruits__.

4. A __brisk__ wind swirled the fallen leaves.

5. Most children __crawl__ before they are able to walk.

6. Moshanda learned to ride a __tricycle__ on her third birthday.

7. The marathon runner __drank__ water continually.

8. Mrs. Kim mixed yellow and blue paint to make __green__.

9. Scott connected the new laser __printer__ to his computer.

10. We have a favorite spot to fish for __trout__.

11. Grandmother poured __gravy__ over her mashed potatoes.

12. Mr. Abert needed four quarters for the __dryer__ at the laundromat.

13. The mason laid the __bricks__ according to the building plans.

14. 1 2/3, 5 7/8 and 10 4/5 are examples of mixed __fractions__.

15. The drapes in the castle ballroom were made of heavy gold __brocade__.

Notes for Home: Your child wrote words with *r*-blends. **Home Activity:** Have your child make a list of *r*-blend words that he or she finds in a magazine article.

74

The consonant blends *bl, cl, fl, gl, pl,* and *sl* stand for the beginning sounds in these words.

blow   **cl**ue   **fl**aw   **gl**eam   **pl**ug   **sl**ip

Write *bl, cl, fl, gl, pl,* or *sl* to complete the word that goes with the definition.

1. **pl**_ant_   put seeds in the ground to grow

   sl_ant_   tilt, lean, or slope

2. **bl**_ame_   to hold someone responsible for doing wrong

   fl_ame_   glowing tongues of fire; to flare, burn, blaze

3. **fl**_ock_   a group of sheep

   cl_ock_   used to measure or show time

4. **fl**_oat_   held up by air or water

   gl_oat_   to brag, often in a spiteful way

5. **bl**_ank_   a space left to be filled in

   pl_ank_   a long, flat piece of timber

6. **gl**_ue_   a sticky substance used to hold things together

   bl_ue_   a primary color; the color of a clear sky in daylight

7. **sl**_ot_   a small, narrow opening often used in machines to take coins

   pl_ot_   scheme or secret plan; a small piece of ground; storyline

8. **sl**_ow_   taking a long time; not fast or quick

   fl_ow_   to move like a current or stream

9. **bl**_oom_   open into flowers, blossom

   gl_oom_   darkness; low spirits

10. **cl**_aw_   a sharp, hooked nail on an animal's foot

   fl_aw_   a slight defect or fault

Notes for Home: Your child completed words with *l*-blends. **Home Activity:** Together with your child make up your own rhyming *l*-blend word groups. Some possibilities are *-ight, -ink, -under, -ush, -ew, -ate, -ump, -ood, -utter, -ip, -ume,* and *-aze.*

75

The consonant blends *bl, cl, fl, gl, pl,* and *sl* stand for the beginning sounds in *blow, clue, flaw, gleam, plug,* and *slip.*

Circle the *l*-blend words used in the following five-day weather forecasts.

MONDAY	1. overcast (gloomy) skies
TUESDAY	2. dark (clouds) with storm front moving in
WEDNESDAY	3. heavy rain; (flash flood) warnings for the entire coast; make travel (plans) accordingly
THURSDAY	4. record west winds; (blustery) all day
FRIDAY	5. skies (clearing) with (slightly) warmer temperatures

Use the *l*-blend words below to complete each daily weather forecast description. You will not use all the words.

flurries	blizzard	pleasant	slight	floods
plunge	clashing	glimpses	blistering	gloomy

MONDAY	6. sunny, mild, and __pleasant__
TUESDAY	7. overcast with brief __glimpses__ of sunshine
WEDNESDAY	8. temperatures will __plunge__ to a record low
THURSDAY	9. light snow __flurries__ throughout the day
FRIDAY	10. __blizzard__ conditions make driving hazardous

Notes for Home: Your child wrote words with *l*-blends. **Home Activity:** Have your child find and circle *l*-blend words used on the weather page of a newspaper.

76

© Scott Foresman 4–6

Answers **199**

Sometimes three consonants stand for the beginning sounds in a word. The three-letter blends *chr, sch, scr, shr, spl, spr, squ, str,* and *thr* stand for the beginning sounds in words such as *school, scream, split, sprain, strike,* and *three.*

Write the word that completes each sentence. Underline the three-letter blend in each word.

1. The toddler __splattered__ paint all over the walls.

   screen   splattered   throw   shred

2. Each actor got a copy of the movie's __script__.

   scrawl   square   script   scribble

3. It is important to __spread__ the fertilizer in a thin, even layer.

   spread   shrink   strand   splice

4. Thea used __string__ to tie the packages together.

   shrivel   string   strap   scraps

5. Doctor Chin __schedules__ appointments every half hour.

   schedules   squeezes   sprinkles   scrambles

6. The sudden appearance of the monster made the audience __shriek__.

   spring   throb   screen   shriek

7. Pablo drew a perfect __square__ using a ruler as his guide.

   square   chronic   string   sprain

8. Sara carefully polished the __chrome__ trim on the new car.

   spring   chrome   scrape   strong

9. We walked single file __through__ the narrow passageway.

   threw   thrown   through   throw

10. The dates on the time line were arranged in __chronological__ order.

   scholarly   chronological   scheduled   chromosome

Notes for Home: Your child wrote words with three-letter blends. **Home Activity:** Help your child look for three-letter blend words in the copy on packages and containers in the kitchen and bathroom.

77

The three-letter blends *chr, sch, scr, shr, spl, spr, squ, str,* and *thr* stand for the beginning sounds in words such as *school, scream, split, sprain, strike,* and *three.*

Write the word that completes each analogy. Circle the three-letter blend in the word.

scream	three	spring	school	squeal
string	chrome	squad	splint	stream
throat	shrub	shrug	strawberries	sprain

1. summer : winter :: fall : __spring__

2. students : __school__ :: audience : theater

3. grapes : vine :: __strawberries__ : bush

4. door : slam :: brakes : __squeal__

5. leg : cast :: finger : __splint__

6. brain : skull :: __throat__ : neck

7. eye : wink :: shoulders : __shrug__

8. twist : ankle :: __sprain__ : wrist

9. __stream__ : river :: path : road

10. actors : cast :: soldiers : __squad__

11. whisper : __scream__ :: flute : tuba

12. frosting : cake :: __chrome__ : car

13. __shrub__ : tree :: hill : mountain

14. __three__ : nine :: four : sixteen

15. __string__ : rope :: guppy : trout

Notes for Home: Your child wrote three-letter blend words to complete analogies. **Home Activity:** Have your child make up analogies using words with three-letter blends. Some analogy relationships are opposites, same uses, and part to whole.

78

Sometimes two consonants stand for the ending sounds in a word. The consonant blends *ct, ld, lf, lk, lt, mp, nd, nt, pt, sk, sp,* and *st* stand for the ending sounds in words such as *hold, silk, stamp, sent, task,* and *last.*

Unscramble the letters to make a final consonant blend word to complete each phrase. Write the word and circle its final consonant blend.

1. got a __cramp__ in my leg   m a c p r

2. a carved, wooden __mask__   s m k a

3. a __gold__ bracelet   l g d o

4. __milk__ and cookies   k l i m

5. boxes stacked on the closet __shelf__   f h s e l

6. a __lamp__ on the end table   p m l a

7. a __belt__ with a buckle   t e l b

8. __first__, second, third   r i s f t

9. line up one __behind__ the other   b h i d e n

10. __perfect__ weather for sailing   t r e c f e p

11. gave a birthday __present__   e p e t n r s

12. __kept__ her promise   p k t e

13. __exact__ measurements of the room   t x c a e

14. stung by a red __wasp__   s p a w

15. saw __myself__ in the mirror   y e l m f s

Notes for Home: Your child wrote words with final consonant blends. **Home Activity:** Take turns with your child scrambling the letters of final consonant blend words and having the other person unscramble the letters.

79

The consonant blends *ct, ld, lf, lk, lt, mp, nd, nt, pt, sk, sp,* and *st* stand for the ending sounds in words such as *hold, silk, stamp, sent, task,* and *fast.*

Underline the final consonant blend in each word. Then write the words to complete the menu.

melt	buttermilk	hand	lump	meant
cold	breakfast	last	crisp	overslept

"THE (1.) __LAST__ STOP DINER"

TODAY'S (2.) __BREAKFAST__ SPECIALS

All your favorite cereals—hot or (3.) __cold__

Our famous oatmeal—"You'll never find a (4.) __lump__"

Blueberry or (5.) __buttermilk__ pancakes

Bacon, served (6.) __crisp__ and hot

Fresh sweet rolls, made by (7.) __hand__ in our kitchen

Double apple pancake—so big, it's (8.) __meant__ to be shared

Waffles with whipped cream—they (9.) __melt__ in your mouth!

Coffee, made strong for those who (10.) __overslept__

Create your own menu. Describe five items you would serve. Use one final consonant blend word in each description.

Menu   Answers will vary.

11. _____

12. _____

13. _____

14. _____

15. _____

Notes for Home: Your child wrote words with final consonant blends. **Home Activity:** Help your child create his or her own menu or add items to those your child has already written. Remember to use a final consonant blend word in each description.

80

© Scott Foresman 4–6

Name _____

Initial Consonant Digraph *ch*

When two consonants stand for one sound, they are called a digraph. The consonant digraph *ch* stands for the beginning sound in these words.

chop   chess   chirp

Underline the consonant digraph *ch* in each word in the box. Then write the words that name the pictures.

chain	checkers	chimney	chin	cherries
chalk	cheese	chicken	chair	check

1. chin

2. cheese

3. chimney

4. chicken

5. cherries

6. chalk

7. check

8. chain

9. chair

10. checkers

Notes for Home: Your child wrote words with the initial consonant digraph *ch*.
Home Activity: Take turns with your child naming other words that begin with *ch*.

81

Initial Consonant Digraph *sh*

The consonant digraph *sh* stands for the beginning sound in these words.

shape   should   shore

Circle the consonant digraph *sh* in each word in the box. Then write the words to complete the sentences.

shell	showed	shared	shower	shelter
shadow	shelf	sheets	short	shop

1. Oscar arranged the books neatly on the __shelf__.

2. Hugo was too __short__ to ride the roller coaster.

3. Juliette __shared__ the pizza with her friends.

4. The frightened turtle pulled its head into its __shell__.

5. Your __shadow__ gets longer in the afternoon.

6. Randell put the new __sheets__ on the bed.

7. Kyoko went to the mall to __shop__ for a gift.

8. Scott __showed__ his art project to the class.

9. After the race, Jessica took a long, hot __shower__.

10. The campers found __shelter__ from the sudden storm.

Notes for Home: Your child wrote words with the initial consonant digraph *sh*.
Home Activity: Have fun with the classic tongue twister: *She sells seashells by the seashore.* Have your child make up his or her own tongue twister with *sh* words.

82

Initial Consonant Digraph *th*

The consonant digraph *th* stands for the beginning sounds in these words.

them   thank

Write the word that completes the phrase and has the beginning sound in *them* or *thank*.

1. ____ book of poems   this   one   this

2. one ____ miles   hundred   thousand   thousand

3. a ____ gift   thoughtful   nice   thoughtful

4. rode ____ bikes   their   our   their

5. rain and ____   lightning   thunder   thunder

6. put a box ____   there   here   there

7. ____ on a rose   thorns   petals   thorns

8. more ____ my sister   for   than   than

9. ____ of hot soup   thermos   bowl   thermos

10. fell with a ____   thud   crash   thud

11. ____ right answer   a   the   the

12. now and ____   then   forever   then

13. ____-four cents   twenty   thirty   thirty

14. ____ red shoes   her   those   those

15. broke my ____   thumb   toe   thumb

Notes for Home: Your child wrote words in which the consonant digraph *th* stands for two different initial sounds. **Home Activity:** Have your child look up *them* and *thank* in a dictionary and note the phonetic respellings for the words. Have your child locate the pronunciation key and find the symbols and example words that explain the respellings.

83

Initial Consonant Digraph *wh*

The consonant digraph *wh* stands for the beginning sound in these words.

whale   whip   while

Find and write the 15 words with initial consonant digraph *wh* in the newspaper article.

Science Fair Winner Chosen

Darnell Wheatly, with the help of his white cat, Snowball, won the science fair on Friday. Darnell wanted to know if face whiskers helped cats sense whether or not they could fit through spaces of different sizes. Darnell used cat treats and three boxes. He put a treat inside the largest box where Snowball could find it easily. Darnell whispered, "Go get it." Snowball whizzed over to the box, quickly went in, and got the treat. Darnell then put a treat in the medium-sized box and whistled for his cat. Snowball whirled around and ran to the box. Then she slowed down, carefully went in, and got the treat. The last box was just smaller than Snowball's body. What would happen? When Snowball put her face near the box, she began to whine and whimper. Darnell knew why she would not try to go in. Snowball's whiskery "antennae" let her sense that the box was too small for her body.

1. Wheatly   2. white   3. whiskers

4. whether   5. where   6. whispered

7. whizzed   8. whistled   9. whirled

10. What   11. When   12. whine

13. whimper   14. why   15. whiskery

Notes for Home: Your child wrote words with the initial consonant digraph *wh*.
Home Activity: Have your child scan a newspaper article and circle words that begin with *wh*.

84

Answers **201**

Name

The consonant digraphs *sh*, *th*, *ch*, and *wh* stand for the beginning sounds in *share*, *thumb*, *cheese*, and *while*.

Write the word that belongs in each group. Circle the letters that stand for the beginning sound.

chin	thunder	ship	cherries	white
whirl	chalk	whale	third	shells
thimble	shovel	chair	sheets	thousand

1. pencil, crayon, _____ (ch)alk
2. ax, hoe, _____ (sh)ovel
3. rain, lightning, _____ (th)under
4. raspberries, blueberries, _____ (ch)erries
5. sand, seaweed, _____ (sh)ells
6. dolphin, shark, _____ (wh)ale
7. bench, stool, _____ (ch)air
8. blanket, pillowcase, _____ (sh)eets
9. turn, spin, _____ (wh)irl
10. first, second, _____ (th)ird
11. sailboat, canoe, _____ (sh)ip
12. ten, hundred, _____ (th)ousand
13. black, brown, _____ (wh)ite
14. nose, mouth, _____ (ch)in
15. needle, thread, _____ (th)imble

Notes for Home: Your child wrote words with the initial consonant digraphs *ch*, *sh*, *th*, and *wh*. **Home Activity:** Have your child add *ch*, *sh*, *th*, and *wh* to these word forms to make as many words as possible: ___*in*, ___*en*, ___*ip*.

85

Name

Two consonants can stand for the ending sound in a word. The consonant digraphs *ch*, *sh*, and *th* stand for the ending sounds in these words.

bench   wash   both

Write the digraph *ch*, *sh*, or *th* to complete the word in each phrase.

1. sandy bea__ch__
2. a wrea__th__ on the door
3. a long, curving pa__th__
4. fre__sh__ homemade bread
5. smoo__th__, not bumpy
6. sat on the cou__ch__
7. pu__sh__, don't pull
8. soup and salad for lun__ch__
9. fla__sh__ of lightning
10. ate a grilled cheese sandwi__ch__
11. fell with a cra__sh__
12. like a mo__th__ to the flame
13. the laun__ch__ of the space shuttle
14. ma__sh__ the potatoes
15. ma__th__ homework

Notes for Home: Your child completed words with the final consonant digraphs *ch*, *sh*, and *th*. **Home Activity:** Divide a sheet of paper into three columns labeled *sh*, *ch*, and *th*. Challenge your child to write as many final *sh* words as he or she can in three minutes. Then do the same for *ch* and *th*.

86

Name

The consonant digraphs *ch*, *sh*, and *th* stand for the ending sounds in *coach*, *dish*, and *south*. The final /ch/ can also be spelled *tch*.

Underline the final consonant digraph in each word. Then complete each sentence with a word that has the same final digraph as the word in dark type.

push	north	wash	math	fish
length	cash	hatch	tenth	teach
branch	teeth	wish	catch	bench

1. I paid ____cash____ for the new **hairbrush** I bought.
2. The **coach** will ____teach____ the team a new play.
3. The opposite direction of **south** is ____north____.
4. Our best baseball player can hit, **pitch**, and ____catch____
5. We sat and ate our **lunch** on a park ____bench____
6. I will ____wash____ and dry each **dish** carefully.
7. It was amazing to **watch** the baby chicks ____hatch____
8. My ____math____ project and my English paper are **both** due today.
9. The plural of **tooth** is ____teeth____
10. Miguel measured the ____length____ and **width** of the window.
11. We saw many ____fish____ jump and **splash** in the water.
12. October is the ____tenth____ **month**.
13. Kim saw the **flash** of a shooting star and made a ____wish____
14. Roberto could not **reach** the highest ____branch____ of the tree.
15. Marie had to ____push____ to get all the **trash** into the can.

Notes for Home: Your child wrote words with the final consonant digraphs *ch*, *sh*, and *th*. **Home Activity:** Ask your child to write a sentence with a final digraph word. Have your child read the sentence aloud without saying the word. You try to guess the word.

87

Name

The consonant digraphs *gh* and *ph* stand for the *f* sound in *laugh* and *elephant*. The consonants *f* and *ff* stand for the *f* sound in *find* and *cliff*.

Write *gh*, *ph*, *f*, or *ff* to complete the word in each phrase.

1. lau__gh__ at a joke
2. rou__gh__, not smooth
3. my niece and ne__ph__ew
4. a tele__ph__one call
5. the lost and __f__ound department
6. names in al__ph__abetical order
7. enou__gh__ money for bus fare
8. li__f__eguard at the pool
9. main idea of the paragra__ph__
10. sneezing and cou__gh__ing
11. too much stu__ff__ in my backpack
12. tou__gh__ hide of an alligator
13. the first-place tro__ph__y
14. wa__ff__les and maple syrup
15. a high __f__ence around the yard

Notes for Home: Your child completed words with the consonant digraphs *gh* and *ph* and the letters *f* or *ff*. **Home Activity:** Have your child make up elephant riddles using a *ph* or *gh* word in each answer. Example: Why did the elephant play the banjo? Because he didn't know how to play the saxophone!

88

© Scott Foresman 4–6

The consonant digraphs *ng* and *nk* stand for the ending sounds in these words.

wrong   sink

Change the underlined word in the sentence to a word with the same final digraph that makes sense in the sentence. *Hint*: The two words will also rhyme.

1. Please <u>sang</u> your clothes in the closet.   hang

2. Bernice took her money to the <u>tank</u>.   bank

3. Xavier and his brother sleep in <u>chunk</u> beds.   bunk

4. It took a <u>gong</u> time for Joseph to fall asleep.   long

5. The <u>sing</u> rode with his knights to the castle.   king

6. The skaters went round and round the <u>sink</u>.   rink

7. <u>Swing</u> an extra towel to the swimming pool.   Bring

8. The baby monkey <u>rung</u> tightly to its mother.   clung

9. The <u>junk</u> lived in the woods.   skunk

10. Latisha <u>gang</u> the bell several times.   rang

11. Reiko climbed the ladder one <u>sung</u> at a time.   rung

12. An elephant uses its <u>bunk</u> like a hand.   trunk

13. Did I <u>sank</u> you for the present?   thank

14. The <u>wing</u> was a plain gold band.   ring

15. The flower is a soft shade of <u>wink</u>.   pink

Notes for Home: Your child wrote words with the final consonant digraphs *ng* and *nk*.
Home Activity: Have your child look through a favorite book for words ending in *ng* and *nk*.

89

Two consonants that stand for one sound are called a digraph. Digraphs, such as *sh, ch, th, wh, ph, gh, ng,* and *nk,* may appear at the beginning, in the middle, or at the end of words.

Complete each word with the digraph *ch, ch, th, wh, ph, gh, nk,* or *ng.*

Dear Grandmo__th__er,

Greeti__ng__s from __Ph__iladel__ph__ia, Pennsylvania, "the city of bro__th__erly love." The first __th__ing I did was go to the Visitors' Center and pick up a sightseeing pam__ph__let. I was in luck! A double-decker tour bus was leavi__ng__ in two minutes. I saw famous historical places every__wh__ere I looked. My favorite was __th__e Liberty Bell. (Yes, it is cracked!) For lun__ch__, I got the famous __ch__eesesteak sandwi__ch__ from a vendor in Independence National Park. I will __sh__ow you all of the __ph__otos I've taken wi__th__ the new camera you gave me (tha__nk__s again!) __wh__en I get back next week. The wea__th__er has been fine—warm with sun__sh__ine duri__ng__ the day but __ch__illy at night. As you can tell, I've done more than enou__gh__ for one day. I'm havi__ng__ a great time. Wi__sh__ you were here.

Love,

Mike

Notes for Home: Your child completed words with consonant digraphs.
Home Activity: Have your child write a brief letter using at least five words with consonant digraphs.

90

The vowel *a* followed by the consonant *r* stands for the vowel sound in these words.

star   carpet

Underline the words that have the vowel sound you hear in *star*.

<u>apart</u>	stairs	collar	<u>darkness</u>	skirt
spare	<u>harden</u>	declare	<u>carton</u>	nearby
<u>remark</u>	bearing	<u>large</u>	<u>hardly</u>	depart
<u>sparkle</u>	corner	rare	deer	<u>argue</u>

Using the underlined words in the box, write the antonym for each word below.

1. small   large

2. together   apart

3. arrive   depart

4. light   darkness

5. soften   harden

Using the underlined words in the box, write the synonym for each word below.

6. glitter   sparkle

7. box   carton

8. scarcely   hardly

9. quarrel   argue

10. comment   remark

Notes for Home: Your child wrote words in which *ar* stands for the vowel sound in *star.*
Home Activity: Have your child scan a newspaper article and draw a star by every word he or she finds that has the vowel sound in *star* spelled *ar.*

91

The letters *ar* stand for the vowel sound in *star* and *carpet.*

Write the words in each phrase in which *ar* stands for the vowel sound you hear in *star*.

1. got a rare bargain on a cardigan   bargain, cardigan

2. partners who are never apart   partners, apart

3. beware of garbage in the harbor   garbage, harbor

4. tracked the departing airplane on radar   departing, radar

5. farmers preparing for the harvest   farmers, harvest

6. an article about a career in the army   article, army

7. fresh pears in a carton at the market   carton, market

8. an artist carving a reindeer   artist, carving

9. startled by the blaring alarm   startled, alarm

10. a barber with a cheerful remark   barber, remark

11. a hare in the garden in our yard   garden, yard

12. repairs needed on the large cargo ship   large, cargo

13. marvel at the clear harmony   marvel, harmony

14. stare at the sparklers in the darkness   sparklers, darkness

15. careful to mark only in the margin   mark, margin

Notes for Home: Your child wrote words in which *ar* stands for the vowel sound in *star.*
Home Activity: Take turns with your child writing phrases with at least one *ar* word and asking each other to identify that word.

92

Page 93

The vowel *o* followed by the consonant *r* stands for the vowel sound in these words.

corn   orbit

Circle the words that have the vowel sound you hear in *corn*.

(assorted)	(escort)	(forward)	borrow	(uniform)
color	(corner)	worry	(stormy)	major
(morning)	effort	(order)	(fortune)	(orchard)

Write the circled words to complete the phrases.

1. depart at 8 o'clock in the ___morning___
2. a dark and ___stormy___ night
3. comes in ___assorted___ colors and sizes
4. made a ___fortune___ in diamonds
5. gave the command "___forward___, march!"
6. many apple trees in an ___orchard___
7. the ___corner___ of the room
8. a police officer's ___uniform___
9. words in alphabetical ___order___
10. ___escort___ the official to the meeting

Notes for Home: Your child wrote words in which *or* stands for the vowel sound in *corn*. **Home Activity:** Think of a clue for one of the *or* words on the page and have your child give an answer. Then have your child think of a clue for you.

93

Page 94

The letters *or* stand for the vowel sound in *corn* and *orbit*.

Write the *or* words to complete the paragraph. Hint: Some words should be capitalized.

performing	absorbed	popcorn	orchard	chorus
forty	auditorium	chord	disorder	organ
hornets	important	unfortunately	normal	gorgeous

The (1.) ___chorus___ usually sings in places like the (2.) ___auditorium___. But today is not a (3.) ___normal___ day. We are (4.) ___performing___ in an unusual place—an apple (5.) ___orchard___. Mrs. Juarez insists that it is a (6.) ___gorgeous___ setting. And it is. The apple blossoms look like fluffy white (7.) ___popcorn___ on the trees and the ground. (8.) ___Unfortunately___, the blossoms attract (9.) ___hornets___. This created some (10.) ___disorder___ among the (11.) ___forty___ of us! But then Mr. Abert played the opening (12.) ___chord___ on the (13.) ___organ___. We began to sing and soon we were (14.) ___absorbed___ in the music. The bugs didn't seem very (15.) ___important___ now. And you know what? Mrs. Juarez was right.

Notes for Home: Your child wrote words in which *or* stands for the vowel sound in *corn*. **Home Activity:** Have your child write a phrase or sentence using each *or* word in the box.

94

Page 95

The vowels *e, i,* and *u* followed by the consonant *r* stand for the vowel sound in these words.

fern   bird   turn

Underline the word in each sentence that has the vowel sound in *fern*. Then write each word under the correct heading.

1. The salty crackers made us very <u>thirsty</u>.
2. <u>Concerned</u> citizens wrote, called, and e-mailed their representatives.
3. The colors of Mardi Gras are gold, green, and <u>purple</u>.
4. The gymnast scored a <u>perfect</u> ten on the balance beam.
5. Hikers need thick socks and <u>sturdy</u> boots.
6. The children sat in a <u>circle</u> around the teacher.
7. I was <u>nervous</u> about making a speech in class.
8. The dancers were <u>whirling</u> around the room.
9. Adding -*ly* to *happy* makes the adjective into an <u>adverb</u>.
10. The <u>purpose</u> of the project is to construct better guardrails.

er as in *herd*	**ir** as in *bird*	**ur** as in *turn*
11. Concerned	15. thirsty	18. purple
12. perfect	16. circle	19. sturdy
13. nervous	17. whirling	20. purpose
14. adverb		

Notes for Home: Your child wrote words in which *er, ir,* and *ur* stand for the vowel sound in *fern, bird,* and *turn*. **Home Activity:** Have your child read a magazine article and highlight words in which *er, ir,* and *ur* stand for the vowel sound in *fern*.

95

Page 96

The letters *er, ir,* and *ur* stand for the vowel sound in *fern, bird,* and *turn*.

Write the word that answers the clue and has the vowel sound you hear in *fern*.

1. illogical, impossible, and silly   ___absurd___
     ridiculous   absurd
2. a kind of tree whose bark peels off   ___birch___
     birch   sycamore
3. a person who knows about a particular subject   ___expert___
     expert   scholar
4. something perfectly round   ___circle___
     sphere   circle
5. number that comes after twenty   ___thirty___
     forty   thirty
6. straight up and down   ___vertical___
     vertical   upright
7. something that generates heat   ___furnace___
     furnace   fireplace
8. on the outside   ___external___
     outward   external
9. a root of a plant eaten as a vegetable   ___turnip___
     carrot   turnip
10. too much of something   ___surplus___
     surplus   extra

Notes for Home: Your child wrote words in which *er, ir,* and *ur* stand for the vowel sound in *fern, bird,* and *turn*. **Home Activity:** Have your child sort the words on the page into categories of *er, ir,* and *ur* words.

96

© Scott Foresman 4–6

r-Controlled Vowels
are, air, ear /âr/; ear, eer /ir/

The vowel-*r* patterns *are*, *air*, and *ear* stand for the vowel sound in these words.

care   chair   bear

The vowel-*r* patterns *ear* and *eer* stand for the vowel sound in these words.

near   deer

Underline a word in each phrase with the vowel sound in *care* or *near*. Then write each word under the picture whose name that has the same vowel sound.

1. four sides of a square
2. the steering wheel of a car
3. appear suddenly
4. house in need of repair
5. fresh, yellow pears
6. share the last apple
7. a career as a lawyer
8. fearful of snakes
9. fell down the stairs
10. wearing jeans and a t-shirt

11. square
12. repair
13. pears
14. share
15. stairs
16. wearing
17. steering
18. appear
19. career
20. fearful

Notes for Home: Your child wrote words with *are*, *air*, *ear*, and *eer*. **Home Activity:** Have your child make lists of rhyming words with the patterns *are*, *air*, *ear*, and *eer*.

97

---

r-Controlled Vowels
are, air, ear /âr/; ear, eer /ir/

The vowel-*r* patterns *are*, *air*, and *ear* stand for the vowel sound in *dare*, *pair*, and *bear*.
The vowel-*r* patterns *ear* and *eer* stand for the vowel sound in *near* and *steer*.

Circle the words in the box that have the vowel sounds you hear in *dare* and *near*. Then combine each circled word with a word below to make a compound word. Write the compound word.

better	marine	wear	greedy	chair
stair	care	merge	cheer	ear
deer	fair	year	target	scare

1. ____grounds   fairgrounds
2. ____free   carefree
3. arm____   armchair
4. ____book   yearbook
5. rein____   reindeer
6. ____ring   earring
7. ____case   staircase
8. under____   underwear
9. ____leader   cheerleader
10. ____crow   scarecrow

Notes for Home: Your child wrote words with *are*, *air*, *ear*, and *eer*. **Home Activity:** Have your child use each circled word in a sentence with another word that has the same pattern for the same vowel sound. Example: The *year* is *nearly* at an end.

98

---

r-Controlled Vowels *ore, our /ôr/*

The vowel-*r* patterns *ore* and *our* stand for the vowel sound in these words.

tore   four

Circle the words that have the vowel sound in *tore*. Then write each word in the group where it belongs.

course	sore	mourn	explorer
rope	source	shout	brought
chore	house	store	court
protect	ignore	harbor	before

1. shop, market, _____ store
2. earlier, previously, _____ before
3. grieve, weep, _____ mourn
4. beginning, origin, _____ source
5. overlook, disregard, _____ ignore
6. pioneer, trailblazer, _____ explorer
7. tender, painful, _____ sore
8. route, path, _____ course
9. job, task, _____ chore
10. field, track, rink, _____ court

Notes for Home: Your child wrote words with *ore* and *our*. **Home Activity:** Have your child write sentences using one *ore* word and one *our* word in each sentence.

99

---

r-Controlled Vowels *ore, our /ôr/*

The vowel-*r* patterns *ore* and *our* stand for the vowel sound in *core* and *four*.

Write the words to complete the sentences. Circle the letters that stand for the vowel sound you hear in *core*.

wore	pouring	ashore	source	foretell
court	snore	course	encore	adores
explore	gourd	ignore	bored	mourned

1. What is the source of your information on fossils?
2. Ted made a birdhouse out of a dried, hollowed-out gourd.
3. Katje wore a dress from her native Netherlands.
4. After six months at sea, the sailors couldn't wait to go ashore.
5. Try to ignore the noise from the party.
6. The children mourned their dog after it died.
7. Who could foretell that the weather would be so bad?
8. The long, dull speech bored the listeners.
9. The cat wants to explore every closet and cupboard in the house.
10. The floods caused the river to change its course.
11. The ball hit the sideline on the left side of the court.
12. Because it is all hers, Corinna adores her new room.
13. The water is pouring out of a hole in the bottle.
14. His snore could be heard three rooms away!
15. The audience called the singer to come back and sing an encore.

Notes for Home: Your child wrote words with *ore* and *our*. **Home Activity:** Have your child write rhymes using the word pairs *four/pour*, *course/source*, *store/chore*, and *more/score*.

100

Name _____

The number of syllables in a word is the same as the number of vowel sounds in the word.

pencil
Number of vowel sounds: 2   (short *e* sound and schwa sound)
Number of syllables: 2

Say each word. Circle 1, 2, or 3 to show how many vowel sounds you hear in the word. Circle 1, 2, or 3 to show how many syllables the word has.

	Number of Vowel Sounds	Number of Syllables
1. school	① 2 3	① 2 3
2. whisper	1 ② 3	1 ② 3
3. yesterday	1 2 ③	1 2 ③
4. city	1 ② 3	1 ② 3
5. grandmother	1 2 ③	1 2 ③
6. until	1 ② 3	1 ② 3
7. admit	1 ② 3	1 ② 3
8. dollars	1 ② 3	1 ② 3
9. hidden	1 ② 3	1 ② 3
10. holiday	1 2 ③	1 2 ③
11. concentrate	1 2 ③	1 2 ③
12. reach	① 2 3	① 2 3
13. computer	1 2 ③	1 2 ③
14. excitement	1 2 ③	1 2 ③
15. straight	① 2 3	① 2 3

Notes for Home: Your child identified the number of vowel sounds and syllables in words.
Home Activity: Have your child list the names of favorite foods and identify the number of syllables in each word.

101

Name _____

Number of syllables in a word = number of vowel sounds in the word

	Number of Vowel Sounds	Number of Syllables
drill	1	1
foun/tain	2	2
mag/net/ic	3	3
fas/ci/na/tion	4	4

Say each word. Write the number of vowel sounds you hear. Write the number of syllables the word has.

	Number of Vowel Sounds	Number of Syllables
1. workbook	2	2
2. stronger	2	2
3. seven	2	2
4. interrupted	4	4
5. following	3	3
6. scratch	1	1
7. umbrella	3	3
8. complete	2	2
9. office	2	2
10. flicker	2	2
11. women	2	2
12. destination	4	4
13. overlap	3	3
14. surface	2	2
15. musical	3	3

Notes for Home: Your child identified the number of vowel sounds and syllables in words.
Home Activity: Have your child make a list of frequently used words with one, two, three, or four syllables.

102

Name _____

Number of syllables in a word = number of vowel sounds in the word.

Circle the words with the same number of syllables as the underlined word. Write one of the circled words to complete the sentence.

1. Remind Tony to close the __window__ quietly.
   cabinet   (window)   door   (letter)

2. The rabbit ate the carrots growing in the __garden__.
   park   (kitchen)   (garden)   balcony

3. Thanksgiving is a holiday in __November__.
   January   July   (November)   (October)

4. The weather forecaster predicts a __blizzard__.
   hurricane   (blizzard)   (danger)   tornado

5. Ana's favorite food is __spaghetti__.
   (spaghetti)   pizza   (umbrella)   yogurt

6. The new art museum is very __beautiful__.
   pretty   (dangerous)   (beautiful)   spacious

7. Pioneer women wore __bonnets__.
   gloves   (bonnets)   jewelry   (helmets)

8. Did you put a __radish__ in the salad?
   tomato   (pencil)   cucumber   (radish)

9. Silver is a precious __metal__.
   ore   mineral   (buckle)   (metal)

10. A __cactus__ is a desert plant.
    (cactus)   marigold   rose   (tulip)

Notes for Home: Your child identified the number of syllables in words.
Home Activity: Have your child count the number of syllables in each word that was *not* circled on the page.

103

Name _____

Adding affixes to words adds syllables to the words.

pack   un/pack   power   pow/er/ful   heat   re/heat/a/ble

Write the number of syllables in the base word. Then add the affix and write the new word and the number of syllables in that word.

1. **pleasant** — 2
   Add *un-*. — unpleasant — 3
   Now add *-ly*. — unpleasantly — 4

2. **grace** — 1
   Add *dis-*. — disgrace — 2
   Now add *-ful*. — disgraceful — 3

3. **help** — 1
   Add *-less*. — helpless — 2
   Now add *-ness*. — helplessness — 3

4. **fill** — 1
   Add *re-*. — refill — 2
   Now add *-able*. — refillable — 4

5. **treat** — 1
   Add *mis-*. — mistreat — 2
   Now add *-ment*. — mistreatment — 3

Notes for Home: Your child added affixes and endings to words and counted the number of syllables in the words. **Home Activity:** Point out words with affixes and endings in a newspaper article and have your child tell you the number of syllables in the words.

104

© Scott Foresman 4–6

Page 105 — Multisyllabic Words

Name _____ **Multisyllabic Words**

Adding an ending to a word may or may not add a syllable. Say these words.

count	count/ed	walk	walked	call	call/ing
talk	talks	cry	cries
star	stars	bench	bench/es

Add the ending to each word in the list. Say the word. Write *Yes* if adding the ending adds a syllable. Write *No* if adding the ending does not add a syllable.

-ed

1. decide **Yes**
2. gather **No**
3. watch **No**
4. guard **Yes**
5. relate **Yes**
6. challenge **No**
7. protest **Yes**
8. realize **No**

-s

9. petal **No**
10. messenger **No**
11. clue **No**
12. insect **No**

-es

13. batch **Yes**
14. radish **Yes**
15. multiply **No**
16. worry **No**

-ing

17. shop **Yes**
18. deny **Yes**
19. depend **Yes**
20. release **Yes**

Notes for Home: Your child added endings to words and counted the number of syllables in the words. **Home Activity:** Together with your child study the words on the page and see what conclusions you can draw about when endings add syllables to words.

105

Page 106 — Schwa Sound

Name _____ **Schwa Sound**

The schwa sound is a vowel sound that is heard in unaccented syllables. The letters *a, e, i, o,* and *u* can spell the schwa sound. This symbol (ə) represents the schwa sound.

| above | effect | cabin | lemon | cactus |

Circle the letter that stands for the schwa sound in each word.

1. minus a e i o (u)
2. robin a e (i) o u
3. dollar (a) e i o u
4. second a e i (o) u
5. walrus a e i o (u)
6. human (a) e i o u
7. fossil a e (i) o u
8. color a e i (o) u
9. seven a (e) i o u
10. zebra (a) e i o u
11. moment a (e) i o u
12. pencil a e (i) o u
13. bottom a e i (o) u
14. wagon a e i (o) u
15. system a (e) i o u
16. about (a) e i o u
17. circus a e i o (u)
18. barrel a e (e) i o u
19. shiver a (e) i o u
20. gremlin a e (i) o u
21. forum a e i o (u)
22. sentence a (e) i o u
23. origin a e (i) o u
24. bonus a e i o (u)
25. mirror a e i (o) u

Notes for Home: Your child identified the letters that stand for the schwa sound in words. **Home Activity:** Have your child look through newspaper ads to find bargains whose names have the schwa sound and make a shopping list of the words.

106

Page 107 — Schwa Sound

Name _____ **Schwa Sound**

The letters *a, e, i, o,* and *u* can spell the schwa sound.

| above | effect | cabin | lemon | cactus |

Circle the letter that stands for the schwa sound in the first word. Then circle other words in the row in which the same letter stands for the schwa sound.

1. finger (water) (clever) deepest
2. margin timing (family) (muffin)
3. ahead (breakfast) (panda) face
4. cotton boat (honor) (bacon)
5. jewel (hammer) peak (eleven)
6. apron solo (bottom) (weapon)
7. goblin (fossil) picnic (carnival)
8. bonus (focus) (walrus) phone
9. zebra last (beggar) (loyal)
10. minus (campus) useless (dreadful)
11. salad sales (allow) (tuna)
12. carol (today) (pilot) stole
13. success (submit) recess (citrus)
14. cabinet mimic (pupil) (minimum)
15. severe (chicken) (hundred) return

Notes for Home: Your child identified words in which the same letters stand for the schwa sound. **Home Activity:** Have your child create a bumper sticker using words that have the schwa sound, such as *loyal, dollar, panda, better, wisdom,* and *fortune.*

107

Page 108 — Schwa Sound

Name _____ **Schwa Sound**

Underline the word in each pair that has the schwa sound. Write the underlined word that answers each clue. Then circle the letter that stands for the schwa sound.

quarter	dime	eleven	thirteen
shack	cabin	zebra	rhino
spider	monkey	team	family
minus	reduce	closet	dresser
inside	bottom	soup	salad

1. It's a small house made of logs. **cabin**
2. It's the opposite of *top.* **bottom**
3. It's worth twenty-five cents. **quarter**
4. This is a striped animal. **zebra**
5. This is part of a meal. **salad**
6. This is a place for clothes. **dresser**
7. It means "less." **minus**
8. It's often made up of parents and children. **family**
9. It spins a web. **spider**
10. It's a number greater than ten. **eleven**

Notes for Home: Your child identified and wrote words that have the schwa sound. **Home Activity:** Have your child read a story and find words that he or she thinks have the schwa sound and then look them up in a dictionary.

108

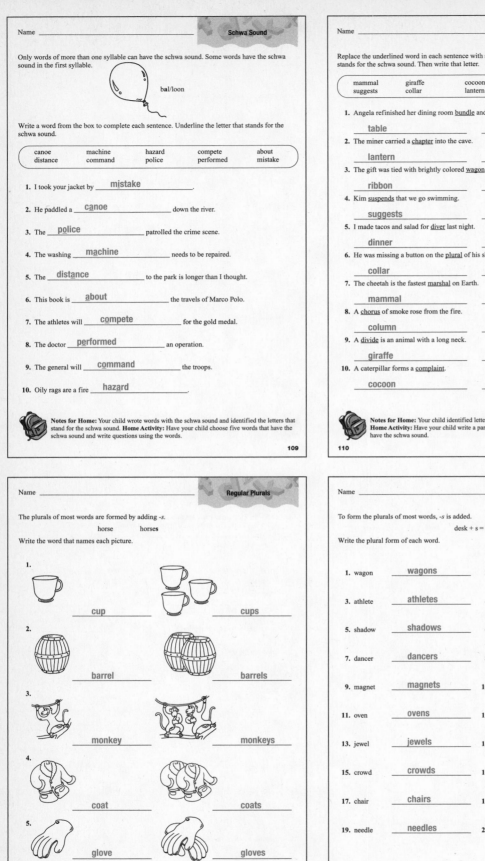

Name _____

Only words of more than one syllable can have the schwa sound. Some words have the schwa sound in the first syllable.

bal/loon

Write a word from the box to complete each sentence. Underline the letter that stands for the schwa sound.

canoe	machine	hazard	compete	about
distance	command	police	performed	mistake

1. I took your jacket by __mistake__.

2. He paddled a __canoe__ down the river.

3. The __police__ patrolled the crime scene.

4. The washing __machine__ needs to be repaired.

5. The __distance__ to the park is longer than I thought.

6. This book is __about__ the travels of Marco Polo.

7. The athletes will __compete__ for the gold medal.

8. The doctor __performed__ an operation.

9. The general will __command__ the troops.

10. Oily rags are a fire __hazard__.

Notes for Home: Your child wrote words with the schwa sound and identified the letters that stand for the schwa sound. **Home Activity:** Have your child choose five words that have the schwa sound and write questions using the words.

109

Name _____

Replace the underlined word in each sentence with a word from the box in which the same letter stands for the schwa sound. Then write that letter.

mammal	giraffe	cocoon	table	dinner
suggests	collar	lantern	ribbon	column

1. Angela refinished her dining room <u>bundle</u> and chairs.
   __table__   e

2. The miner carried a <u>chapter</u> into the cave.
   __lantern__   e

3. The gift was tied with brightly colored <u>wagon</u>.
   __ribbon__   o

4. Kim <u>suspends</u> that we go swimming.
   __suggests__   u

5. I made tacos and salad for <u>diver</u> last night.
   __dinner__   e

6. He was missing a button on the <u>plural</u> of his shirt.
   __collar__   a

7. The cheetah is the fastest <u>marshal</u> on Earth.
   __mammal__   a

8. A <u>chorus</u> of smoke rose from the fire.
   __column__   u

9. A <u>divide</u> is an animal with a long neck.
   __giraffe__   i

10. A caterpillar forms a <u>complaint</u>.
    __cocoon__   o

Notes for Home: Your child identified letters that stand for the schwa sound. **Home Activity:** Have your child write a paragraph about an adventure using words that have the schwa sound.

110

Name _____

The plurals of most words are formed by adding -s.

horse   horses

Write the word that names each picture.

1. __cup__   __cups__

2. __barrel__   __barrels__

3. __monkey__   __monkeys__

4. __coat__   __coats__

5. __glove__   __gloves__

Notes for Home: Your child formed the plurals of words by adding -s. **Home Activity:** Have your child choose five household objects and write the plural forms of their names.

111

Name _____

To form the plurals of most words, -s is added.

desk + s = desks

Write the plural form of each word.

1. wagon __wagons__   2. gift __gifts__

3. athlete __athletes__   4. paper __papers__

5. shadow __shadows__   6. turtle __turtles__

7. dancer __dancers__   8. cave __caves__

9. magnet __magnets__   10. football __footballs__

11. oven __ovens__   12. lecture __lectures__

13. jewel __jewels__   14. plumber __plumbers__

15. crowd __crowds__   16. instruction __instructions__

17. chair __chairs__   18. narrator __narrators__

19. needle __needles__   20. journal __journals__

Notes for Home: Your child formed the plurals of words by adding -s. **Home Activity:** Have your child write sentences using the words on this page.

112

The plurals of words that end in *x, s, ss, ch,* or *sh* are formed by adding *-es.*

box   boxes   watch   watches

Write the word that names the picture.

1.
fox   foxes

2.
dress   dresses

3.
dish   dishes

4.
peach   peaches

5.
bus   buses

Notes for Home: Your child formed the plurals of words ending in *x, s, ss, ch,* or *sh* by adding *-es.* **Home Activity:** Have your child choose five words from the page and write a clue for each word.

113

To form the plural of a word ending with a consonant and *y,* the *y* is changed to *i,* and *-es* is added.

party   parties

Write the plural form of a word in the box to complete each sentence.

| factory | memory | mystery | grocery | cavity |
| charity | country | ceremony | hobby | baby |

1. I have many good _____ memories _____ of my trip to Alaska.

2. The two _____ babies _____ splashed in the wading pool.

3. All cultures have _____ ceremonies _____ to mark important occasions.

4. I was dismayed when the dentist said I had two _____ cavities _____.

5. Several _____ factories _____ opened in the new industrial park.

6. Her _____ hobbies _____ are stamp collecting and rock climbing.

7. My favorite books are _____ mysteries _____ set in foreign places.

8. The leaders of the two _____ countries _____ signed the trade agreement.

9. Anya carried four bags of _____ groceries _____ into the kitchen.

10. Several _____ charities _____ joined together for a fund-raising campaign.

Notes for Home: Your child formed the plurals of words ending in a consonant and *y* by changing *y* to *i* and adding *-es.* **Home Activity:** Have your child write questions using the plural forms of words on the page.

114

Write the plural form of each word in the box in the correct list.

party	girl	vase	glass	picture
daisy	country	nurse	box	sandwich
wagon	diary	gas	brush	enemy

Add -s

1. wagons
2. girls
3. vases
4. nurses
5. pictures

Add -es

6. gases
7. glasses
8. boxes
9. brushes
10. sandwiches

Change y to i and add -es

11. parties
12. daisies
13. countries
14. diaries
15. enemies

Notes for Home: Your child formed the plurals of words by adding *-s* and *-es.* **Home Activity:** Have your child write riddles for five plural words on the page.

115

Write the plural form of a word from the list to answer each clue.

garden	string	knee	ranch	album
pencil	fox	marsh	dictionary	emergency
address	melody	battery	chorus	speech

1. These are wild animals.   foxes

2. These are joints between the upper and lower legs.   knees

3. You pluck these on a guitar to make sounds.   strings

4. These go on the front of envelopes.   addresses

5. These are several groups of singers.   choruses

6. Flowers and vegetables grow in these.   gardens

7. You look up words in these.   dictionaries

8. These are wetlands.   marshes

9. Cattle are raised on these.   ranches

10. These call for a cool head and quick action.   emergencies

11. Politicians make a lot of these.   speeches

12. You put pictures in these.   albums

13. Lots of toys need these.   batteries

14. Songs have these.   melodies

15. These are writing tools.   pencils

Notes for Home: Your child has formed the plurals of words by adding *-s* and *-es.* **Home Activity:** Have your child make lists of things found in the city and the country and write the plural of each word.

116

Worksheet 1 (page 117)

The plurals of words that end in a vowel and *o* are formed by adding *-s*.

radios

The plurals of some words ending in a consonant and *o* are formed by adding *-s;* others by adding *-es*. Some words add either *-s* or *-es*.

cellos   potatoes   banjos or banjoes

Add *-s* or *-es* to each word to make the plural form of the word.

1. piano   **pianos**

2. hero   **heroes**

3. tornado   **tornadoes or tornados**

4. patio   **patios**

5. soprano   **sopranos**

6. volcano   **volcanoes or volcanos**

7. video   **videos**

8. ratio   **ratios**

9. tomato   **tomatoes**

10. stereo   **stereos**

Notes for Home: Your child formed the plurals of words ending in *o* by adding *-s* and *-es*.
Home Activity: Have your child check the spelling of each of the plural words on the page in a dictionary.

117

Worksheet 2 (page 118)

The ending *-s* is added to a word ending in a vowel and *o* to form the plural.

The ending *-s* or *-es* is added to a word ending in a consonant and *o* to form the plural.

Write the plural forms of the words to complete the puzzle.

echo   soprano   photo   alto   patio
torpedo   radio   hero   piano   video

Across
2. women's lowest singing voices
3. large metal tubes containing explosives
8. brave people
9. things you can watch on a television
10. women's highest singing voices

Down
1. musical instruments with keys
4. places for outdoor dining
5. repeated sounds
6. pictures taken with a camera
7. machines that pick up or send sound

Crossword:
```
      P
      I
  A L T O S
      N
  T O R P E D O E S
  S   A       C
      T       H   P
  R   I       O   H
  A   O     H E R O E S
  V I D E O S   S   T
  I           S   O
  S O P R A N O S   S
  S
```

Notes for Home: Your child formed the plurals of words ending in *o* by adding *-s* or *-es*.
Home Activity: Have your child choose five words from the page and write a sentence for each one.

118

Worksheet 3 (page 119)

To form the plurals of some words ending in *f* or *fe*, the *f* or *fe* is changed to *v*, and *-es* is added. To form the plurals of words ending in *ff*, the ending *-s* is added.

half   hal**ves**   muff   muffs

Choose a word from the box and write the plural form to complete each sentence.

| calf | wife | loaf | sheriff | life |
| cliff | leaf | knife | thief | shelf |

1. Be very careful when handling sharp **knives**.

2. The travelers were robbed by a band of **thieves**.

3. Ben raked four bags of **leaves**.

4. A cat is said to have nine **lives**.

5. The farmer put the **calves** in the pasture.

6. The heavy books made the **shelves** sag in the middle.

7. The trail led us to the edge of some sheer **cliffs**.

8. Women who are married are called **wives**.

9. Many **sheriffs** came to the law-enforcement convention.

10. The baker took the **loaves** of bread out of the oven.

Notes for Home: Your child formed the plurals of words ending in *ff, f,* or *fe*.
Home Activity: Have your child form the plurals of *elf, wolf,* and *cuff* and then write a sentence using each word.

119

Worksheet 4 (page 120)

Some words form their plurals in a special way.

goose—geese   mouse—mice   ox—oxen
woman—women   man—men   child—children

Some words have the same form for both singular and plural.

deer   sheep   moose   salmon

Write the answer to each clue to complete the puzzle.

Across
3. large animals that live in the woods, bigger than deer
7. domestic cattle used for farm work
8. large fish
10. young girls and boys

Down
1. woolly animals
2. large birds, like ducks
4. adult males
5. adult females
6. graceful animals that live in the woods
9. small rodents

Crossword:
```
                              S
        G               W     H
  M O O S E       M       W   E
        E         E   D   O X E N
  S A L M O N     E   E   M   P
        E     I   N   E   E
              C H I L D R E N
              E
```

Notes for Home: Your child used the plurals of irregular words to complete a puzzle.
Home Activity: Have your child write two sentences using the words from the page that have the same form for both plural and singular.

120

Compound words are made by combining two smaller words.

doghouse = dog + house

Write the two words that make up each compound word.

1. myself = __my__ + __self__
2. everything = __every__ + __thing__
3. clothesline = __clothes__ + __line__
4. thumbtack = __thumb__ + __tack__
5. sunshine = __sun__ + __shine__
6. footprints = __foot__ + __prints__
7. blindfold = __blind__ + __fold__
8. drawbridge = __draw__ + __bridge__
9. stepladder = __step__ + __ladder__
10. spellbound = __spell__ + __bound__
11. watermelon = __water__ + __melon__
12. password = __pass__ + __word__
13. oatmeal = __oat__ + __meal__
14. wristwatch = __wrist__ + __watch__
15. cloudburst = __cloud__ + __burst__

Notes for Home: Your child identified words that make up compound words.
Home Activity: Have your child make a list of frequently used compound words and then identify the two words that make up each compound word.

121

A compound word is made up of two smaller words.

rain + coat = raincoat

Choose a word to finish the compound word in the sentence. Write the word.

1. She put the letter in the mail__box__.
   box   back   spot
2. Miguel wrote his assignment in his note__book__.
   house   book   place
3. I stacked the logs in the fire__place__.
   stand   snake   place
4. Tall sun__flowers__ grew in the garden.
   cases   flowers   glasses
5. The rattle__snake__ was ready to strike.
   flake   drop   snake
6. The volley__ball__ team was undefeated.
   ball   wall   line
7. Val planted zinnias in the flower__pots__.
   coats   pots   books
8. Put the silver__ware__ on the table.
   line   writing   ware
9. I carry my books in a back__pack__.
   pack   ground   home
10. We ate dinner at a road__side__ inn.
    shore   side   by

Notes for Home: Your child put words together to make compound words.
Home Activity: Have your child write the following words on cards and sort them to make compound words: *birth, text, house, horse, hand, day, writing, work, book, back.*

122

A compound word is formed by putting two smaller words together.

every + thing = everything

Draw a line from a word in Column A to a word in Column B to make a compound word. Write the compound words.

Column A   **Column B**

1. out   ball
2. wild   by
3. base   side
4. arm   teller
5. any   born
6. sea   chair
7. through   flowers
8. new   shell
9. story   out
10. near   thing

11. __outside__   12. __wildflowers__
13. __baseball__   14. __armchair__
15. __anything__   16. __seashell__
17. __throughout__   18. __newborn__
19. __storyteller__   20. __nearby__

Notes for Home: Your child put words together to make and write compound words.
Home Activity: Have your child make compound words by adding words to *sand, earth, light,* and *day.*

123

Some compound words are written as one word. Other compound words are written as two words.

everybody   all right

Write a compound word from the box to complete each sentence.

| high school | peanut butter | downstairs | remote control | first aid |
| wristwatch | spacecraft | no one | pen pal | flashlight |

1. He ate a __peanut butter__ and jelly sandwich.
2. The championship game was played in the __high school__ gym.
3. It's a good idea to know __first aid__ if you are going camping.
4. Does your __wristwatch__ have a second hand?
5. We saw __no one__ we knew at the carnival.
6. Betty received a letter from her __pen pal__ in Scotland.
7. The __spacecraft__ orbited the moon.
8. The children went __downstairs__ to play.
9. Use the __remote control__ to change the television channel.
10. Keep a __flashlight__ handy in case of emergency.

Notes for Home: Your child wrote one- and two-word compound words to complete sentences. **Home Activity:** Encourage your child to keep a list of compound words that are written as two words.

124

© Scott Foresman 4–6

Answers **211**

Compound words may be written as one word or two words.

        lifeguard   life raft

Choose two words to make a compound word that matches each clue. Check a dictionary to see whether each compound word is one word or two. Write the compound word.

birth	ground	high	snow	bird
flakes	way	day	bathing	camp
back	window	port	room	box
suit	living	car	bone	watcher

1. the spine in a body   backbone

2. garment worn for swimming   bathing suit

3. shelter for an automobile   carport

4. room for general family use   living room

5. the day you were born   birthday

6. container for plants on a windowsill   window box

7. person who observes wild birds   bird watcher

8. a public road   highway

9. falls from the sky in winter   snowflakes

10. a place where you sleep in a tent   campground

Notes for Home: Your child wrote one- and two-word compound words.
Home Activity: Have your child choose five words from the page and write a sentence for each one.

A contraction is a short way of writing two words. An apostrophe (') is used in place of the letter or letters omitted in the contraction. Sometimes the spelling will change.

     we are   →   we're   will not   →   won't

     she is   →   she's

Write the contraction for each pair of words.

1. he has   he's

2. we will   we'll

3. they are   they're

4. would not   wouldn't

5. must not   mustn't

6. I am   I'm

7. they will   they'll

8. did not   didn't

9. are not   aren't

10. where is   where's

11. she would   she'd

12. you have   you've

13. I have   I've

14. that is   that's

15. let us   let's

Notes for Home: Your child formed contractions from pairs of words.
Home Activity: Have your child look through a newspaper and highlight words that could be written as contractions.

An apostrophe (') takes the place of the letter or letters omitted in a contraction.

     let us   let(u)s   let's

Write the two words from which each contraction was formed.

1. doesn't   does   not

2. hasn't   has   not

3. you've   you   have

4. I'll   I   will

5. we've   we   have

6. here's   here   is

7. haven't   have   not

8. she'll   she   will

9. we're   we   are

10. won't   will   not

11. it's   it   is

12. who's   who   is

13. shouldn't   should   not

14. wouldn't   would   not

15. isn't   is   not

Notes for Home: Your child identified the words from which contractions are formed.
Home Activity: Have your child look through a newspaper or magazine, find contractions, and identify the two words used to form each contraction.

A contraction is a short way to write two words.   I will   I'll

Write a contraction for the underlined words in each sentence.

1. We will make pizza for lunch.

    We'll

2. He could not have painted the house without your help.

    couldn't

3. Who is going to the concert this evening?

    Who's

4. We are planning a trip to Mexico this summer.

    We're

5. Our dog does not like to be bathed.

    doesn't

6. She would like a camera for her birthday.

    She'd

7. You will have to study for the math test tonight.

    You'll

8. They are planting a garden in the yard.

    They're

9. It is the first day of spring.

    It's

10. That is the funniest thing I've ever heard!

    That's

Notes for Home: Your child combined words to form contractions. **Home Activity:** Have your child make a set of cards that can be combined to make contractions using the following words: *he, she, I, you, they, is, are, will, have, had.*

© Scott Foresman 4-6

Sometimes two words can be combined to form a contraction.

Who is going to make dinner?   **Who's** going to make dinner?

Circle the words in each sentence that can be combined to make a contraction. Write the contraction.

1. (He will) represent the class at the student council meeting.

   He'll

2. I (did not) invite my friend for lunch.

   didn't

3. (You have) visited many countries over the summer.

   You've

4. (It is) a good day for skiing.

   It's

5. I hope (they will) like the movie.

   they'll

6. (She has) read many new books.

   She's

7. I knew (you would) like the museum.

   you'd

8. We (could not) find Dad's car keys.

   couldn't

9. (They are) going to soccer practice after school.

   They're

10. (I would) like to learn to play the guitar.

    I'd

Notes for Home: Your child identified words that can be combined to form contractions. **Home Activity:** Have your child read a story and look for words that can be combined to form contractions.

129

Underline the two contractions in each sentence. Write the words from which the contractions are formed.

1. You haven't told me when she'll be arriving.

   have   not   she   will

2. I don't understand why there's no answer.

   do   not   there   is

3. I'll meet you at the restaurant, and we'll have dinner together.

   I   will   we   will

4. Wouldn't you like to know who's going to give the keynote speech?

   Would   not   who   is

5. They're going to the art museum while I'm at the planetarium.

   They   are   I   am

6. Although she'd like to be on the team, she hasn't been coming to practice.

   she   would   has   not

7. You're working on your report, aren't you?

   You   are   are   not

8. He won't tell me where he's hidden the key.

   will   not   he   has

9. Here's what he said: he'll pick you up at the airport.

   Here   is   he   will

10. He's in the band, and she's on the tennis team.

    He   is   she   is

Notes for Home: Your child identified the words that make up contractions. **Home Activity:** Have your child write a short dialogue without using any contractions and then rewrite it using contractions whenever possible.

130

Sometimes a base word doesn't change when -ed or -ing is added.

shout   shout**ed**   shout**ing**

If a base word ends in e, the e is dropped before -ed or -ing is added.

chase   chas**ed**   chas**ing**

Add the ending to each word and write the new word.

1. invite (-ing)   **inviting**   2. paint (-ed)   **painted**

3. stay (-ed)   **stayed**   4. turn (-ed)   **turned**

5. try (-ing)   **trying**   6. live (-ed)   **lived**

7. graze (-ing)   **grazing**   8. read (-ing)   **reading**

9. flicker (-ed)   **flickered**   10. follow (-ing)   **following**

11. cover (-ed)   **covered**   12. enter (-ed)   **entered**

13. come (-ing)   **coming**   14. write (-ing)   **writing**

15. illustrate (-ed)   **illustrated**   16. hear (-ing)   **hearing**

17. arrive (-ing)   **arriving**   18. receive (-ing)   **receiving**

19. skate (-ed)   **skated**   20. jump (-ing)   **jumping**

Notes for Home: Your child added -ed and -ing to base words. **Home Activity:** Ask your child to choose five words from the page and write a sentence using each word.

131

The ending -es is added to words that end in ch, sh, s, x, or z.

pinch   pinch**es**

Add -es to the words in the box and write the new words to complete the sentences.

dash	wish	teach	fix	march
buzz	relax	finish	guess	miss

1. My sister **wishes** she had a kitten.

2. Dad **teaches** high school math.

3. She **guesses** that it will be evening before our company arrives.

4. After exercising, I find a warm bath really **relaxes** me.

5. Jesse usually **finishes** his homework before dinnertime.

6. The bee **buzzes** around the flowers.

7. After three weeks at camp, Kerry **misses** her family.

8. The runner **dashes** for the finish line.

9. The school band **marches** in parades several times a year.

10. A handy person **fixes** things around the house.

Notes for Home: Your child added -es to words ending in ch, sh, s, x, or z. **Home Activity:** Ask your child to choose a sentence from the page and write a story that begins with the sentence.

132

Add the ending to each word in the set. Write the new words.

Add -es

1. stretch _____ stretches _____
2. watch _____ watches _____
3. push _____ pushes _____
4. dress _____ dresses _____
5. wax _____ waxes _____

Add -ed

6. tax _____ taxed _____
7. pour _____ poured _____
8. replace _____ replaced _____
9. start _____ started _____
10. describe _____ described _____

Add -ing

11. type _____ typing _____
12. send _____ sending _____
13. finish _____ finishing _____
14. light _____ lighting _____
15. compete _____ competing _____

Notes for Home: Your child added -es, -ed, and -ing to base words.
Home Activity: Have your child write phrases using ten words from this page.

Add -es, -ed, or -ing to the base word to make a word that completes the sentence. Write the new word.

hatch 1. The chick is _____ hatching _____ from the egg.

saddle 2. She wanted to ride, so she _____ saddled _____ her horse.

reach 3. He is thirsty, so he _____ reaches _____ for a glass.

laugh 4. Are you _____ laughing _____ at the clown's antics?

save 5. Cara has _____ saved _____ enough money for a new CD player.

graze 6. The cattle are _____ grazing _____ on the prairie.

patch 7. Tim _____ patched _____ the holes in the wall yesterday.

skate 8. Have you _____ skated _____ on the frozen pond?

wave 9. The candidate _____ waved _____ at the people, who cheered loudly.

serve 10. Luke is _____ serving _____ pizza to his friends.

rush 11. Because she is late, Hanna _____ rushes _____ through breakfast.

limit 12. I am _____ limiting _____ my phone calls to five minutes each.

stress 13. Mrs. Yan always _____ stresses _____ the need for patience.

remove 14. I had a hard time _____ removing _____ the label from the disk.

borrow 15. Kevin _____ borrowed _____ that book several weeks ago.

Notes for Home: Your child added -es, -ed, and -ing to base words.
Home Activity: Have your child add a different ending to each word on the page.

The ending -er is used to compare two things. The ending -est is used to compare more than two things.

long   longer than that one   longest of them all

Add -er or -est to the base word. Write the new word to complete the phrase.

high 1. _____ highest _____ of all the mountains

bright 2. _____ brighter _____ than a star

sweet 3. _____ sweetest _____ apple of all

low 4. _____ lowest _____ branch on the tree

warm 5. _____ warmer _____ than yesterday

tall 6. _____ taller _____ than his brother

cold 7. _____ coldest _____ month of the year

loud 8. _____ louder _____ than a whisper

quick 9. _____ quickest _____ route to school

small 10. _____ smaller _____ than a basketball

smooth 11. _____ smoother _____ than a silk scarf

cool 12. _____ coolest _____ day since last spring

short 13. _____ shorter _____ of the two ponies

kind 14. _____ kinder _____ than she was before

fast 15. _____ fastest _____ runner on the team

Notes for Home: Your child added -er and -est to base words. **Home Activity:** Have your child write -er and -est words comparing things he or she might see at a carnival.

The endings -er and -est are used to compare things. If a base word ends in e, the e is dropped before -er or -est is added.

safe   safer than the other one   safest of all

Add -er or -est to the base word. Write the new word to complete the phrase.

large 1. _____ largest _____ elephant in the whole herd

pale 2. _____ palest _____ shade of pink I've ever seen

close 3. _____ closest _____ park to our school

white 4. _____ whiter _____ than a snowflake

cute 5. _____ cutest _____ puppy in the litter

wise 6. _____ wiser _____ than an owl

blue 7. _____ bluer _____ than the sky

late 8. _____ later _____ than an hour ago

fine 9. _____ finest _____ meal I've ever eaten

brave 10. _____ bravest _____ soldier in the army

nice 11. _____ nicer _____ than our old house

pure 12. _____ purer _____ than other brands of soap

severe 13. _____ severest _____ sentence allowed by law

rude 14. _____ ruder _____ than any salesclerk should be

lame 15. _____ lamest _____ excuse I have ever heard

Notes for Home: Your child added -er and -est to words ending in e.
Home Activity: Have your child use -er and -est words to compare TV shows, books, or movies.

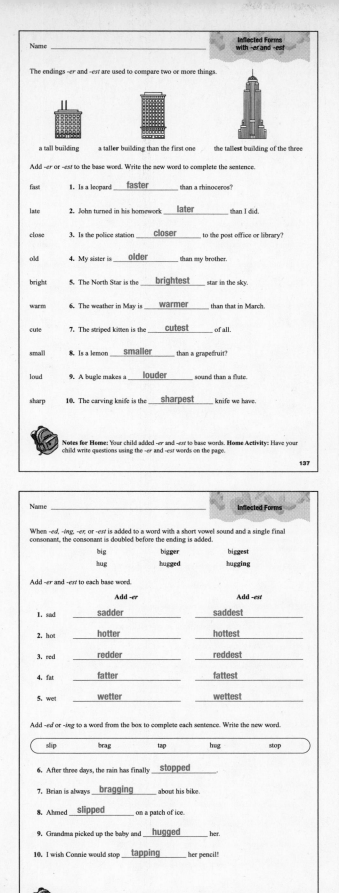

Name _____

The endings -er and -est are used to compare two or more things.

a tall building   a tall**er** building than the first one   the tall**est** building of the three

Add -er or -est to the base word. Write the new word to complete the sentence.

fast   **1.** Is a leopard ___**faster**___ than a rhinoceros?

late   **2.** John turned in his homework ___**later**___ than I did.

close   **3.** Is the police station ___**closer**___ to the post office or library?

old   **4.** My sister is ___**older**___ than my brother.

bright   **5.** The North Star is the ___**brightest**___ star in the sky.

warm   **6.** The weather in May is ___**warmer**___ than that in March.

cute   **7.** The striped kitten is the ___**cutest**___ of all.

small   **8.** Is a lemon ___**smaller**___ than a grapefruit?

loud   **9.** A bugle makes a ___**louder**___ sound than a flute.

sharp   **10.** The carving knife is the ___**sharpest**___ knife we have.

Notes for Home: Your child added -er and -est to base words. **Home Activity:** Have your child write questions using the -er and -est words on the page.

137

Name _____

When -es, -ed, -er, or -est is added to a base word ending in y, the y is changed to i before the ending is added. When -ing is added, the y remains.

If the base word is an adjective, add -er and -est and write both words. If the base word is a verb, add -es, -ed, and -ing and write all three words.

1. early ___**earlier, earliest**___

2. worry ___**worries, worried, worrying**___

3. lazy ___**lazier, laziest**___

4. deny ___**denies, denied, denying**___

5. merry ___**merrier, merriest**___

6. carry ___**carries, carried, carrying**___

7. pretty ___**prettier, prettiest**___

8. try ___**tries, tried, trying**___

9. silly ___**sillier, silliest**___

10. hurry ___**hurries, hurried, hurrying**___

11. apply ___**applies, applied, applying**___

12. happy ___**happier, happiest**___

13. study ___**studies, studied, studying**___

14. funny ___**funnier, funniest**___

15. easy ___**easier, easiest**___

Notes for Home: Your child added endings to base words that end in y. **Home Activity:** Have your child use words with endings from the page in oral sentences.

138

Name _____

When -ed, -ing, -er, or -est is added to a word with a short vowel sound and a single final consonant, the consonant is doubled before the ending is added.

big	big**ger**	big**gest**
hug	hug**ged**	hug**ging**

Add -er and -est to each base word.

	Add -er	**Add -est**
1. sad	sadder	saddest
2. hot	hotter	hottest
3. red	redder	reddest
4. fat	fatter	fattest
5. wet	wetter	wettest

Add -ed or -ing to a word from the box to complete each sentence. Write the new word.

slip	brag	tap	hug	stop

6. After three days, the rain has finally ___**stopped**___.

7. Brian is always ___**bragging**___ about his bike.

8. Ahmed ___**slipped**___ on a patch of ice.

9. Grandma picked up the baby and ___**hugged**___ her.

10. I wish Connie would stop ___**tapping**___ her pencil!

Notes for Home: Your child added endings to base words. **Home Activity:** Have your child make a list of other words in which the final consonant is doubled before endings are added.

139

Name _____

Add the ending to each word in the list. Write the new word.

Add -es		**Add -ed**	
1. copy	copies	6. reply	replied
2. fly	flies	7. marry	married
3. supply	supplies	8. clip	clipped
4. spy	spies	9. fry	fried
5. scurry	scurries	10. trot	trotted

Add -ing	
11. shop	shopping
12. plot	plotting
13. cry	crying
14. trap	trapping
15. plan	planning

Add -er		**Add -est**	
16. empty	emptier	21. scary	scariest
17. sad	sadder	22. lonely	loneliest
18. busy	busier	23. wet	wettest
19. thin	thinner	24. red	reddest
20. healthy	healthier	25. easy	easiest

Notes for Home: Your child added endings to base words. **Home Activity:** Take turns with your child writing a phrase with each word on the page.

140

© Scott Foresman 4-6

Possessive nouns show who or what owns something. To make a singular noun possessive, an apostrophe (') and an *s* are added to the word.

the wheels of the car   the car's wheels

Write a possessive noun to complete each phrase.

1. the glasses of my grandmother   my __grandmother's__ glasses
2. the helmet of the soldier   the __soldier's__ helmet
3. the streets of the city   the __city's__ streets
4. the principal of the school   the __school's__ principal
5. the rays of the sun   the __sun's__ rays
6. the news of the year   the __year's__ news
7. the toys of the child   the __child's__ toys
8. the troops of the commander   the __commander's__ troops
9. the purse of her mother   her __mother's__ purse
10. the oceans of Earth   __Earth's__ oceans
11. the scarf of Manuel   __Manuel's__ scarf
12. the desk of the teacher   the __teacher's__ desk
13. the backpack of Emiko   __Emiko's__ backpack
14. the roof of the building   the __building's__ roof
15. the trip of our friend   our __friend's__ trip

Notes for Home: Your child added *'s* to singular nouns to make their possessive forms.
Home Activity: Have your child write the name of each family member, add *'s*, and then write the name of an item to show ownership.

141

To make the possessive form of a plural noun that ends in *s*, an apostrophe (') is added to the word.

the desks of the students   the students' desks

Write a possessive noun to complete each phrase.

1. the jackets of the girls   the __girls'__ jackets
2. the collars of the dogs   the __dogs'__ collars
3. the branches of the trees   the __trees'__ branches
4. the books of the teachers   the __teachers'__ books
5. the caves of the bears   the __bears'__ caves
6. the racquets of the players   the __players'__ racquets
7. the pictures of the artists   the __artists'__ pictures
8. the brushes of the painters   the __painters'__ brushes
9. the eggs of the hens   the __hens'__ eggs
10. the boots of the hikers   the __hikers'__ boots
11. the yards of the houses   the __houses'__ yards
12. the ropes of the climbers   the __climbers'__ ropes
13. the sales of the stores   the __stores'__ sales
14. the jokes of the boys   the __boys'__ jokes
15. the tails of the cats   the __cats'__ tails

Notes for Home: Your child added an apostrophe to plural nouns ending in *s* to make their possessive forms. **Home Activity:** Have your child write five phrases from the page as sentences.

142

To make the possessive form of a plural noun that does not end in *s*, an apostrophe (') and an *s* are added to the word.

the bikes of the women   the women's bikes

Add *'s* to each word.

1. feet   __feet's__
2. men   __men's__
3. teeth   __teeth's__
4. children   __children's__
5. mice   __mice's__
6. geese   __geese's__
7. oxen   __oxen's__

Write a possessive noun to complete each phrase.

8. the kites of the children   the __children's__ kites
9. the hats of the men   the __men's__ hats
10. the beaks of the geese   the __geese's__ beaks
11. the roots of the teeth   the __teeth's__ roots
12. the yokes of the oxen   the __oxen's__ yokes
13. the feet of the mice   the __mice's__ feet
14. the cheers of the people   the __people's__ cheers
15. the laughter of the women   the __women's__ laughter

Notes for Home: Your child added *'s* to plural nouns that do not end in *s* to make their possessive forms. **Home Activity:** Have your child write sentences using the possessive nouns in items 1–7.

143

Singular nouns — *'s*   girl's
Plural nouns ending in *s* — '   dogs'
Plural nouns not ending in *s* — *'s*   teeth's

Circle the correct possessive form of the noun to complete the sentence.

1. The (**cities'**, city's) connecting road made it easy to travel between them.
2. The (children', **children's**) bicycles were in the garage.
3. The tour (**guides'**, guide's) colorful uniforms stood out in a crowd.
4. One (**boy's**, boys') notebook was missing.
5. The mechanic repaired the (airplanes', **airplane's**) engine.
6. The (**campers'**, camper's) tents were pitched around the fire.
7. The (womens', **women's**) group meets on Thursday evening.
8. The (foxes', **fox's**) tail was large and bushy.
9. The (**beekeeper's**, beekeepers') hat was covered with netting.
10. The three lab (**assistants'**, assistant's) reports were very accurate.
11. The (student's, **students'**) scores on the test ranged from 83 to 99.
12. The (jobs', **job's**) salary was higher than she had expected.
13. The map showed Allen where the (**men's**, mens') locker room was.
14. Mr. Kronsky used heavy tape to secure the (**boxes'**, box's) lids.
15. Rosa tried to ignore the (geese', **geese's**) loud honking.

Notes for Home: Your child identified the correct possessive noun in sentences.
Home Activity: Have your child write sentences using any correct possessive nouns *not* circled on the page.

144

Page 145 — Possessives

Name _____

Possessives

Add an apostrophe and *s* or an apostrophe to make the correct possessive form of each noun. Then write the words to complete the sentences.

1. elephants ___**elephants'**___
2. men ___**men's**___
3. tourist ___**tourist's**___
4. table ___**table's**___
5. guests ___**guests'**___
6. people ___**people's**___
7. schools ___**schools'**___
8. dress ___**dress's**___
9. mice ___**mice's**___
10. Edison ___**Edison's**___

11. Samantha really liked the ___**dress's**___ color.

12. The wooden staircase had been damaged by the ___**mice's**___ gnawing.

13. The ___**table's**___ legs were made of oak.

14. Last year the ___**men's**___ ski team won the gold medal.

15. Each month the ___**schools'**___ principals meet to share information.

16. Did you know that all ___**elephants'**___ tusks are ivory?

17. The politician worked hard to gain the ___**people's**___ support.

18. The light bulb and phonograph are among ___**Edison's**___ inventions.

19. The ___**tourist's**___ lost camera was found in the airport.

20. All of the ___**guests'**___ coats were hanging in the closet.

Notes for Home: Your child wrote possessive forms of nouns to complete sentences.
Home Activity: Have your child make a list of things found in a school and then write words that show ownership of each item.

145

Page 146 — Base Words

Name _____

Base Words

A base word is a word to which other word parts, or affixes, may be added to make new words. Affixes may be endings, prefixes, or suffixes.

wash	**wash + ed**	**re + wash**
base word	base word + ending	prefix + base word

Divide each word into its base word and affix.

	Base Word		**Affix**
1. careful	care	+	ful
2. building	build	+	ing
3. quickly	quick	+	ly
4. enjoyment	enjoy	+	ment
5. darkness	dark	+	ness
6. thoughtless	thought	+	less
7. laughable	laugh	+	able
8. freedom	free	+	dom

	Affix		**Base Word**
9. recall	re	+	call
10. disagree	dis	+	agree
11. pretest	pre	+	test
12. misunderstood	mis	+	understood
13. unpaid	un	+	paid
14. impolite	im	+	polite
15. nonsense	non	+	sense

Notes for Home: Your child divided words into base words and affixes.
Home Activity: Have your child look in a newspaper to find at least six words made up of a base word and affix and write the base word and affix for each word.

146

Page 147 — Base Words

Name _____

Base Words

Affixes are word parts that have meaning. They may be added to the beginning or end of the base word.

Draw a line from each affix in Column A to a base word in Column B. Then write the new word.

A	**B**	**New Word**
1. -ly	hope	softly
2. -dom	soft	kingdom
3. -or	king	actor
4. -less	act	hopeless

5. re-	possible	reheat
6. non-	heat	nonsense
7. im-	like	impossible
8. dis-	sense	dislike

9. -ment	teach	assignment
10. -er	slow	teacher
11. -ful	assign	hopeful
12. -est	hope	slowest

13. sub-	legal	subway
14. im-	way	impatient
15. il-	patient	illegal

Notes for Home: Your child combined base words and affixes to make new words.
Home Activity: On a sheet of paper, write four affixes at the top of four columns. Challenge your child to list as many words with that affix as possible given one minute for each column.

147

Page 148 — Base Words

Name _____

Base Words

When the affix or affixes are removed, only the base word remains.

Write the affix or affixes in each word. Then write the base word.

	Affix(es)	**Base Word**
1. kindness	ness	kind
2. faster	er	fast
3. pretested	pre, ed	test
4. smallest	est	small
5. helpful	ful	help
6. recalled	re, ed	call
7. crying	ing	cry
8. childish	ish	child
9. unacceptable	un, able	accept
10. freedom	dom	free
11. midnight	mid	night
12. illegal	il	legal
13. effortless	less	effort
14. insincerely	in, ly	sincere
15. healthy	y	health

Notes for Home: Your child identified base words and affixes in words.
Home Activity: Have your child build as many new words as possible by adding affixes to these words: *pay, build, teach, polite, deep.*

148

Worksheet 1 (page 149) — Base Words

Different affixes can be added to a base word to give the word different meanings.

paint　　　repaint　　　painting　　　unpainted　　　painter

Choose an affix to add to the base word to form a new word that completes the sentence. Write the new word.

write　　1. Please __rewrite__ your rough draft.
　　　　　　sub-　　　re-　　　non-

play　　2. The puppies were very __playful__.
　　　　　　-est　　　-ing　　　-ful

loud　　3. Morris raised the volume to the __loudest__ setting.
　　　　　　-est　　　-ment　　　-ly

sense　　4. I could not understand the baby's __nonsense__ words.
　　　　　　pre-　　　mis-　　　non-

spell　　5. Many people __misspell__ the word *receive*.
　　　　　　mis-　　　il-　　　dis-

match　　6. Monique sorted the socks into __matching__ pairs.
　　　　　　-ful　　　-ing　　　-ish

heat　　7. The baking directions said to first __preheat__ the oven.
　　　　　　pre-　　　inter-　　　sub-

effort　　8. Mia made the difficult dive seem __effortless__.
　　　　　　-less　　　-ish　　　-ing

buckled　9. The passengers __unbuckled__ their seat belts after takeoff.
　　　　　　non-　　　dis-　　　un-

act　　10. The young __actor__ auditioned for the play.
　　　　　　-ion　　　-or　　　-ing

Notes for Home: Your child formed and wrote words by adding affixes to base words. **Home Activity:** Have your child look for words with affixes in printed directions. Talk together about how the meaning of the directions would change if the affixes in the words were changed.

149

Worksheet 2 (page 150) — Base Words

A base word can have an affix at the beginning or at the end. A base word can have more than one affix.

Start at *First Base*. Draw a line between the affix(es) and the base word. Write the base word. Follow the numbers to *Second Base*, *Third Base*, and *Home Plate* until you have written all the base words.

Home Plate

16. illegal __legal__
17. scoreless __score__
18. placement __place__
19. previewing __view__
20. disgraceful __grace__

First Base

1. recalled __call__
2. camping __camp__
3. neatness __neat__
4. laughable __laugh__
5. catcher __catch__

Third Base

11. unlikely __like__
12. preschool __school__
13. unbreakable __break__
14. imperfect __perfect__
15. mistrust __trust__

Second Base

6. shorten __short__
7. immature __mature__
8. national __nation__
9. nonsense __sense__
10. thankful __thank__

Notes for Home: Your child identified and wrote the base words in words with affixes. **Home Activity:** Have your child scan a newspaper article and underline the base words in ten or more words with affixes in the article.

150

Worksheet 3 (page 151) — Prefix re-

A prefix is a word part added to the beginning of a word that changes the word's meaning. The prefix *re-* means "again."

re + paint = **re**paint　　　to paint again

Add *re-* to make new words. Then write the words to complete the sentences.

__re__cycles　__re__fill　__re__new　__re__read　__re__told
__re__elected　__re__heat　__re__organized　__re__set　__re__united
__re__enter　__re__loaded　__re__place　__re__tie　__re__view

1. Tanya stopped skating to __retie__ her laces.
2. Our mayor was __reelected__ for a second term.
3. I had to __replace__ the glass that I dropped and broke.
4. The critic gave that movie a good __review__.
5. Our community __recycles__ paper, plastic, and aluminum.
6. Grandma __retold__ the story of her coming to America.
7. Last Sunday, I cleaned out and __reorganized__ my closet.
8. I quickly read the notice; then I __reread__ it more slowly.
9. The colonists' rifles had to be __reloaded__ after every shot.
10. After a long separation, Kate was __reunited__ with her cousin.
11. Joseph will __reheat__ the leftovers in the microwave.
12. The price of a bucket of popcorn includes one free __refill__.
13. We needed to show our ticket stub to __reenter__ the theater.
14. Jasmine __reset__ the alarm on her clock radio.
15. Emilio needed to __renew__ the overdue library book.

Notes for Home: Your child added the prefix *re-* to base words and wrote those words in sentences. **Home Activity:** Have your child find ten action words (verbs) in a magazine or newspaper article. Add *re-* to the words and talk about how this changes the meaning of the article.

151

Worksheet 4 (page 152) — Prefix mis-

The prefix *mis-* means "bad," "wrong," or "incorrect."

mis + use = **mis**use　　　to use in the wrong way

Welcome to the first annual Miss *Mis-* Contest! Read the statement by each of our ten "contestants." Then write the *mis-* word that best describes that contestant.

Contestant #1: "I use an eraser to correct these."
I am Miss __Mistakes__.　Mistakes　Miscount　Mislead

Contestant #2: "I bought a CD at the music store without checking for a sale price."
I am Miss __Misspent__.　Misapply　Misfit　Misspent

Contestant #3: "I can't find my homework!"
I am Miss __Misplace__.　Misuse　Mistrust　Misplace

Contestant #4: "Sometimes I say words incorrectly."
I am Miss __Mispronounce__.　Misjudge　Mispronounce　Misspell

Contestant #5: "I ran out of gas because I didn't figure the mileage correctly."
I am Miss __Miscalculate__.　Misapply　Miscalculate　Misfit

Contestant #6: "I'm a 12-year-old actress but was given the role of a grandmother."
I am Miss __Miscast__.　Miscast　Mistrust　Misjudge

Contestant #7: "I get lost a lot because I can't read and follow directions."
I am Miss __Misread__.　Mistrusted　Misread　Miscount

Contestant #8: "I like wearing a striped shirt with a plaid skirt and polka dot socks."
I am Miss __Mismatched__.　Misused　Misjudged　Mismatched

Contestant #9: "Magazines and newspapers never print exactly what I say."
I am Miss __Misquoted__.　Misquoted　Mistrust　Misbehave

Contestant #10: "I was given the wrong information about the store's return policy."
I am Miss __Misinformed__.　Misinformed　Misfire　Mishandle

Notes for Home: Your child wrote words with the prefix *mis-*. **Home Activity:** Help your child make up "contestant" descriptions using *mis-* words that were not used on the page.

152

The prefix *un-* means "not" or "opposite of."

un + happy = **un**happy   not happy, opposite of *happy*

Write the word with *un-* that matches each meaning. Then write the words to complete the sentences.

1. not true **untrue**
2. not paid **unpaid**
3. not equal **unequal**
4. not pleasant **unpleasant**
5. opposite of *lock* **unlock**
6. not safe **unsafe**
7. opposite of *pack* **unpack**
8. not usual **unusual**
9. opposite of *load* **unload**
10. not fair **unfair**

11. The overdue bill was **unpaid**
12. Use the key to **unlock** the door.
13. Let's **unpack** our suitcases later.
14. Going out of turn is **unfair**.
15. A pint and a quart are **unequal** amounts.
16. Riding without using a seat belt is **unsafe**
17. A skunk's odor is very **unpleasant**
18. A lie is **untrue**
19. Snow in May is **unusual**
20. She will **unload** the boxes from the truck.

Notes for Home: Your child wrote words with the prefix *un-*. **Home Activity:** Have your child think of "un-" advertising slogans based on the opposite qualities of items or products. For example: Dogs—the "uncats"—great pets that don't choke on fur balls!

153

The prefixes *non-* and *un-* mean "not."

non + profit = **non**profit   not for profit   un + happy = **un**happy   not happy

Add *non-* or *un-* to make new words. Then write the words to complete the sentences.

unsure   **un**tidy   **un**lucky   **un**tied   **non**fat
nonsense   **non**stop   **un**comfortable   **un**seen   **non**fiction
unknown   **un**familiar   **non**flammable   **non**violence   **un**solved

1. Renaldo **untied** the ribbon before opening the gift.
2. The lumpy mattress was very **uncomfortable**.
3. The true identity of the suspect is **unknown** at this time.
4. Skim milk is used to make **nonfat** yogurt.
5. I promised to clean up my **untidy** room.
6. The hidden camera was **unseen** by the shoppers.
7. Reginald was **unsure** of the correct answer.
8. The toddler spoke only **nonsense** words.
9. Joe felt **unlucky** after he lost his wallet and got a flat tire.
10. After years of investigation, the mystery is still **unsolved**
11. Biographies are **nonfiction** books.
12. The express train runs **nonstop** from here to downtown.
13. Children's pajamas are made of **nonflammable** materials.
14. Pablo was **unfamiliar** with his new school.
15. Dr. Martin Luther King, Jr. believed in **nonviolence**

Notes for Home: Your child wrote words with the prefixes *un-* and *non-*. **Home Activity:** Take turns with your child naming words with *non-* and *un-* and writing them in two lists.

154

The prefix *pre-* means "before."

pre + approved = **pre**approved   approved before

The prefix *dis-* means "not" or "opposite of."

dis + similar = **dis**similiar   not similar, opposite of *similar*

Add *dis-* or *pre-* to each base word to make a word that makes sense in the sentence.

1. **dis**agreed   The coach **disagreed** with the referee.
2. **pre**test   Our teacher gave us a **pretest**.
3. **dis**continued   Terrell **discontinued** his magazine subscription.
4. **dis**approves   Al **disapproves** of watching too much TV.
5. **pre**view   We saw a sneak **preview** of the movie.
6. **dis**comfort   The icy winds added to our **discomfort**
7. **dis**organized   My desk drawer is very **disorganized**
8. **pre**teen   Twelve is the last year you are a **preteen**
9. **dis**honest   Stealing is **dishonest**
10. **pre**school   Ana went to **preschool** before kindergarten.
11. **pre**paid   Mrs. Panek **prepaid** her rent for two months.
12. **dis**qualified   Felice was **disqualified** after misspelling a word.
13. **dis**appeared   The setting sun **disappeared** from the sky.
14. **pre**heat   First **preheat** the oven to 350°.
15. **dis**connected   Sometimes I am **disconnected** from the Internet.

Notes for Home: Your child wrote words with the prefixes *pre-* and *dis-*. **Home Activity:** Have your child draw pictures to illustrate the meanings of two or more *dis-* or *pre-* words from the page.

155

The prefix *sub-* means "under," "nearly," or "again."

sub + title = **sub**title   a title under the main title

The prefix *en-* means "to make or cause to be."

en + circle = **en**circle   make a circle around

The prefix *mis-* means "bad," "wrong," or "incorrect."

mis + use = **mis**use   use incorrectly

Draw a line to connect the prefix to the correct base word. Write the new word next to its definition.

1. mis- / way — A. railroad under the ground **subway**
   sub- / joy — B. be happy with **enjoy**
   en- / read — C. see words incorrectly **misread**

2. sub- / behave — A. act badly **misbehave**
   mis- / close — B. put a wall around **enclose**
   en- / marine — C. underwater ship **submarine**

3. mis- / large — A. make bigger **enlarge**
   sub- / spell — B. use the wrong letters **misspell**
   en- / divide — C. break apart again **subdivide**

4. mis- / danger — A. put in a harmful position **endanger**
   en- / inform — B. give incorrect information **misinform**
   sub- / urban — C. near the city **suburban**

5. mis- / total — A. nearly the final amount **subtotal**
   sub- / tangle — B. get twisted; caught in **entangle**
   en- / trust — C. doubt, not be sure of **mistrust**

Notes for Home: Your child wrote words with the prefixes *sub-*, *en-*, and *mis-*. **Home Activity:** Have your child look for advertisements in magazines or newspapers that use words with *sub-*, *en-*, or *mis-*. Have your child create his or her own ad using one or more words with those prefixes.

156

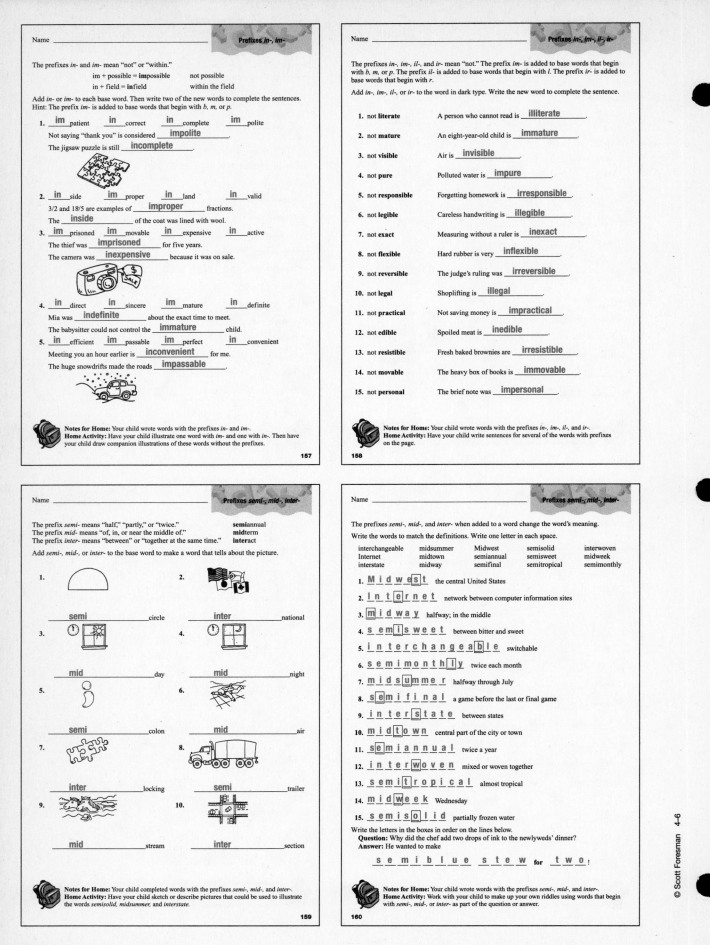

Name _____ Prefixes *in-, im-*

The prefixes *in-* and *im-* mean "not" or "within."

im + possible = **im**possible — not possible
in + field = **in**field — within the field

Add *in-* or *im-* to each base word. Then write two of the new words to complete the sentences.
Hint: The prefix *im-* is added to base words that begin with *b, m,* or *p.*

1. __im__patient __in__correct __in__complete __im__polite
   Not saying "thank you" is considered __impolite__.
   The jigsaw puzzle is still __incomplete__.

2. __in__side __im__proper __in__land __in__valid
   3/2 and 18/5 are examples of __improper__ fractions.
   The __inside__ of the coat was lined with wool.

3. __im__prisoned __im__movable __in__expensive __in__active
   The thief was __imprisoned__ for five years.
   The camera was __inexpensive__ because it was on sale.

4. __in__direct __in__sincere __im__mature __in__definite
   Mia was __indefinite__ about the exact time to meet.
   The babysitter could not control the __immature__ child.

5. __in__efficient __im__passable __im__perfect __in__convenient
   Meeting you an hour earlier is __inconvenient__ for me.
   The huge snowdrifts made the roads __impassable__.

Notes for Home: Your child wrote words with the prefixes *in-* and *im-*.
Home Activity: Have your child illustrate one word with *im-* and one with *in-*. Then have your child draw companion illustrations of these words without the prefixes.

157

Name _____ Prefixes *in-, im-, il-, ir-*

The prefixes *in-, im-, il-,* and *ir-* mean "not." The prefix *im-* is added to base words that begin with *b, m,* or *p.* The prefix *il-* is added to base words that begin with *l.* The prefix *ir-* is added to base words that begin with *r.*

Add *in-, im-, il-,* or *ir-* to the word in dark type. Write the new word to complete the sentence.

1. not **literate**   A person who cannot read is __illiterate__.
2. not **mature**   An eight-year-old child is __immature__.
3. not **visible**   Air is __invisible__.
4. not **pure**   Polluted water is __impure__.
5. not **responsible**   Forgetting homework is __irresponsible__.
6. not **legible**   Careless handwriting is __illegible__.
7. not **exact**   Measuring without a ruler is __inexact__.
8. not **flexible**   Hard rubber is very __inflexible__.
9. not **reversible**   The judge's ruling was __irreversible__.
10. not **legal**   Shoplifting is __illegal__.
11. not **practical**   Not saving money is __impractical__.
12. not **edible**   Spoiled meat is __inedible__.
13. not **resistible**   Fresh baked brownies are __irresistible__.
14. not **movable**   The heavy box of books is __immovable__.
15. not **personal**   The brief note was __impersonal__.

Notes for Home: Your child wrote words with the prefixes *in-, im-, il-,* and *ir-*.
Home Activity: Have your child write sentences for several of the words with prefixes on the page.

158

Name _____ Prefixes *semi-, mid-, inter-*

The prefix *semi-* means "half," "partly," or "twice." **semi**annual
The prefix *mid-* means "of, in, or near the middle of." **mid**term
The prefix *inter-* means "between" or "together at the same time." **inter**act

Add *semi-, mid-,* or *inter-* to the base word to make a word that tells about the picture.

1. __semi__circle
2. __inter__national
3. __mid__day
4. __mid__night
5. __semi__colon
6. __mid__air
7. __inter__locking
8. __semi__trailer
9. __mid__stream
10. __inter__section

Notes for Home: Your child completed words with the prefixes *semi-, mid-,* and *inter-*.
Home Activity: Have your child sketch or describe pictures that could be used to illustrate the words *semisolid, midsummer,* and *interstate.*

159

Name _____ Prefixes *semi-, mid-, inter-*

The prefixes *semi-, mid-,* and *inter-* when added to a word change the word's meaning.

Write the words to match the definitions. Write one letter in each space.

interchangeable midsummer Midwest semisolid interwoven
Internet midtown semiannual semisweet midweek
interstate midway semifinal semitropical semimonthly

1. M i d w e s t the central United States
2. I n t e r n e t network between computer information sites
3. m i d w a y halfway; in the middle
4. s e m i s w e e t between bitter and sweet
5. i n t e r c h a n g e a b l e switchable
6. s e m i m o n t h l y twice each month
7. m i d s u m m e r halfway through July
8. s e m i f i n a l a game before the last or final game
9. i n t e r s t a t e between states
10. m i d t o w n central part of the city or town
11. s e m i a n n u a l twice a year
12. i n t e r w o v e n mixed or woven together
13. s e m i t r o p i c a l almost tropical
14. m i d w e e k Wednesday
15. s e m i s o l i d partially frozen water

Write the letters in the boxes in order on the lines below.
Question: Why did the chef add two drops of ink to the newlyweds' dinner?
Answer: He wanted to make

s e m i b l u e s t e w for t w o !

Notes for Home: Your child wrote words with the prefixes *semi-, mid-,* and *inter-*.
Home Activity: Work with your child to make up your own riddles using words that begin with *semi-, mid-,* or *inter-* as part of the question or answer.

160

© Scott Foresman 4–6

A suffix is a word part added to the end of a word that changes the word's meaning.

The suffix *-ful* means "full of." hope + ful = hope**ful** full of hope
The suffix *-less* means "without." hope + less = hope**less** without hope

Add *-ful* and *-less* to the base word. Write the two new words to complete the sentences.

1. **hope** Sighting land made the sailors feel __hopeful__.
   Being lost at sea had made them feel __hopeless__.

2. **thought** It was __thoughtful__ of you to remember my birthday.
   How __thoughtless__ of you to forget my birthday!

3. **color** The all white room seemed __colorless__.
   The __colorful__ room was painted red and purple.

4. **rest** Sitting in rush hour traffic makes me __restless__.
   Lying on a beach is very __restful__.

5. **help** The climbers were __helpless__ without a rope.
   The tour guide offered __helpful__ suggestions.

6. **use** First aid training is very __useful__.
   Without batteries, the flashlight was __useless__.

7. **care** Be __careful__ with that hot water!
   Hurrying will result in __careless__ work.

8. **thank** Cleaning the bathroom is a __thankless__ task.
   I am __thankful__ I wasn't hurt in the accident.

9. **fear** The __fearful__ child hid under the covers.
   The __fearless__ firefighter ran into the burning building.

10. **harm** He explained how to approach a __harmless__ snake
    and how to avoid a __harmful__ one.

Notes for Home: Your child wrote words with the suffixes *-ful* and *-less*.
Home Activity: Have your child list other base words that have opposite meanings when the suffixes *-ful* and *-less* are added. Examples: *meaning, power, joy.*

161

The suffix *-or* or *-er* means a person or thing that does something.

instruct + or = instruct**or** person who instructs
mix + er = mix**er** thing that mixes

Add *-er* or *-or* to the word in dark type to make a word that describes the picture. You will need to drop letters before adding a suffix. Use a dictionary to check the spellings of *-er* and *-or* words.

1. person who **sings** singer
2. person who **dances** dancer
3. machine that **blends** blender
4. person who **drives** driver
5. person who **acts** actor
6. person who **farms** farmer
7. person who **sails** sailor
8. person who is elected to the **Senate** Senator
9. person who serves on a **jury** juror
10. machine that **prints** printer

Notes for Home: Your child wrote words with the suffix *-er* or *-or*.
Home Activity: Have your child find occupations or items listed in the Yellow Pages® business directory that end in *-or* or *-er.*

162

The suffix *-y* added to a word makes the word an adjective.
   snow + y = snowy It is a snowy day.
The suffix *-ly* added to a word makes the word an adjective or an adverb.
   dangerous + ly = dangerously He is driving dangerously.

Add *-y* or *-ly* to each word. Then write the words to complete the sentences.

patient __ly__ friend __ly__ mess __y__ slow __ly__ dirt __y__
wind __y__ loud __ly__ water __y__ sweat __y__ time __ly__

1. Michael organized his __messy__ desk.
2. The turtle crawled __slowly__ across the room.
3. Paul loaded the __dirty__ clothes into the washer.
4. The fans cheered __loudly__ for their team.
5. We were hot and __sweaty__ after an hour of exercising.
6. Terasita waited __patiently__ for the store to open.
7. Shaking hands is a __friendly__ gesture.
8. The tasteless soup was thin and __watery__.
9. The __timely__ warning of the alarm kept me from being late.
10. Meeko likes to fly kites on __windy__ days.

Notes for Home: Your child wrote words with the suffixes *-y* and *-ly.*
Home Activity: Have your child look through a magazine or newspaper article, find three words with the suffix *-y* and three words with the suffix *-ly*, and identify the base word in each one.

163

The suffixes *-ment, -ness, -ation, -ion,* and *-dom* added to words make the words nouns.

argue + ment = argu**ment** collect + ion = collect**ion**

Combine a base word from the box with the suffix given to make a word that fits in the definition. You may need to drop a letter before adding the suffix.

imagine	invite	free	king	elect
state	quick	pollute	arrange	wise
bore	examine	educate	agree	ill

1. a test; __examination__ (-ation)
2. an understanding; a contract; __agreement__ (-ment)
3. a request to come to a party or event; __invitation__ (-ation)
4. position or a certain order; __arrangement__ (-ment)
5. state of being fast or swift; __quickness__ (-ness)
6. schooling; learning; training; __education__ (-ion)
7. country ruled by a king or queen; __kingdom__ (-dom)
8. making choices by voting; __election__ (-ion)
9. disease; an unhealthy condition; __illness__ (-ness)
10. dirty air, water, and land; __pollution__ (-ion)
11. thinking and acting as you want; __freedom__ (-dom)
12. something said; a type of sentence; __statement__ (-ment)
13. knowledge based on experience; __wisdom__ (-dom)
14. ability to picture ideas in your mind; __imagination__ (-ation)
15. nothing to do; __boredom__ (-dom)

Notes for Home: Your child wrote words with the suffixes *-ment, -ness, -ation, -ion,* and *-dom.* **Home Activity:** Challenge your child to think of another word with each of the suffixes *-ment, -ness, -ation, -ion,* and *-dom.*

164

© Scott Foresman 4-6

The suffixes -al, -ic, -ive, -ish, -ible, and -able added to words make the words adjectives.

profession + al = professional   sense + ible = sensible

Add the base word and the suffix to make an adjective. You may need to change the spelling of the base word before you add the suffix. Then write the words to complete the phrases.

1. wash + able = **washable**   2. artist + ic = **artistic**

3. self + ish = **selfish**   4. enjoy + able = **enjoyable**

5. nation + al = **national**   6. colony + al = **colonial**

7. flex + ible = **flexible**   8. base + ic = **basic**

9. rely + able = **reliable**   10. support + ive = **supportive**

11. our **national** government

12. a **selfish** child who would not share

13. exercises to keep your body strong and **flexible**

14. a **reliable** clock that keeps perfect time

15. a relaxing and **enjoyable** vacation

16. **washable** fabric that shouldn't be dry cleaned

17. a young sculptor with **artistic** talent

18. a re-creation of a town in **colonial** America

19. being **supportive** when someone needs help

20. the **basic** equipment needed for scuba diving

Notes for Home: Your child wrote words with the suffixes -al, -ic, -ive, -ish, -ible, and -able. **Home Activity:** Have your child write one more word with each of the six suffixes on this page.

165

Look at these words.

ham/mer   star/ry

Each word has two like consonants after the first vowel. The first vowel is between two consonants. This vowel usually stands for the short vowel sound unless it is followed by r.

Divide each word into syllables as you write the word. Put an X by each word with a short vowel sound in the first syllable.

1. letter **let/ter** X   2. rabbit **rab/bit** X

3. yellow **yel/low** X   4. puppet **pup/pet** X

5. worry **wor/ry**   6. horror **hor/ror**

7. tunnel **tun/nel** X   8. ribbon **rib/bon** X

9. butter **but/ter** X   10. jelly **jel/ly** X

11. lettuce **let/tuce** X   12. drummer **drum/mer** X

13. pepper **pep/per** X   14. cotton **cot/ton** X

15. hurry **hur/ry**   16. furry **fur/ry**

17. pillow **pil/low** X   18. current **cur/rent**

19. cabbage **cab/bage** X   20. button **but/ton** X

Notes for Home: Your child divided words with two like consonants in the middle into syllables. **Home Activity:** Help your child make a list of other words with two like consonants in the middle.

166

Look at these words.

bas/ket   car/ton

Each word has two unlike consonants after the first vowel. The first vowel is between two consonants. This vowel usually stands for the short vowel sound unless it is followed by r.

ta/ble   ap/ple

Each word ends in a consonant + le. The first vowel can stand for the long or short vowel sound. Do not divide words between the consonant and le.

Divide each word into syllables as you write the word. Put an X by each word with a short vowel sound in the first syllable.

1. sister **sis/ter** X   2. corner **cor/ner**

3. dentist **den/tist** X   4. mustard **mus/tard** X

5. perfect **per/fect**   6. uncle **un/cle** X

7. cattle **cat/tle** X   8. service **ser/vice**

9. window **win/dow** X   10. custard **cus/tard** X

11. pencil **pen/cil** X   12. picture **pic/ture** X

13. market **mar/ket**   14. puddle **pud/dle** X

15. cable **ca/ble**   16. carpet **car/pet**

17. public **pub/lic** X   18. thirteen **thir/teen**

19. blanket **blan/ket** X   20. bugle **bu/gle**

Notes for Home: Your child divided words with two unlike consonants in the middle or a consonant + le pattern into syllables. **Home Activity:** Help your child make up sentences for some of the two-syllable words on the page.

167

Use the words in the box to answer the questions. Write each syllable of the word on a line.

turkey	hammer	letter	rabbit	garbage
candle	tunnel	picture	circus	hornet
carpet	mittens	ladle	simmer	bargain

1. Where can you see a clown? **cir** / **cus**

2. What is a type of floor covering? **car** / **pet**

3. What is something you write to a friend? **let** / **ter**

4. What is another name for trash? **gar** / **bage**

5. What is something that has a low price? **bar** / **gain**

6. What gives off light? **can** / **dle**

7. What means "to boil gently"? **sim** / **mer**

8. What is a tool that a carpenter uses? **ham** / **mer**

9. What might a train travel through? **tun** / **nel**

10. What is a large cup-shaped spoon? **la** / **dle**

11. What animal says "gobble"? **tur** / **key**

12. What do you wear to keep your hands warm? **mit** / **tens**

13. What animal hops around? **rab** / **bit**

14. What can you put in a frame and hang on a wall? **pic** / **ture**

15. What animal can sting? **hor** / **net**

Notes for Home: Your child divided words with two like or unlike consonants in the middle or a consonant + le into syllables. **Home Activity:** Have your child look through a newspaper to find other words with two consonants in the middle.

168

© Scott Foresman 4–6

Complete each sentence with a two-syllable word. Circle the word. Then write the word and divide it into syllables.

1. We had _____ pie at dinner.
   peach (custard)
   cus / tard

2. The _____ lived in the woods.
   snake (rabbit)
   rab / bit

3. Dad washed the _____.
   floor (window)
   win / dow

4. We put _____ books on the shelf.
   (fifteen) three
   fif / teen

5. The _____ sweater had a flower on it.
   green (yellow)
   yel / low

6. The _____ shaker needed to be filled.
   (pepper) salt
   pep / per

7. I spoke to the _____ about my cold.
   nurse (doctor)
   doc / tor

8. We put all the food in a _____ basket.
   (picnic) green
   pic / nic

9. The _____ was on the big porch.
   swing (hammock)
   ham / mock

10. The girl has two _____ in her hair.
    bows (ribbons)
    rib / bons

Notes for Home: Your child divided words with two like or unlike consonants in the middle into syllables. **Home Activity:** Choose four two-syllable words from the page and create a sentence using each word.

169

Look at these words.

pi/lot   ro/bot

Each word has one consonant after the first vowel. The first vowel stands for the long vowel sound. The first syllable ends with that vowel.

Divide each two-syllable word into syllables as you write the word. If it has only one syllable, *do not* write the word.

1. flavor fla/vor
2. final fi/nal
3. hotel ho/tel
4. razor ra/zor
5. clock _____
6. spider spi/der
7. lazy la/zy
8. clover clo/ver
9. legal le/gal
10. trunk _____
11. boat _____
12. major ma/jor
13. paper pa/per
14. black _____
15. motor mo/tor
16. bacon ba/con
17. cocoa co/coa
18. trick _____
19. stack _____
20. soda so/da

Notes for Home: Your child divided words with a long vowel sound into syllables. **Home Activity:** Have your child write phrases using ten words from the page.

170

Look at these words.

sev/en   riv/er

Each word has one consonant after the first vowel. The first vowel stands for the short vowel sound. The words are divided after the consonant that follows this vowel.

Divide each two-syllable word into syllables as you write the word. If it has only one syllable, *do not* write the word.

1. melon mel/on
2. ever ev/er
3. travel trav/el
4. robin ro/bin
5. think _____
6. crust _____
7. lemon lem/on
8. petal pet/al
9. never nev/er
10. damage dam/age
11. spill _____
12. palace pal/ace
13. visit vis/it
14. blank _____
15. cabin cab/in
16. medal med/al
17. model mod/el
18. wagon wag/on
19. crack _____
20. camel cam/el

Notes for Home: Your child divided words with a short vowel sound into syllables. **Home Activity:** Challenge your child to make a list of ten two-syllable words that have a short vowel sound and divide them into syllables.

171

Write a word from the box to complete each sentence. Then write each syllable of the word on a line.

| finish | river | camel | limit | pilot |
| lilac | medal | solid | hotel | music |

1. The __pilot__ landed the airplane on the runway.
   pi / lot

2. The __lilac__ bush blooms every spring.
   li / lac

3. The firefighter was awarded a __medal__ for bravery.
   med / al

4. The crowd applauded as the runner crossed the __finish__ line.
   fin / ish

5. My brother listens to __music__ when he studies.
   mu / sic

6. A __camel__ can travel a long distance without food or water.
   cam / el

7. During the winter, the lake was frozen __solid__.
   sol / id

8. The driver was ticketed for exceeding the speed __limit__.
   lim / it

9. The __hotel__ had over five hundred rooms.
   ho / tel

10. A large amount of rain caused the __river__ to overflow.
    riv / er

Notes for Home: Your child divided words into syllables based on the vowel sound in the first syllable. **Home Activity:** Have your child write a riddle for each word in the box.

172

Answers **223**

Complete each sentence with a two-syllable word that has a long vowel sound. Circle the word. Then write the word, dividing it into syllables.

1. We had _____, toast, and eggs for breakfast.
   (bacon)   melon
   ba / con

2. The _____ lived by the tall grass on the plateau.
   (tiger)   camel
   ti / ger

3. The _____ crawled along the rocks.
   lizard   (spider)
   spi / der

4. I wanted to buy a _____ at the store.
   wagon   (paper)
   pa / per

5. The _____ in the movie was very pretty.
   (music)   palace
   mu / sic

6. We got a new _____ for my bike.
   pedal   (license)
   li / cense

7. I heard the _____ tell about her career.
   (pilot)   doctor
   pi / lot

8. The _____ was built on the side of a hill.
   (hotel)   cabin
   ho / tel

9. The ad was in the _____ paper.
   city   (local)
   lo / cal

10. The _____ was located near the center of town.
    (station)   river
    sta / tion

Notes for Home: Your child divided words with long vowel sounds into syllables.
Home Activity: Challenge your child to make up movie titles using two-syllable words with long vowel sounds.

173

---

1. Two-syllable words with two like or unlike consonants after the first vowel

ham/mer   bas/ket

2. Two-syllable words with one consonant after the first vowel

pi/lot   sev/en

3. Two-syllable words with a consonant + *le*

ap/ple   ta/ble

On the first line, write the number of the rule that tells how to divide the word. Then write the word and divide it into syllables.

1. gallop	1	gal/lop		2. copper	1	cop/per
3. cancel	1	can/cel		4. music	2	mu/sic
5. minute	2	min/ute		6. siren	2	si/ren
7. litter	1	lit/ter		8. cozy	2	co/zy
9. muscle	3	mus/cle		10. crazy	2	cra/zy
11. razor	2	ra/zor		12. channel	1	chan/nel
13. vanish	2	van/ish		14. maple	3	ma/ple
15. pillow	1	pil/low		16. wisdom	1	wis/dom
17. motor	2	mo/tor		18. petal	2	pet/al
19. paddle	3	pad/dle		20. locate	2	lo/cate

Notes for Home: Your child divided two-syllable words into syllables.
Home Activity: Have your child write the rules for dividing words on paper and write new words for each rule.

174

Choose a two-syllable word to replace the underlined one-syllable word. Write the word and divide it into syllables.

carton   jungle   river   carpet   apple
bonnet   music   lemon   bacon   hammer
robin   lantern   bugle   paddle   rabbit

1. The <u>sour</u> drops were in a fancy bag.
   lem / on

2. Our new <u>rug</u> was a light brown color.
   car / pet

3. I used the <u>oar</u> to move the canoe.
   pad / dle

4. The <u>tune</u> had a very fast rhythm.
   mu / sic

5. The soldier played a <u>horn</u>.
   bu / gle

6. The <u>stream</u> overflowed its banks.
   riv / er

7. I ate a green <u>grape</u>.
   ap / ple

8. The <u>bird</u> pulled a worm out of the ground.
   rob / in

9. The driver delivered a large <u>box</u>.
   car / ton

10. The <u>hare</u> ran across the yard to the woods.
    rab / bit

11. The tiger wandered through the <u>grass</u>.
    jun / gle

12. The camper had a gas <u>light</u>.
    lan / tern

13. We had <u>pork</u> for breakfast with our eggs.
    ba / con

14. This <u>tool</u> will help fix the broken door.
    ham / mer

15. The actress wore a green <u>hat</u> with feathers.
    bon / net

Notes for Home: Your child divided two-syllable words into syllables.
Home Activity: Work with your child to write sentences with one-syllable words that can be changed to two-syllable words. Read the sentences to family members.

175

Two-syllable words that are divided between two consonants are usually accented on the first syllable.

ham´ mer   win´ dow

Divide each word into syllables as you write it. Then mark the accented syllable.

1. carrot   **car´/rot**   2. yellow   **yel´/low**

3. robber   **rob´/ber**   4. cabbage   **cab´/bage**

5. lantern   **lan´/tern**   6. narrow   **nar´/row**

7. valley   **val´/ley**   8. temper   **tem´/per**

9. velvet   **vel´/vet**   10. bottom   **bot´/tom**

11. lumber   **lum´/ber**   12. letter   **let´/ter**

13. practice   **prac´/tice**   14. elbow   **el´/bow**

15. pepper   **pep´/per**   16. pencil   **pen´/cil**

17. ladder   **lad´/der**   18. walrus   **wal´/rus**

19. winter   **win´/ter**   20. mitten   **mit´/ten**

Notes for Home: Your child divided words into syllables and marked the accented syllable.
Home Activity: Make a list of two-syllable words with two like or unlike consonants in the middle and ask your child to identify the accented syllable in each word.

176

---

224 Answers

© Scott Foresman 4-6

Worksheet 1 (page 177)

Name _____

Syllabication

Two-syllable words with one consonant after the first vowel are divided before or after the consonant and are usually accented on the first syllable. The first vowel can stand for the long or the short vowel sound.

pi´ lot   sev´ en

Divide each word into syllables as you write it. Then mark the accented syllable.

1. open   o´/pen
2. shovel   shov´/el
3. bacon   ba´/con
4. gravel   grav´/el
5. moment   mo´/ment
6. humid   hu´/mid
7. second   sec´/ond
8. shiver   shiv´/er
9. robot   ro´/bot
10. radar   ra´/dar
11. notice   no´/tice
12. unit   u´/nit
13. never   nev´/er
14. radish   rad´/ish
15. music   mu´/sic
16. pupil   pu´/pil
17. bison   bi´/son
18. camel   cam´/el
19. tiger   ti´/ger
20. robin   rob´/in

Notes for Home: Your child divided words into syllables and marked the accented syllable.
Home Activity: Have your child write the words on the page in alphabetical order.

177

Worksheet 2 (page 178)

Name _____

Syllabication

Two-syllable words with a prefix or suffix are usually accented on the base word.

play´ ing   un lock´   play´ ful

Divide each word into syllables as you write it. Then mark the accented syllable.

1. slower   slow´/er
2. nonfat   non/fat´
3. thankful   thank´/ful
4. talking   talk´/ing
5. friendly   friend´/ly
6. careful   care´/ful
7. rewrite   re´/write
8. crying   cry´/ing
9. hardest   hard´/est
10. reread   re/read´
11. untie   un/tie´
12. impure   im/pure´
13. distrust   dis/trust´
14. nonstop   non/stop´
15. windy   wind´/y
16. unsure   un/sure´
17. misty   mist´/y
18. prepay   pre/pay´
19. unfit   un/fit´
20. lucky   luck´/y

Notes for Home: Your child divided words into syllables and marked the accented syllable.
Home Activity: Have your child make a list of base words and add *un-*, *pre-*, *re-*, *dis-*, *-ing*, and *-ful* to make new words. Ask your child to divide each new word into syllables and mark the accented syllable.

178

Worksheet 3 (page 179)

Name _____

Syllabication

When an affix is added to a word that has more than one syllable, the accent often shifts to a syllable nearer to the affix.

mag´ net → mag net´ ic

Write each word in syllables and mark the accented syllable.

1. fantasy   fan´/ta/sy   fantastic   fan/tas´/tic
2. product   prod´/uct   production   pro/duc´/tion
3. divide   di/vide´   division   di/vi´/sion
4. real   re´/al   reality   re/al´/i/ty
5. person   per´/son   personality   per/son/al´/i/ty
6. memory   mem´/or/y   memorial   me/mo´/ri/al
7. patriot   pa´/tri/ot   patriotic   pa/tri/ot´/ic
8. irrigate   ir´/ri/gate   irrigation   ir/ri/ga´/tion
9. communicate   com/mu´/ni/cate   communication   com/mu/ni/ca´/tion
10. equal   e´/qual   equality   e/qual´/i/ty

Notes for Home: Your child identified the accented syllables in pairs of related words.
Home Activity: Have your child choose five pairs of related words and write sentences using each pair.

179

Worksheet 4 (page 180)

Name _____

Syllabication

Mark the accent in each word. Write the longer word in each pair to complete the sentence.

1. The Alamo is a __historic__ site.
   his´tory   histor´ic
2. The __publicity__ committee for the concert put up posters at school.
   pub´lic   public´ity
3. The __political__ party held its convention in Dallas, Texas.
   pol´itics   politi´cal
4. Soccer is Ted's favorite after-school __activity__.
   ac´tive   activ´ity
5. The __musician__ is a member of the community orchestra.
   mu´sic   musi´cian
6. Machine parts were made by the __production__ department.
   prod´uct   produc´tion
7. The __location__ of the new library will be decided by the city council.
   lo´cate   loca´tion
8. Terry's new suit required extensive __alteration__.
   al´ter   altera´tion
9. The police conducted an __investigation__ of the traffic accident.
   inves´tigate   investiga´tion
10. Planning the school carnival requires a great deal of __organization__.
    or´ganize   organiza´tion

Notes for Home: Your child identified the accented syllables in pairs of related words.
Home Activity: Have your child write sentences for the shorter word in each pair on the page.

180